SKULL
· IN THE ·
ASHES

MURDER, A GOLD RUSH MANHUNT,
AND THE BIRTH OF CIRCUMSTANTIAL
EVIDENCE IN AMERICA

🌿 🌿 🌿

PETER KAUFMAN

University of Iowa Press
Iowa City

University of Iowa Press, Iowa City 52242
Copyright © 2013 by the University of Iowa Press
www.uiowapress.org
Printed in the United States of America

Design by April Leidig

The University of Iowa Press is a member of Green Press
Initiative and is committed to preserving natural resources.

Printed on acid-free paper

Library of Congress Cataloging-in-Publication Data
Kaufman, Peter.
Skull in the ashes: murder, a gold rush manhunt, and the birth
of circumstantial evidence in America / Peter Kaufman.
p.   cm.
Includes bibliographical references and index.
ISBN: 978-1-60938-188-2, 1-60938-188-2 (pbk.)
ISBN: 978-1-60938-213-1, 1-60938-213-7 (e-book)
1. Homicide investigation—Iowa—Walford.   2. Trials (Murder)—
Iowa—Walford.   3. Evidence, Circumstantial—Iowa—Walford.
4. Novak, Frank—Trials, litigation, etc.   I. Title.
HV8079.H6K38   2013
364.152'3 — dc23   2013010115

FOR DAN, PEG, AND ANNA

CONTENTS

PART ONE

FIRE AND ICE

ONE

•————————————————•

Death in Flames

Walford, Iowa, February 3, 1897. Martin Loder woke up. It was about 1:30 AM and someone was shouting at him.

It was his wife Emma.

"Martin, get up!" she screamed. "The store's on fire!" The Loders lived about one hundred yards down the street.

Dressing quickly, Loder jammed his feet into a pair of boots. At the same time, he sent his brother-in-law to rouse the Novaks, who lived a few blocks away, since their son, Frank Novak, owned the dry goods store along with Charles Zabokrtsky. Loder knew that Novak was in the habit of sleeping in the place. In fact, he had last seen Novak behind the counter about an hour and a half ago, preparing to close for the night and then go upstairs to sleep on a small cot. The store had been burglarized about two years ago and Novak had vowed it wouldn't happen again, so he and his partner, whom everyone called Charley Zeb, had been taking turns sleeping there, guarding the store in case the robbers returned.[1]

Loder ran through the blowing snow to the two-story store, the largest building in the little town of Walford. Twenty-three-year-old Joe Strened had already woken up the Novaks and was right behind him. Both men saw the flames flash brightly, breaking out of the second floor window, and Loder could hear the wood cracking and popping. It was then that Strened yelled to Loder that Frank Novak was still inside.[2]

The whole scene was a nightmare. The tavern owner tried opening the heavy front doors, but they were both locked. He picked up a large wooden plank and worked to pry them open, but the plate glass shattered and the doors held fast. A strong odor of gas poured through the broken glass and drove Loder back. Thinking fast, he ran around to the other side of the building and tried several times to raise a ladder to the second floor. It was then that he noticed something curious. The cellar door was open. This was odd, he thought, since he had always known Frank Novak to keep that door locked. Loder dropped the ladder and made a few attempts to enter the cellar but was driven back by the heat and the fear that the gas-fired boiler might explode at any moment.[3]

Now the spreading fire raced through the rest of the building, burning everything in the general store—shelves full of blue work shirts from the nearby Amana colony, overalls, heavy winter jackets, food supplies, tobacco plugs, and other materials.[4] The flames rose high into the night. As the townspeople gathered, there was little to do but stand and watch. Some of the men brought water from a nearby creek in wooden buckets, but their efforts were in vain as the fire raged with an angry ferocity, tearing through the building as if it were some hungry animal with a life of its own, consuming all of the goods on the shelves and eagerly engulfing the row of coffins stacked neatly in one corner on the second floor.

After a while, the firefighting efforts stopped and the townspeople stood by, helpless, the sloshing water in their buckets cooling as they watched the wood frame succumb to the flames. The south wind blew the fire around to the other side of the building and soon the entire structure was ablaze. Everyone began to move back slowly, as if in a trance, staring as the conflagration burned all night, lighting the sky for miles across Benton County.

No one slept very much during the early morning hours of February 3. Most of the hundred or so residents of Walford[5] watched the flames, while a few men worked to keep the fire from spreading to the other buildings in the town, which consisted of a hardware store, saddle and harness business, a small lumber yard, and a creamery.[6] Through the work of the townspeople, these structures were saved but the store and its adjoining bank building were lost.[7]

In the morning, when the weak slanting rays of the winter sun lit the bleak Iowa countryside, everyone saw that the store and bank were destroyed, with nothing left standing but a portion of a blackened brick wall. Someone had hooked up a small hose and was listlessly playing a stream of water back and forth across the wreckage, but the smoke continued to billow, mixing with the short, staccato puffs of air emerging from the townspeople's mouths, giving them the appearance of little steam locomotives.

And Frank Novak was still missing.

Then, on the afternoon of that day, Lars Norland, an implement dealer from nearby Norway, was hosing down the ashes when he saw what appeared to be part of a human ribcage sticking out from the rubble. Martin Loder, Tom Davin, Knute Sampson, and a few others climbed cautiously over the pieces of still-smoldering wood, picking their way past the drifting snow and ice mixed with a thick layer of ashes as Norland helped clear off the debris with his hose.

The body was a few feet from the boiler, lying on the cot that Loder assumed had fallen from the balcony, since that was where Novak usually slept. The remains were unrecognizable, since the corpse's legs were completely burned off, one arm was gone, and the flesh around the scorched face was missing, leaving only a ghastly grimacing skull.

Despite the poor condition of the body, no one doubted that it was Frank Novak's corpse, especially after the searchers discovered several of his personal items under the cot: a pair of pocket scissors, his penknife, and a small metal identification check—#3522—that matched the one Novak always wore on his suspenders. The men also found a partial dental bridge that apparently had fallen from the corpse's mouth onto the dirt floor.[8] This scattering of personal items confirmed what Martin Loder already knew: that Frank Novak had slept in the store that night, as he often did. They gently carried the remains to a shed about fifty feet away from the burned-out basement.

Everyone else in town and in the county, including Benton County Sheriff Sam Metcalf, also assumed that the disfigured corpse found in the ashes was Frank Alfred Novak. How could it have been anyone else? One newspaper report from the town stated that Novak's father was so distraught that he had attempted suicide.[9]

So it was quite a shock when W. I. Endicott, a city editor for the *Cedar Rapids Evening Gazette*, received an urgent telegram from Walford on the afternoon on February 3. A reporter wrote that William Murray, an eighty-three-year-old retired farmer, claimed that his son Edward had not returned home the night before. This was strange, William Murray believed, since he had expected his son back at the farm. He asked many in Walford about Edward's whereabouts, but no one had seen him since the previous evening.

The news that Edward Murray was missing threw the little town into confusion. With the store ruins still smoking, half of the people were convinced that the body was Novak's while the other half now thought that perhaps Edward Murray had died in the fire. The arguments raged all day; some insisted it was Novak because of the four clues found under the corpse and because they knew that he had been sleeping in the store lately; others were positive that the body was Murray's, because the young farmer had been in Novak's store just a few hours before it burned down. A few people were sure that *both* men had died in the flames, and even fewer believed that the bank had been robbed again, and that the burglars decided to cover their tracks by burning down the bank and the store as well.

Soon enough, the authorities stepped in to investigate the fire and the man it had killed. M. J. Tobin, the thirty-two-year-old newly elected Benton County attorney, hustled down from Vinton, about twenty-seven miles north of Walford. The son of Irish immigrants at a time when they faced significant prejudice, Tobin was self-conscious of his background, and although his name was Michael James, he insisted that everyone called him M. J. to obscure his ethnic identity.[10]

Tobin was sharp, streetwise, and stubborn as a terrier. Described as "brilliant" during his years at Cornell College, he had received a law degree from Columbia University several years earlier.[11]

At the scene in Walford, the young attorney had much work to do. He needed to identify the corpse first, but just as important, he also had to determine the sequence of events in the store on Tuesday night.

🖋 🖋 🖋

Tobin knew he'd have to turn to forensics to obtain these answers. Utilizing "science as it pertains to the law,"[12] forensics can include virtually anything pertaining to a crime—from handwriting analysis, bone fragments, and bloody fingerprints to hair samples, shotgun pellets, and DNA. Forensic experts are much more than scientists. They serve as "archaeologists of the near past, who use scientific comparison to recreate plausible scenarios and dismiss implausible ones."[13]

Although the origins of forensic science can be traced back at least 2700 years, it did not begin to be used by law enforcement until about the middle of the nineteenth century. In 1840, during the murder trial of a Frenchwoman named Maria LaFarge, the Marsh Test—used to detect the presence of certain chemicals such as arsenic—was employed, and evidence from this test helped result in a murder conviction of Mrs. LaFarge. It was one of the first times that scientific analysis played such a critical role in a case.[14]

Another invention during that time that had immediate benefits for forensic scientists was Louis Jacques Daguerre and Henry Fox Talbot's process of capturing images through use of a polished silver-plated copper sheet with a thin coating of iodine. These daguerreotypes were the forerunner of photographs. The images caught the eye of a young American writer named Edgar Allan Poe, who wrote several essays on this new invention.[15]

One of the first men to advocate the use of photography to identify and apprehend criminals was a Chicago deputy sheriff named Allan Pinkerton, a Scotch immigrant who later founded the famous detective agency that bore his name. Known as "The Eye" because of his constant search for clues, Pinkerton documented the physical appearance of hundreds of suspects—tattoos, birthmarks, and any other obvious characteristics. Other police departments followed his lead, and the use of photographs to identify criminals became more prevalent. In 1859, the United States became the first country to use photographs as evidence in court.[16]

By the latter part of the nineteenth century, the evolving field of forensic science was becoming more advanced, especially in Austria and France. While some attribute the spread of modern forensics to men like Hans Gross, a scientist and professor of law at the University of Graz in Austria, Dr. Jean-Alexandre-Eugene Lacassagne also was recognized as a pioneer. In 1881, as a professor of forensic medicine at the University of Lyon in France, Lacassagne was one of the first to employ scientific research and specific medical procedures at the crime scene. He discovered that in many criminal cases, "death leaves a signature, and [the students] would learn to read the meaning: a peaceful death versus a violent one, a death by accident, suicide or crime."[17]

Lacassagne understood the significance of bullet strike marks and was among the first scientists to match a bullet with the gun that fired it. He also learned that the pattern of bloodstains could divulge important information.[18] His practice of utilizing scientific methodology at crime scenes became recognized in other countries and by the 1890s, some American forensic experts had many weapons in their arsenal. Among these were handwriting analysis, forensic dentistry, chemical testing, and even photomicrography, the study of photographs taken through a microscope.

🌿 🌿 🌿

With all of these techniques for amassing evidence available to him, County Attorney Tobin immediately took charge of the scene in Walford. He organized a coroner's inquest, gathering several eyewitnesses while also sending for three more people: a dental assistant from Cedar Rapids who had treated Frank Novak, and two physicians. One of the doctors, Benton County Coroner C. B. Chenoweth, had already come from Newhall to preside at the inquest, which was held in the poolroom of Martin Loder's saloon. The other man, a prominent Cedar Rapids doctor named Wencil Ruml, arrived the following day.[19]

To establish a timetable for the events that led up the fire in the early morning of February 3, Tobin called a number of locals to testify before the coroner's jury, beginning with Loder. The saloon-keeper recalled that he had seen Frank Novak and Edward Murray twice that Tuesday night—first in his tavern at about 9:00 PM and then again in Novak's store at about 11:00 PM. The second time occurred when a couple of farm boys, Jake Haage and Mike Houser, had come into town on a horse-drawn sleigh. They woke up Loder and told him they were having a party and wanted to buy some beer and tobacco. Since Loder did not sell tobacco, he suggested that they all walk over to the general store, where Haage and Houser purchased some chewing tobacco, candy, and cigars from Novak. The boys talked to Ed Murray for a little while and then followed the saloonkeeper back to his tavern, where he sold them a small keg of beer. Loder also thought it was worth mentioning that there was some bad blood between Ed Murray, Murray's brothers, and Frank Novak.[20]

Then Tobin showed Loder a pocketknife, an identification check, and a pair of scissors. The saloonkeeper wasn't sure about the knife but swore that the scissors and identification check belonged to Novak. After examining the corpse's mouth and remains, Loder said that there was absolutely no doubt it was the body of his neighbor.[21]

After a few more witnesses, one of whom testified that the gas boiler in the store's basement had been shut off and probably had not contributed to the fire, Nellie Murray Shea was called before the coroner's jury. A widow who lived on a farm outside of Walford, Nellie Shea was one of Edward Murray's sisters, and she disagreed with Loder about the corpse's identity. Mrs. Shea had been convinced that the body was Ed Murray's as soon as she saw it carried out of the store's cellar on the afternoon of February 3. At that time, she had spotted a scrap of cloth under the corpse's neck and noticed that the color and pattern of the fabric matched that of a shirt her brother often wore. That shirt, she recalled, was blue, made of a drilled material, and had a pattern of stars and crescent moons. She also had noticed remnants of a St. Joseph's cord, a thin white rope worn around the waist by Catholics as a sign of chastity.[22]

Then Louis Hasek testified before the three-man jury. Hasek was only eighteen years old but had already spent four years in Cedar Rapids as a dental assistant for two dentists named Drs. Brotherton and Whelply. Although he had no dental degree or certificate at the time, Hasek had been employed at the practice for so long that he was an expert at plate work and general dentistry. Hasek added that whenever the dentists were busy, he would do the examinations and determine what was needed. The dental assistant also knew Novak well and had been in Walford only two weeks before, having had supper at the older man's house on January 19.[23] At that time, Novak had showed Hasek some bridgework and had asked the young man to repair it for him. This bridge, Hasek testified, consisted of a molar, bicuspid, and two open-faced caps on the upper right side. He also noted that two bicuspids were missing from the left side of Novak's mouth, where he had and placed a new bridge.[24]

Tobin leaned forward intently.

"Doctor, examine this bridgework on which a black thread is tied . . . and tell this jury what it is."

Hasek didn't hesitate.

"This is the bridgework of the upper left side, that on the nineteenth day of January I fitted in Frank Novak's mouth," he said, adding that "it was the bridge made to take the place of the two upper bicuspids on the left side."

Tobin next asked Hasek to inspect the skull in front of him. He did so, pausing for a moment before saying, "I now find from an examination of the upper jaw of this corpse, . . . which was taken from the ruins of the Novak fire, that it has the two bicuspids on the upper left jaw there." Hasek also stated that "to the best of my judgment as an assistant dentist and one who has examined the mouth of Frank Novak, the upper jaw of this corpse is not that of Frank Novak. . . . I further find that the bridge which would fit Frank Novak's upper right-hand jaw will not fit the upper right-hand jaw of the corpse before the coroner's jury." Hasek concluded, "From my examination of Frank Novak's mouth on the nineteenth day of January 1897, and the examination which [I] have made on this fourth day of February 1897 of the mouth of the said corpse before the coroner's jury, I solemnly swear that the jaw and head on the corpse before the coroner's jury is not the jaw and head of Frank Novak."[25]

Dr. Ruml, the Cedar Rapids physician, also testified. After first demanding twenty-five dollars in "expert fees" from the coroner, Ruml examined the corpse, confirming Hasek's finding that two incisors were missing from the upper left jaw. The doctor added that they had been gone for a long time. Turning the skull over carefully in his hands to examine the scorched bone, Ruml was surprised to find a fracture on the left side, which had resulted in a fist-sized clot of baked blood.

"That blood clot would suggest to me that there was bleeding within the skull," he noted.

"From your examination of the skull at the present time, would you consider the man received an injury previous to death?" Tobin asked.

"On account of the severe mutilation of the remaining portions of the skull, it is impossible for me to state," Dr. Ruml replied. He refused to say, based on the evidence before him, whether a blow to the skull had occurred prior to death.[26]

The next day, after listening to testimony from many other eyewitnesses, including Novak's business partner and brother-in-law Charles Zabokrtsky, Tobin had only one question for the coroner's jury: "Whose body lies before you here?"

The answers from the three Walford men on the jury—A. J. Riley, Henry Tuttle, and W. B. Russell—were unanimous:

"Ed Murray."

TWO

•————————————————————•

The Bohemian Immigrant's
Clever Son

For as long as he could remember, Frank Alfred Novak, the oldest of John and Anna Novak's four children, believed that he was better than anyone else. He was clever and possessed of a mind that churned out intricate moneymaking schemes as fast as a hay baler. Even as a young boy, Frank knew that he was destined for great things, and was determined to do whatever he could to achieve his dreams. But he began his life in humble circumstances. Like so many of the farmers in and around the Cedar Rapids area, his parents were immigrants from Bohemia. This area of Europe, part of the Austro-Hungarian Empire in the 1830s and now the Czech Republic, produced hundreds of thousands of immigrants in the nineteenth century.[1] Many of them journeyed from the East Coast by train to settle in Johnson and Linn Counties in Iowa.

Jan Nowak, renamed John Novak after he came to the United States, was born in Rychnov nad Kneznou, a small town in northeastern Bohemia, on April 4, 1839.[2] Situated in the foothills of the Orlicke Mountains, about 150 miles east of Prague, Rychnov could trace its origins back to the first millennium BC, but the town was not officially included in any records of the area until 1258 AD. Although it prospered due to its location on the trade route to Kladsko and Slezsko, in many ways, nothing ever seemed to change in this part of Bohemia. In fact, the town's medieval wooden structures, old-style shops scattered around the town square, and trade guilds survived for hundreds of years.[3]

In 1848, Austria eliminated serfdom and the area received its first constitution.[4] Most of the newly minted citizens were illiterate farmers and laborers who lived in great poverty. What began as a trickle of immigrants heading for America soon became a torrent. They made their way from the German port city of Bremen to the United States, initially settling in the state of Wisconsin, in towns with strange-sounding names like "Milvanky [Milwaukee]" and "Rezyna [Racine]." By 1860, there were about seven thousand Bohemian immigrants in that area.[5] But they also fanned out to other states, including Texas, Minnesota, Nebraska, and Iowa. To many of these immigrants, Iowa, with its rich soil, was indeed the Promised Land.[6] Thousands of Bohemians lived in Cedar Rapids and Iowa City, and in Howard, Johnson, Jones, Linn, Tama, Washington, and Winneshiek counties. In fact, the last-named county was home to so many Bohemians that the famed Bohemian composer Antonin Dvorak spent a summer in the town of Spillville, Iowa, where he composed his well-known Symphony No. 9 in E Minor, "From the New World."[7]

The first Bohemians came to Linn County in about 1852, when many of them began working at the T. M. Sinclair meat packing plant in Cedar Rapids.[8] At the time, the place was no more than a small village; there were no railroads or even a bridge over the Cedar River yet. In fact, Cedar Rapids did not have any brick buildings until about three years later.[9] While some Bohemians worked in the city, others became farmers, applying the few hardscrabble agricultural skills they had learned in their native land to the fertile black soil of Iowa.

Jan Nowak was one of those early immigrants. When he was about sixteen years old, Nowak secured passage to the United States and in 1855 settled in Johnson County, southeast of Cedar Rapids. Somewhere during this time, like so many other immigrants, he anglicized the pronunciation and spelling of his name to John Novak. The surname was and still is very common in eastern Iowa. In fact, according to a current resident of the area, "you can't swing a dead cat around here without hitting a Novak."[10]

After working for other farmers, John Novak managed to save enough money to purchase a tract of about eighty acres in Linn County.[11] He worked this land for two years, then sold the parcel and bought two hundred sixty acres, also in Linn County. The soil of his new property turned out to be quite rich even by Iowa standards, and the acreage became extremely valuable. For seventeen years, Novak thrived by raising crops and livestock. In 1880, the census listed the prosperous immigrant as living in Clinton Township with his wife, Anna (Cherveny), whom he had married in 1864. They had four children—sixteen-year-old Frank, born in Solon on April 5, 1864; Blanch, thirteen; Milo, nine; and Anna, six.[12] But John Novak was restless by nature and was never content with his current business interests. He was confident that he could make more money exploring new opportunities beyond the sphere of farming or land speculation.

The little settlement of Terry caught his eye. Located in the southwestern corner of Benton County, a short distance from the Amana Colonies, the area was relatively unpopulated, having been last surveyed on May 27, 1884, by W. W. Sheldon. In that year, the Chicago, Milwaukee and St. Paul Railway had established a secondary line to Terry from Marion, Iowa. Five years later, on November 11, 1889, the town's name was officially changed to Walford, because the U.S. Post Office was having trouble delivering the mail; thanks to the fancy handwritten "P's" and "T's" of the time, letters and packages for Terry were consistently sent to the town of Perry, Iowa, by mistake.[13] Oddly enough, no reason why the name of Walford was selected has ever been verified. No one in the immediate vicinity was named Walford and the only other places with that name are a town and a parish in Herefordshire, England. Like the trademarked name of Betty Crocker, Walford appears to have been a name of convenience, possibly coined by the U.S. Post Office.

The availability of cheap land parcels in Walford must have

dazzled John Novak, but he wasn't thinking about farming. He was quick to see the advantage in having a business close by a railroad terminus. So Novak sold his prosperous farm, took on a new associate, and in 1891 established a grain and lumber business in Walford. His new business partner was enthusiastic, driven, and charming. Residents of Walford and Cedar Rapids were generally impressed with the young man's enthusiasm. He was polished, seemed to be a good businessman, and could talk the ears off a stalled mule. Anyone who met him could see that he was different from most of the other farmers' sons, since he had plans and aspirations far beyond that of a little settlement on the Iowa plains. Clearly destined for success beyond Walford, this young man was primed and ready to make his mark on the world. As one newspaper put it, John Novak's business partner was a "good fellow, the best of the kind in all the country for miles around and that reputation brought him business."[14]

The new business associate was John Novak's oldest son, twenty-seven-year-old Frank, whose future looked limitless based on his own energy and initiative, especially when coupled with his father's considerable wealth.

🌿 🌿 🌿

The promising young entrepreneur Frank Novak had a mostly happy childhood, although one curious incident occurred when he was about four years old. While playing with some matches next to a stack of dried wheat, he tossed a lit match into a sheaf, starting a large fire.[15] The story was that his father was so upset that he threw young Frank into the flames to teach him a lesson. In reality, his angry father had only threatened to pitch Frank into the burning wheat. Although he vehemently denied it later, the young Novak's infatuation with fire exceeded that of other boys and girls; in fact, he never outgrew it. Later in his life, he became a suspect in several mysterious fires. Novak simply liked to watch things burn.

It was quickly apparent that Novak did not have the constitution of a hard-working farm boy. Physically, he was bow-legged, had weak

ankles, and was somewhat frail. Moreover, he despised farm work.[16]
He was an indolent boy, especially when it came to hard work. Initially, as the oldest male in the family, he was expected to become
a farmer like his father, but Frank did not believe that he was cut
from the same cloth as his plodding Old World forebears. Perhaps
he thought of his father and grandfather as powerful draught horses,
dully plowing through the endless rolling fields, while he saw himself
as a fast, spirited thoroughbred. From an early age, he displayed a
quick mind and infectious enthusiasm, and it seemed clear to everyone who met him that Frank Novak was destined for success. He
had something that made him different from the other farm boys,
something that set him apart. It was raw ambition—the desire to
make his mark in the world—that pushed him, and Frank knew that
he couldn't achieve anything as long as he was trapped on that farm.
Just the possibility of remaining on the farm sickened him, and he
might have wished for wings so that he could float above the dull
green cornstalks and reach for the greatness that appeared to be just
out of his grasp.

His father understood. He knew that his oldest son's future did not
lie in raising corn or wheat and so John Novak made every attempt to
make sure that Frank was prepared for a career in business. Novak
attended school in Cedar Rapids and also may have taken a business
course at Iowa City. As a young man, his first job was as a salesman
for F. J. Upton & Company, a Cedar Rapids firm that managed the
enormous Star Wagon factory.[17]

After his marriage to childhood sweetheart Mary Shunka on February 14, 1888, Novak moved from Cedar Rapids to Walford, which
was still named Terry, and began working for Miner & Company as
a grain purchaser. But he was not one to stay with one company for
very long, nor was he particularly interested in working for someone else. Restless by nature like his father, he decided that he would
rather start his own grain business and use the granary as a stepping-
stone for other, larger companies. His zeal for adding new business
ventures was coupled with a keen, rapacious mind that absorbed

everything around him. In 1891, Novak convinced his father to invest in a lumber company. Along with the grain business, it was the beginning of what Frank Novak envisioned would be a boom in the small town. Located in what one newspaper referred to as a "hilly wilderness," the rolling terrain around Walford reminded some people of New York State's Catskill Mountains.[18]

The little town seemed to have a lot going for it. Walford already had a post office, and of course Novak made sure that he became its postmaster. Both Novaks realized that Walford held the promise of a bright future primarily because it was located on a railroad spur line and surrounded by lush farmland, land that was plowed by hardworking Bohemian, German, and Norwegian immigrants. But much more than his father, Frank Novak saw money—lots of it, in gold and silver—lying just beneath the surface of the dark soil, like seeds of corn sown the year before waiting to be cultivated and harvested.

He seemed to have an insatiable appetite for any new business endeavors. Novak quickly made the little town his own Corn Belt fiefdom, both on a business and social level. He became active in political circles, traveling constantly between Walford and Cedar Rapids. His name popped up frequently in the Cedar Rapids papers, with the *Cedar Rapids Evening Gazette* duly noting his comings and goings on a regular basis.[19] Novak was clever about publicity and loved seeing his name in print. He made sure to drop by the newspaper offices whenever he was in town. The *Gazette* obliged by listing him in the society column, marking the frequent times that the Walford businessman "Sundayed in the city."[20]

In addition to all of his business efforts, Novak always set aside time for social activities as well. He was a popular guest at parties, an accomplished violinist who was much sought after for dances. Whether it was in Walford or Cedar Rapids, Novak attended many parties, playing his violin, tapping out the beat with his shoe to help liven up the long Iowa winters. Many of the women at these dances looked upon Novak with warmth and affection, admiring his cleverness and his pleasing personality. He made a sharp contrast to their boring husbands, men who did little but work in the fields for six days a week.

He also dressed the part of a wealthy merchant. John Novak's son wore "diamonds of the first magnitude . . . drove the finest horses and spent with a lavish hand." His way of life was becoming "extravagant," according to one newspaper account.[21] Young Frank also dabbled in politics and joined the Republican Party. One of the party's candidates he supported was a thirty-two-year-old Vinton attorney who was running for Benton County attorney. The young lawyer's name was M. J. Tobin.[22]

Thanks to these efforts, Benton County residents counted Frank Novak as one of its rising young businessmen, a man with a bright future that stretched far over the horizon, away from the small town on the spur line, possibly to the national stage. Supremely confident, Novak believed that there was nothing he couldn't accomplish. He had big ideas and was eager to implement them. Going into the lumber business in Walford with his father was just the beginning. In addition, he was now investing in the grain market on his own, scrutinizing the daily fluctuations on the Chicago Board of Trade.[23] One way or another, he was going to amass a fortune. Nothing, he probably thought, was going to stop him.

But five years after moving to Walford, he felt frustrated. For no matter how hard he worked, none of his business plans seemed to go smoothly. The money seemed to go out much faster than it was entered into his ledger. His lumber and creamery businesses were not very profitable. Although he still operated a granary—and played the Chicago grain market on the side—he must have believed that he was wasting his time and that none of these commercial enterprises would ever make much money. He needed to diversify his businesses, so after assessing the needs of the town, he decided to open a general store with his brother-in-law, a man named Wencil Jilek, who also was the son of a Bohemian immigrant.

This time Novak's business sense was on the mark. The new store was an instant success and quickly became a vital part of Walford, not only for its inventory but also as a social gathering place for the town. But soon after the store was built, Jilek died in a freak train accident on a trip to Chicago. Less than two years later, the Novak & Jilek store burned to the ground.

Undaunted, Novak decided to build a new, larger store, and threw himself into the project, engaging some builders and contractors to draw up the blueprints.[24] He wanted to make sure that this structure would not only have everything that the former store lacked, but would be bigger and better, using the best construction materials available. Novak wanted to utilize this new place as a springboard for other business opportunities. The new general store would be two stories high, with a second floor gallery that could be used for meetings and dances where Novak could play his violin.[25] Maple wood was used for much of the flooring; the thick doors were built of solid wood while the windows were constructed out of expensive plate glass. The place would have room to sell clothing made at the nearby Amana Community along with dozens of other necessities that a general store typically stocked—about three hundred bags of flour, a variety of foods such as cured hams and sausages, dried fruit, tobacco, and candy.[26] All told, the new store had about six thousand dollars worth of inventory.[27]

Perhaps the most important feature of the new building, which measured twenty-two feet in height by twenty-four feet in width by seventy-two feet deep,[28] was the independent lighting and heating system, something still quite innovative for a small town. Novak employed a man named M. D. Snavely to install a gas plant in the basement for light along with a boiler that would provide coal-powered heat throughout the store. The gas plant was considered a real technological advance, as most rural Iowans still used kerosene lamps to light their homes and businesses.

Next to the store was Novak's pride and joy, a small building that would serve the community as a bank. For a long time, Walford had needed its own bank, or at least someone who could handle financial transactions for the farmers and local businesses. Cedar Rapids,

about twelve miles away to the northeast, was simply too far to go by
horse and buggy on a regular basis for business or personal bank-
ing. Novak had done some informal money transactions in the past,
using the old store's safe, and it just made sense, as he was rebuilding
anyway, to draw up plans for a small adjoining bank building. This
addition was just large enough for a safe, a counter, and a small con-
sultation room.

With his new place opened in late April of 1896, the Walford businessman was apparently content, for he not only ran the store but
also operated the only bank for miles around.[29] He also still helped
his father run a lumber business and creamery and even sold a few insurance policies.[30] To almost everyone in town, it seemed as if Novak
had fully recovered from the death of his business partner Jilek in
1893 and the fire that destroyed the store.

He was on top again.

Then one day in the spring of 1896, a farmer named James Havlicek sold some livestock for about five thousand dollars. Naturally,
Havlicek was worried about possessing such a large sum of money
and was not sure where he could keep it safely. He asked Frank Novak
if the money could be held in the store's bank until later, when the
farmer would decide what to do with it. Certainly, Novak replied, that
would not be a problem, and he deposited the money in the large safe.

That same night, on May 4, 1896, burglars robbed the bank, blew
open the safe and made off with all of the money, including the poor
farmer's newly deposited cash.[31] What was strange, many of the townspeople thought, was that although the money was gone, the account-
ing books were all intact.[32]

Shaken by this robbery, Novak told his friends that he had devised
a plan to thwart any future burglaries. He and his new business partner Charles Zabokrtsky—like Jilek, one of Novak's brothers-in-law—
would take turns guarding the place, sleeping on a small cot on the
second floor. But Novak also wanted revenge and dreamed up a
clever scheme in case the burglars should ever return. In either late

December 1896 or early January 1897, he met with a doctor in Cedar Rapids, a fellow Bohemian named F. J. Woitishek, and asked him for a favor. Apparently, when the burglars struck Novak's store earlier, they drank from a bottle of whiskey that he had kept behind the counter. If they ever returned, Novak wanted to set a trap for them, and planned to add morphine to a bottle of whiskey.

How much of this drug, Novak asked the physician, would it take to "lay a man out?"[33] Dr. Woitishek answered that about one-eighth to half a grain of morphine—a grain being a small unit of weight equal to 1/438th of an ounce—would be sufficient, but that Novak had to be extremely careful, as someone else might drink from the bottle by mistake.

Novak persisted. Would one grain put someone to sleep?

Yes, the doctor answered.

Would two or three grains of morphine kill a man?

Certainly, Dr. Woitishek replied.

Novak then asked the physician to obtain some morphine for him. Dr. Woitishek refused but because Novak was so insistent, he mentioned that morphine could be obtained from a druggist without a prescription, as long as the purchaser signed what was called a poison register. This was a detailed ledger that listed the names of individuals, types of poison they purchased, and the intended use of each substance.[34]

Now satisfied, Novak left Cedar Rapids and returned to Walford. It is not known whether he purchased any morphine at that time.

Back home, he worked out a schedule for Charley Zeb and himself. They would alternate months sleeping at the store. Zabokrtsky had taken December and Frank had slept in the store in January. February was supposed to be Charley's turn, but since his wife—Frank's sister Anna—was pregnant, Frank graciously offered to sleep at the store in February as well. He also suggested that the two partners take turns every three months instead of every month, with Novak handling the first three-month shift, beginning in February.

To be sure, Charley Zeb was pleased with Novak's offer. Novak's brother-in-law didn't relish the idea of sleeping on a narrow cot if he could help it. Iowa winters are long and cold, and even though the store had four radiators and a coal-fired boiler, it could be drafty. Moreover, the crude cot, which he had built himself, was barely large enough for a man, measuring only twenty-four inches across and about six feet long. He much preferred sleeping at his father-in-law's warm, comfortable house.

On February 2, 1897, after a bitterly cold day with howling winds and blowing, drifting snow, Charley Zeb counted the store's till, which amounted to roughly three hundred dollars.[35] He and Novak locked up the place at about 9:00 PM and walked over to Martin Loder's tavern, where they had a few glasses of beer with some other customers, one of whom was a drifter named Edward Murray.

It wasn't surprising that Murray was at Loder's place. Anyone who spent any time with Ed Murray quickly learned two things about him: he possessed an insatiable need for any kind of alcohol and he had a terrible set of teeth. His mouth was in such bad shape that his father constantly urged him to have some false teeth made, but the son never did. The best he could manage was to grow a beard, which helped draw attention from the missing left upper incisors.[36] But despite Ed's whiskers, one could still see the jagged holes in his mouth. Perhaps he would have liked to purchase a dental bridge, but he never seemed to have any money. Ed Murray hadn't always been poor, but for the past eight years or so, bad luck had been his constant companion.

Edward Murray was born on February 9, 1865. His father, William, an Irish immigrant, owned a farm about a mile or so west of Walford and had lived there for many years with his wife and nine children. Ed Murray grew up on the family farm, but became restless and decided to strike out on his own. In 1886, when he was twenty-one, Murray traveled out to western Iowa and began farming near Portsmouth, close to the Nebraska border.[37] One of his sisters, Alice, had moved there several years earlier and Murray had decided to follow her lead.

After a few years, trouble began to stalk Edward Murray. First, he lost all of his crops to a hailstorm. Then the hogs he was raising died of cholera and the young farmer "got despaired," as his father said later. Edward decided to sell whatever he had left and support himself as an itinerant laborer.[38] Before he left the Portsmouth area, Alice gave him a St. Joseph's cord, something that devout Catholics wore around the waist. The cord had seven knots, each one symbolizing the joys and sorrows of Jesus at the time of his crucifixion. According to Catholic tradition, the cord was supposed to be especially important to the wearer at the time of death.[39] Ed Murray was pleased with this gift. He thanked his sister and dutifully tied the St. Joseph's cord around his waist. Even though he may not have been an especially religious man, he would wear the cord for the rest of his life.

By this time, Murray had become a serious drinker. Although it's possible people noted his drinking in part because it fit the nineteenth-century stereotype of Irish men, many reports named him "a hard-drinking sort of fellow"[40] or a "heavy-drinking bachelor,"[41] someone who was "a sort of simple fellow . . . a man who was given to his cups" and someone who "would take a drink when he got a chance."[42]

After going out on the road, Ed Murray drifted for years and spent a little time in the Benton County jail as well as the prison in Cedar Rapids, returning to the Walford area in about 1894 or 1895. He was a good worker, especially as a cornhusker. His father later said that Ed had worked for him off and on for many years and had husked all of the corn on the Murray farm during the 1896 harvesting season. By that time, William Murray was retired and living in Cedar Rapids, but he still owned the farm outside of Walford, where his thirty-six-year-old daughter Nellie lived.[43] Since Ed had nowhere else to stay, he had been living with her and their forty-seven-year-old brother

James, helping out with the chores around the farm. The work was hard, but things slowed down somewhat during the winter months after the crops had been harvested. Since he lived so close to Walford, Ed Murray liked to go and socialize with his friends. The night that Novak's store burned down, Ed Murray went into town to have a drink.

THREE

Down on the Ground

At the end of the initial hearing, Tobin had the physical evidence of the body, the dental bridge and other personal items found under the cot, Louis Hasek's statement that the skull was not Frank Novak's, and expert testimony from Dr. Ruml on the condition of the skull, especially concerning what appeared to be a fracture and subsequent clotted blood. He also recorded the statement of Nellie Murray Shea, who swore that the charred corpse still had remnants of a shirt that Ed Murray had worn, along with a few pieces of a St. Joseph's cord. Finally, the county attorney had established a timeline—leading up to sworn testimony that Frank Novak and Edward Murray were last seen together in the store on the night of February 2, less than a few hours before the fire broke out.

Tobin did some more digging and discovered that Frank Novak had taken out twenty-seven thousand dollars in life insurance policies from five different companies. In further discussions with some of Novak's acquaintances as well as some employees from a Cedar Rapids bank, Tobin learned that the Walford businessman was heavily in debt, a longtime loser in the Chicago grain market, and a compulsive gambler who was a fixture at Cedar Rapids card tables and roulette wheels for years. One paper described him as "a plunger and like all plungers not backed by great resources, was a loser."[1]

Reports published in the *Gazette* also raised questions about a string of puzzling incidents that had happened to Novak over the years. For example, there was the 1893 death of his business partner and brother-in-law Wencil Jilek, who fell from a train while he and Novak were traveling together to the Chicago World's Fair. It was rumored that Novak had taken out a life insurance policy on Jilek, but no proof was ever found regarding this story.[2]

At about the same time, Novak was accused of stealing money from a safe at the Walford train station, but once again nothing was proven and no charges were ever filed. Then, in 1895, while his father and mother were on vacation in Bohemia, came the fire that burned down the Novak and Jilek general store, destroying everything inside. The theory was that burglars had entered the place, blown open the small safe inside, and then set fire to the building to eliminate any evidence. Thousands of dollars in currency was missing—money that Novak had been holding for local farmers—as well as the store's cash box. The money was never recovered, although a number of bonds were later found in woods nearby.

After finding out about these events, combined with Novak's alleged debt problems and the life insurance policies, Tobin concluded that the Walford man had a strong motive for murder. He believed that Novak had concocted a plan to kill someone of a similar height and weight, destroy the body, and start a new life. If he could get away with this scheme, his wife would receive the insurance money and Novak would be freed from his current financial burdens.

But something still didn't add up, especially to his family and friends. It seemed incomprehensible to many of them that Novak didn't resort to conventional business practices as a means to pay off his debtors. As a businessman, he certainly must have realized that he could avoid bankruptcy by establishing payment schedules. "But why," one of his friends asked a reporter, "did he not protect local creditors, settle outside claims the best that he could and go on with business? The people of Walford thought everything of him and would have stood by him to the end."[3]

Moreover, his friends claimed that any past problems that had plagued Novak were not due to illegal activities. According to them, he had just had a run of bad luck. His supporters agreed that he was a popular man, well liked by many in Walford and Cedar Rapids, and simply had more bad breaks than most people. Despite Tobin's discoveries, Novak remained a highly regarded figure in Walford, a man who was active socially and had "given liberally to church and school entertainments . . . his name was the synonym for all that was good and chivalrous."[4]

But others disagreed with this assessment. An anonymous detective told a *Gazette* reporter that Novak had a long history of operating outside the law. Besides allegations of Novak's improprieties as postmaster of Walford, this detective may have been referring to an 1891 case in Cedar Rapids, where some money was stolen from an office safe.[5]

"I can hardly understand how Frank Novak was permitted to continue his career for as long as he did. Six years ago, I investigated some of his conduct and at once advised his arrest. Because the evidence in the case was largely circumstantial the parties interested failed to prosecute, but there was no question in my mind as to his guilt."[6]

Amid all of the allegations and rumors, the main question now was where Frank Novak had gone. If it was true that the body removed from the ruined store was that of Edward Murray, some people proposed that there must be a second corpse in the rubble. That theory was quickly discounted. No shred of evidence—bone fragments or anything else—of another body was ever discovered. Outside of a small circle of Novak's family and friends, most Iowans believed that Novak was still alive and had simply disappeared, vanishing into the cold February night. In all, the sequence of events in Walford was, as one newspaper concluded, a "mystery boundless and fathomless."[7]

Determined to solve this mystery, the Benton County attorney forged ahead. It was, some people thought later, as if he was put on the earth for the express purpose of gathering evidence in this case. Persistent and tenacious to the point of obsession, Tobin was well suited to the task.

Michael James Tobin was born in Oswego, New York, on May 1, 1865, a first-generation American like millions of others in the late nine-teenth century.[8] His parents, Richard and Catherine, had fled the Irish potato famine in about 1840. The times were so terrible in Ire-land that both of Richard Tobin's parents had died of starvation.[9] Richard, the oldest of the five orphaned children, managed to scrape together enough money to immigrate to the United States, and after he settled in Oswego, brought the next eldest sibling to America, and the next, until finally all five brothers and sisters were in this country.

M. J. grew up in Oswego with three brothers and one sister. He was educated in the public school system as well as the Oswego Normal School. By the time he was about sixteen or seventeen, he attended classes during the day and worked at the Empire telephone office on West Utica Street at night. After he graduated from the Normal School in 1882, at the age of seventeen, Tobin traveled west to Vinton, Iowa, where his uncle, the Reverend Thomas Tobin, was principal of Tilford Academy, which he had founded in 1871. In fact, M. J. Tobin's older brother Thomas, named for their uncle, also worked at the school as a teacher.[10]

M. J. Tobin taught at Tilford for several years and saved whatever money he could for college tuition. He may have taken some college level courses at Tilford, for he entered Cornell College as a sopho-more in 1885 and quickly rose to prominence. He was elected presi-dent of his class for that year and served as a delegate for a collegiate convention in Des Moines in 1887 while still employed as a professor of elocution and gymnastics at Tilford. By his senior year, he was president of the Amphictyon Literary Society and clearly had made his mark at the college. According to the *Sibylline*, the 1888 yearbook for Cornell College, "M. J. Tobin, of Vinton, is becoming celebrated as a Historiographer and Physicist."[11]

Tobin graduated from Cornell College in 1888 and was accepted into Columbia University School of Law in New York. After graduat-ing, he returned to Iowa with his degree and was accepted into the Iowa bar in 1893. The driven young attorney quickly set up a small law office in Vinton.

Three years later, in 1896, Tobin was elected Benton County attorney. Although Frank Novak had voted for him, it was pure coincidence that the Walford case was Tobin's first as an elected official. Despite his lack of experience, Tobin attacked the Novak case with his customary relish, assimilating each piece of evidence from the fire, knowing that he had his work cut out for him.[12]

       ᵂ ᵂ ᵂ

Back in Walford, despite the results of the coroner's inquest, some doubts still lingered regarding the identity of the body discovered in the ashes. Despite the medical forensics and the testimony given, Novak's parents still believed that the corpse was their son Frank. On the other hand, Murray's relatives insisted that the body was Edward's. The anger between the two families was palpable, and seemed capable of escalating into violence.

Tobin knew there was no time to lose. After the coroner's jury had decided that the body was Ed Murray, the attorney immediately ordered the Benton County sheriff, Sam Metcalf, to disseminate information on Novak. Metcalf had a flyer printed and telegraphed across the country, making sure that it went out to a number of large cities and seaports:

$200.00 REWARD!

Frank Novak is wanted at Vinton, Iowa, being charged with Murder and Arson. He is a Bohemian; about 32 years old; weight about 175-lbs; heighth [sic] 5 feet 8 inches; has seal brown hair; large brown eyes; short mustache, slightly sandy; broad forehead. When last seen was wearing a hunting jacket under an overcoat; wore German socks. Carried a double barrel shot gun. Wore a diamond ring on right hand.

The above reward will be paid by the undersigned in addition to what the Governor of the state may offer for his arrest and delivery.

Wire all information to S. H. METCALF, Sheriff,

I. S. S. A.   Vinton, Iowa.[13]

Meanwhile, Tobin continued his investigation.

He found that many eyewitnesses had seen Novak's cousin, Jo, along with Frank's business partner Charley Zeb, slip into the bank vault after the fire and remove some papers. Jo Novak had taken some of these documents to a Cedar Rapids attorney named Clemons, who was keeping them for the Novak family. Jo also was vigorously pursuing payment of Frank Novak's insurance policies through the five different insurance companies. Like the rest of the family and many people in eastern Iowa, Jo Novak was unimpressed by the results of the coroner's inquest and remained adamant that the body found in the store's ruins was Frank Novak.[14]

🌿 🌿 🌿

Despite the doubts after the coroner's jury ruling, M. J. Tobin released the burned corpse to William Murray, who brought it back to the family farm outside of Walford. The old man spent most of Friday night and all day Saturday keeping a vigil by his son's coffin. Then on Sunday, the family traveled a few miles west to the little town of Norway, where they were parishioners at St. Michael's Catholic Church. Just outside of Norway was the church's cemetery, built on a small hill overlooking a few large farms. A grave had been dug in the family plot and after a few prayers Edward Murray was buried next to his brother Daniel, who had been killed by a train the year before. As he stood on the hill overlooking the snow-covered Iowa fields, William Murray no doubt was thinking about the crushing loss of two of his sons within a six-month period. He was especially aggrieved over this recent death, since Ed's thirty-second birthday would have been just a few days later, on February 9.

The disfigured body was not destined to remain undisturbed for long. A few days after the burial, William Murray was back at St. Michael's Cemetery, along with Tobin, Dr. Chenoweth, and Sheriff Metcalf. Tobin had decided that the corpse should be exhumed, since he might need the skull and the stomach for evidence.

Tobin, Murray, and the others watched as the gravediggers dug down through the frozen earth, lifted the coffin out of the hole, and raised the lid. The coroner grimly severed the head from the spine, removed the corpse's stomach, and gave both body parts to Tobin, who placed them into a satchel. He had decided to keep the disfigured skull himself because he wanted another physician to examine it, someone with more experience than Dr. Chenoweth. Tobin was particularly interested in the shriveled brain and a small amount of baked blood inside the cranium. The attorney also knew that the skull and its missing teeth would be an integral part of any future trial and he did not want to risk the chance of it being stolen or misplaced in the upcoming weeks or months.

Tobin returned to Vinton and took the skull to Dr. C. C. Griffin, a practicing physician and surgeon for three decades.[15] In the next few days, Griffin and Dr. J. P. Whitney, his associate, performed a detailed examination of the skull, brain, and stomach to determine if a blow to the head had caused the skull to shatter. Both physicians also analyzed the stomach, but it was badly burned and its contents had long since evaporated. Just to be sure, however, Tobin sent the stomach to a laboratory for analysis.[16]

Of course, none of the events at Walford and the subsequent investigation went unnoticed by the press. Even as the fire burned, reporters in eastern Iowa hurried to file their stories. The newspapers of the era were fiercely competitive and they each tried to outdo the others with sensational headlines and lurid descriptions of the scene. "Death in Flames" shouted one headline from the *Marshalltown Evening Times Republican* in the immediate aftermath. The paper bemoaned Novak's run of misfortunes, noting that he had suffered a similar fire two years ago and burglary last year. In addition, the paper speculated that robbers had returned to the store, looted it again, and decided to burn down the building to cover up their crime. The *Cedar Rapids Evening Gazette*'s editors slugged their first story, "To His Death," and reported that Novak had indeed perished in the terrible conflagration.[17]

A city editor of the *Evening Gazette*, a rail-thin, balding man with the patrician-sounding name of Washington Irving Endicott, cer-

tainly knew a good story when he saw one. Endicott, whom everyone called W. I. (like many individuals in this story, he detested his
first and middle names) and who bore a remarkable resemblance to
his namesake's fictitious character, Ichabod Crane, had been in the
newspaper business since he was nineteen years old. He began at the
Gazette as a compositor, wrote some blurbs for several years until he
eventually worked his way into the news department.[18] To be sure,
W. I. was nobody's fool and like most city editors had a sixth sense
about what makes a good story.

   He knew instantly that this had the potential of being an especially
colorful one, a long piece or perhaps even a series of articles, each
with enough intriguing details to grab the readers' attention. Acting
quickly, Endicott dispatched a reporter and artist to Walford. The
artist was important, since photography was still rare in newspapers
and most editors relied on ink drawings for both news stories and
portraits. Endicott himself may have gone to the scene and poked
around the rubble and ashes.

   This intense interest in the terrible occurrences in Walford reflected the increase of crime reporting in America. Almost daily,
hundreds of papers across the country emblazoned their front page
with a spectacular murder. When Lizzie Borden murdered both of
her parents with a hatchet in 1892, it was hardly an isolated incident.
In Iowa alone, the papers regularly ran stories about axe murders,
shotgun slayings, poisonings, and stabbings.

   The surge in crime reporting was one aspect of the rise of a new
brand of journalism in the United States. This was yellow journalism,
a style of writing that consisted of "sensationalism, distorted stories,
and misleading images for the sole purpose of boosting newspaper
sales and exciting public opinion."[19]

   Its most famous proponent was William Randolph Hearst, owner
of a chain of newspapers, including the *San Francisco Chronicle* and
New York Journal. In fact, the term "yellow journalism" came from a
character in a *New York World* comic called the Yellow Kid, created by
a cartoonist named Robert Outcault.[20]

Hearst was constantly engaged in circulation fights with competing papers, and he loved these types of stories, especially when they involved gruesome crimes. He knew bad news, and crime in particular, was a surefire way to sell more papers. Larger cities like New York, Chicago, and San Francisco set the tone for this new type of journalism, and smaller circulation dailies and weeklies eagerly followed suit. To them, there was nothing like a "good murder," and if it was bathed in mystery and intrigue, so much the better.

More and more, newspapers picked up on these crime stories and gave them prominent front-page display. The expression "if it bleeds, it leads" may have originated in radio broadcasting in the early twentieth century, but the slogan had its roots in the yellow journalism of the late 1800s. The public craved these stories and the newspapers and magazines delivered them with breathless, staccato prose.[21]

Newspapers caught up in this tide of yellow journalism were the ancestors of today's tabloids. Editors were well aware that long, lurid articles, replete with grim sketches of the corpse by staff artists, sold papers. Any modicum of restraint was lost whenever a kidnapping or murder case broke. More and more, newspaper coverage was becoming similar to the crime melodramas playing on the local stages or opera houses, as "loud headlines, catchy phrases and a hint of blood and mystery, lure on the reader."[22]

This unquenchable thirst for blood and mystery, mixed with righteous retribution, proved to be a potent spur for even more newspaper coverage, from the large circulation papers to the small ones published in towns in villages in the hinterlands. People liked to follow the now-familiar linear framework of a story—from the murder and examination of clues to the subsequent arrest of the guilty party.

Newspapers also sometimes serialized fictional accounts of detectives investigating crime. Whenever a real case broke, the dailies were filled with page after page about the exploits of real detectives in breathless prose. But despite the flood of books and stories, not everyone was enthralled with the techniques of these modern sleuths. In an essay, "The Detective Business," which was highly critical of the rise of the modern-day operative, Robin Dunbar complained, "hardly a noted crook is captured, dies or escapes . . . but some detective is given a boost and an advertisement as to his wonderful man-hunting and catching ability." He added that there seemed to be no end to the demand for these stories, since "The public greedily swallows such stuff and calls for more."[23]

This was certainly the case with the fire at Walford, which was turning out to be the most sensational news story in Iowa in years. To inveterate newshounds like Endicott and other editors, this mysterious tale of a burned corpse discovered in a cellar had everything for their readers—murder, mystery, and best of all, no end in sight. Anyone who had ever set a line of type could tell that it was a newspaperman's dream. This story had legs.

"The Greatest Excitement Prevailing in the Little Town and the Surrounding Country," claimed a headline from the *Cedar Rapids Daily Republican* on February 4, adding, "All sorts of wild rumors are in circulation and nothing else is talked about in the town." The paper also hinted that "there may be some startling developments in a few days."[24] The rival *Gazette* devoted many articles to the story and described the case as "a diabolical plot" and "the greatest mystery ever known in this section of Iowa."[25]

A week after the fire, most people believed that it was Ed Murray who died in the flames, but Frank Novak's whereabouts were still unknown. It seemed that everyone was either talking about Frank Novak or searching for the murder suspect. Riding the crest of the excitement, people in large cities and the smallest of crossroad settlements intensified their searches, as each town in eastern Iowa wanted to become famous for finding and catching the fugitive.

"Novak mania" swept through the state. The *Waterloo Daily Courier* noted that he was "omnipresent" in that city and mentioned that it had received messages from "a dozen corners of the town telling with minute description of the appearance of Novak at back doors. . . . [He] is wandering like a lost spirit under the noses of Waterloo's 'finest.'"[26]

Novak seemed to be everywhere in the state—lurking behind a coal shed, asleep in the corn stubble, or hiding in a back alley somewhere. Few photographs of him were published, so besides the quick newspaper sketches of a mustached man in hunting clothes carrying a shotgun, his actual size and physical characteristics were largely left up to one's imagination. Anyone wearing a hunting jacket or toting a shotgun became a suspect. Two hobos dressed in clothing similar to those of the Walford fugitive were held at the Waterloo police station, but "they were not Novaks," the paper exclaimed disconsolately, and the men were released.[27] Jittery Iowans were now suspicious of almost every Bohemian adult male, since even if a man did not resemble Novak, he might have information on the fugitive's whereabouts.

The search soon focused on a man later identified as either Karl or Charles Kroulik. Also a Bohemian, Kroulik lived close to Cedar Rapids and had many friends in that city. Sometime in early February, he had decided to return to Bohemia to run his father's mill. A conductor spotted him on the train to Cedar Rapids and alerted the police, confident that the man was Frank Novak. However, as soon as the officers confronted Kroulik, he presented his papers and they released him.[28]

Following up on leads, Tobin seemed to be everywhere, flying around cities and towns like a barn swallow. First, the county attorney was spotted in Walford, then Cedar Rapids, and again at Vinton, hustling throughout Linn and Benton counties, trying to collect evidence while researching law textbooks for any legal precedence in past cases. Tobin understood from the beginning that, since he had no suspect under arrest, the prosecution's case would rest solely on circumstantial evidence and he had to make sure that he could gather as much of it as possible. But the dynamic attorney always seemed to feel that he should be doing more. Tobin read many of the major Iowa papers assiduously, keeping abreast of what was written about the case, gleaning articles for any potential leads or clues. He also was acutely aware that Frank's somewhat unsavory cousin,

Jo Novak, who had been in trouble with the law before, had traveled from Iowa City to Cedar Rapids to hire the legal firm of Hubbard & Dawley. The lawyers immediately filed suit against the five insurance companies, demanding that the amount of twenty-seven thousand dollars in Frank Novak's life insurance policies be awarded to his family.[29] They argued that despite the forensic evidence presented at the coroner's inquest and the eyewitnesses' testimony, the Novak family remained convinced that Frank Novak had perished in the fire. For his part, Tobin suspected that Jo Novak might have been directly involved in the murder or at least had some knowledge of Frank's plan. In a letter to W. I. Endicott at the *Gazette*, Tobin wrote, "If the officers had watched Jo Novak from the time Frank disappeared, they would have [Frank] now. Jo is interested in this case. I wish he was watched."[30]

Even before the Novaks filed suit, the insurance companies that issued policies to Frank took an interest in the case. John Way, an agent for the Travelers Insurance Company in St. Louis, read about the Walford fire in the *Globe-Democrat* and remembered that Novak had applied for life insurance on September 17, 1896, with the policy being issued a few weeks later. Way also recalled that Novak had been a noncommercial agent for Travelers but had done little business with the insurance agency.[31]

Way wrote to Travelers president Dr. J. B. Lewis in Hartford, Connecticut, and explained the situation in Iowa, especially the timing of the fire and Novak's life insurance policy with the company. Way also enclosed a clipping he had seen in a St. Louis newspaper, which was enough to raise the suspicions of Dr. Lewis, a no-nonsense businessman with an intuitive feel for gauging any situation. Lewis then received a second letter and newspaper clipping from Way, detailing the accusation that Novak had robbed the safe of the Upton Company years earlier. Way also urged Travelers to investigate Novak's business accounts at the Cedar Rapids National Bank. Lewis, who simply signed his letters with the word "Adjuster," was as curious as Tobin about the case, and on February 8, just five days after the

Walford fire, he contacted Bayard P. Holmes, manager of the Thiel Detective Agency's New York City office. Besides investigating burglaries, shadowing railroad conductors, and engaging in strikebreaking activities, by the close of the nineteenth century, more and more detective agencies were working with large corporations in fraud or embezzlement cases.

In a letter to Holmes, Dr. Lewis explained his doubts about the origins of the fire. "The newspaper item has a suspicious look," he wrote, and then added dryly, "and I am inclined to think that the insured is not so badly burned as his disappearance would indicate."[32]

He wasn't alone. Next, Lewis received a letter dated February 8 from Frank Thornburg, secretary of the Economic Life Association of Clinton, Iowa, another insurance company. Having heard about the ten-thousand-dollar life insurance policy that the Hartford insurance company had on Novak, Thornburg wrote to inform the company that Novak also had taken out a life insurance policy for two thousand dollars with the Economic. In the letter, Thornburg mentioned that the Economic had already hired its own detective, for two reasons: first, because the Benton County sheriff, Sam Metcalf, was "not a very active man in his line of business and I do not think very much has been done to learn the whereabouts of Novak,"[33] and second, since the town of Walford comprised mainly Bohemians who depended on Novak and his businesses, Thornburg believed that they were covering up the truth—that Frank Novak was trying to scam the insurance agencies. Therefore, he felt that a detective was needed to ferret out the details regarding the fire, which he considered highly suspicious. Based on Thornburg's recommendation, the Economic dispatched a detective—whose name has been lost to history—to Walford. After asking questions for a few days, the detective agreed with the results of the coroner's inquest. Thornburg was now certain that Novak had gotten Murray drunk, killed him, and burned down the store.[34]

Dr. Lewis was encouraged by Thornburg's letter. On March 1, 1897, he sent letters to the Economic Life Association, the Northwestern

Mutual Life Association of Milwaukee, the Bankers Life Association of Des Moines, and the U.S. Casualty of New York asking if they would help defray the cost of any Novak investigation. Using a phrase he would later regret, Lewis explained that finding Novak "would be of comparatively little cost to any of [the companies]."[35]

The response to his letters was tepid at best. One agency didn't even bother to answer until September, while the other companies expressed reservations about cooperating on the case. Besides, as Andrew Van Wormer, adjuster for the U.S. Casualty Company pointed out, "it seems that we all have a good defense in that the body found in the burned building can be conclusively shown to be that of one Edward Murray."[36] He argued that the coroner's inquiry had proved that Novak was still alive. Thus, he concluded, none of the insurance companies would have to pay off the policies.

While Travelers waited for responses from the other insurance firms, Bayard Holmes, the manager of the Thiel Detective Agency's New York office, moved forward with the investigation. Holmes had contacted the founder and president of the agency, Gustavus H. "Gus" Thiel, regarding the Novak case and the two men had discussed the situation in some detail.

FOUR

•——————————————————————•

Thiel's Men Move In

Gus Thiel, president of the Thiel Detective Agency, was an odd little man with brown eyes, dark hair, high cheekbones, and a perpetual deadpan expression. It made sense that he had cultivated this impassive look since he was a man who had spent much of his life keeping his emotions a secret, constantly working in the shadows. Thiel had the furtive appearance of a spy, which was not surprising since he had served as one for years.

Little is known about Thiel's early life, but his professional career began when he worked for Allan Pinkerton during the Civil War. Pinkerton had organized the United States Secret Service, and Thiel was one of its first employees, acting as an undercover agent for the Union while providing information for the Army of the Potomac in Virginia. In 1868, three years after the war ended, Thiel moved to Pinkerton's Chicago headquarters where he was employed as superintendent.[1] Then in 1873, the two men had a disagreement, and Thiel formed his own detective company. Much to Pinkerton's everlasting chagrin, Thiel's business prospered and quickly became a strong competitor to the famous detective's agency. Headquartered in St. Louis, Thiel's company grew to seven offices in cities from New York to Portland, Oregon, by the late 1890s.[2]

Thiel devoted much of his agents' efforts to spying on railroad workers. The undercover agents watched the conductors to prevent them from pocketing fares or absconding with freight. The detectives who worked on the railroads referred to themselves as "testers," so named because they tested the honesty of the employees. The railroad men used another, less savory term, for the company dicks. They called them spotters.[3]

Thiel's spotters were "more prevalent than any other's covering as they did every state and territory in the Union as well as most of the provinces of British America, from Nova Scotia to Vancouver Island." They were universally despised by conductors and other railroad employees, who hated being under constant surveillance. The conductors tried desperately to discover the detectives' identities. A piece of doggerel survives that highlights the animosity between the spotter and the railroad men:

> Dear Spotter:
> The conductor yearns to yank thee
> To his brawny breast and squeeze
> Thy palpitating gizzard
> Through thy vest.[4]

In fact, Thiel and his men proved so vexing to railroad employees that, in 1889, a man working under the pseudonym of Martin P. Wheeler wrote a philippic against Thiel's agents. In his book *Judas Exposed: or, The Spotter Nuisance*, Wheeler attacked the detective firm, giving it the pseudonym of "Zeal's Railway Inspection Service." He was particularly incensed with a man he named "Mr. Zeal," a thinly disguised reference to Gus Thiel, and noted sarcastically that once the company began its operation in St. Louis, "a genius had burst upon the world"; and that "Mr. Zeal . . . by his prowess, prudence and experience would frighten every evil-doer in the country."

Judas Exposed expressed the author's low opinion of detectives by printing a false advertisement for "Zeal's" Portland office that read:

The confidential business to consist of following up young men earning beggar's wages and crawling under beds to get evidence against a husband or wife. . . . The kind of men who follow this business are the kind that most men or judges would not believe under oath. They will swear to any or everything in order that they might gain their point and fee. No honorable man would have any connection with this style and mode of business.[5]

Each Thiel office was manned by rough-and-ready, hard-bitten men who were used to operating outside the law to achieve their employers' goals. They not only ascribed to the "shoot first, ask questions later" philosophy, but also were known to "shoot first, and then shoot again." In addition to conducting surveillance of railroad employees, detectives protected the railroad against "hijackers, hooligans, resentful farmers and angry homesteaders."[6] The Thiel detectives, like the Pinkertons, worked as informers, and they also played a key role in the bloody Pullman strike, an 1894 walkout by workers at the Pullman Palace Car Company that slowed railroad traffic across the country. Thiel's men were active in the western mining districts, organizing groups of paid vigilantes to attack protesting miners in several states. One of the most famous incidents occurred during the Cripple Creek strike, also in 1894, when detectives rounded up a small army of thugs in an attempt to intimidate the miners. While Thiel himself was never as famous as Pinkerton, he was nevertheless a resourceful and sometimes cold-blooded man who ran his national detective agency with a ruthlessness that bordered on maniacal. The single-minded Thiel passed on this determination to his cadre of detectives and drove them hard. They responded in kind, and their efforts, particularly as strikebreakers, often resulted in bloodshed. Whenever violence occurred, Gus Thiel shrugged. To him, it simply came with the territory.

A prime example of the quintessential Thiel man was John F. Farley, manager of the Denver office. Prickly as a cactus and tough as rawhide, Farley was a former member of Company K, Third U. S. Cavalry, and saw extensive action in the Apache Indian wars from 1867 to 1872, when he was still a teenager. He fought in many battles, including one at Apache Pass in the Arizona Territory; in that skirmish, Farley was wounded and retired from the army shortly thereafter. In 1873, he began a business relationship with Gus Thiel that would last for about fifteen years. Farley helped Thiel establish the company's New York branch and then moved on to St. Paul, Minnesota, where he founded an office in 1876. The last Thiel bureau that Farley organized was Denver's in 1885.[7]

After that, Farley served as police chief of Denver. He moved to the West Coast in 1907 and rejoined Thiel, becoming a general agent in the company's San Francisco office at the age of 58. The *San Francisco Examiner* reported that "Farley is a veteran of the [detective] service. He joined it 35 years ago and has seen it expand from a small concern with one office in Saint Louis to an institution with agencies in all the large cities of the United States, Canada and Mexico."[8]

Although today's private investigators—both real and fictional—have descended from a long line of progenitors like Dashiell Hammett, himself a former Pinkerton agent, they had little in common with real-life ops like Gus Thiel and John Farley, working at the close of the nineteenth century.

☙ ☙ ☙

In St. Louis, Gus Thiel had been reading the correspondence between his New York office and Travelers regarding the Novak case. He decided that there was no time to waste and dispatched an agent to Walford. A Thiel operative from Kansas City named Hurst arrived in town on February 14, a little less than two weeks after the fire. In his report, Hurst wrote that he was unimpressed with the little burg, which he described as "a small town of about 50 to 60 inhabitants, one hardware store and Post Office."[9] He interviewed people in town and read the coroner's inquest. Then the agent met with Mrs. Frank Novak, who seemed unclear as to how much insurance her husband was carrying at the time of the fire. After that meeting, in which she shed little light on the case, the frustrated Hurst concluded that Mrs. Novak was "not very intelligent."[10]

Then Hurst traveled to the Murray farm outside of town and talked to Ed Murray's sister, Nellie Murray Shea, who had identified scraps of the corpse's shirt as belonging to her brother. The detective also commented on the remnants of a St. Joseph's cord, which he believed proved that the body was Murray and not Novak, since the Bohemian was not Catholic.[11]

After interviewing Frank's father John Novak and many Walford residents, Hurst decided that far from being the genial, well liked store owner and the wealthiest man in town as he was often portrayed, Novak had a long history of shady incidents. Hurst wasn't alone in beginning to question Novak's reputation. One newspaper account printed at about the time of Hurst's visit to Walford highlighted Novak's rather "queer business methods."[12] It was possible, the article continued, that Novak had been involved in the death of his business partner and brother-in-law Wencil Jilek, although nothing was ever proven. He had collected six thousand dollars in insurance money when the first Novak and Jilek store burned down in 1895; garnered an additional seven hundred dollars when items were allegedly stolen from his safe; owed money to a number of people in Cedar Rapids and Walford; had embezzled hundreds of dollars from his own father; and in all owed almost four thousand dollars in notes and mortgages. In fact, John Novak, who had bankrolled all of Frank's business endeavors for years, was now broke. He exclaimed to the detective, "My God, how could he ruin his old parents and his sisters?"[13]

At one point, the younger Novak had served as the postmaster of Walford. In an interview with Hurst, the current postmaster told him that Novak had done some "crooked work" while in that office. To find out the details, he urged the operative to contact the Post Office supervisors in Washington.[14]

The Thiel operative also found out about Frank Novak's compulsive gambling and lavish lifestyle. One account later labeled Novak "a spendthrift . . . who fancied race horses, fancy clothes and diamonds."[15] By most accounts, he was an easy mark for professional gamblers.

Novak was not the only member of his family to have had a somewhat scurrilous past. His cousin, Jo Novak, who was pursuing Frank's

life insurance money settlement in court, also had a history of skirt-
ing the law. He dabbled in numerous moneymaking ventures, including real estate, loan sharking, and a few law cases. Hurst thought little
of Jo's legal knowledge and referred to him in his report to Thiel as
a "jack-leg lawyer."[16]

After gathering whatever information he could at Walford, Hurst
traveled to Cedar Rapids to meet with W. I. Endicott, the *Gazette* editor who was still running daily articles on the case. Endicott claimed
that he had inside information on the story and was eager to discuss
motives with the detective, who reported that the editor envisioned
himself as an amateur sleuth and had done some detective work on
the side. Endicott had followed the case from the beginning and in
fact had urged the dental assistant, Louis Hasek, to give testimony
to the coroner's jury regarding the condition of Novak's teeth. The
Thiel agent called Endicott "very bright" and was impressed that although his paper printed that Novak perished in the fire, Endicott
said he never believed it and reported it as a "blind."[17]

Endicott explained that he had taken a personal interest in the
Novak case, going so far as to travel down to Walford and interview
some witnesses. The editor also said that he had an informant in the
town who reported that Novak's wife was involved in the scheme, and
that she and Frank had shared a rather cryptic good-bye on the night
of February 2. He urged Hurst to investigate Martin Loder, as Endicott believed that the Walford saloonkeeper should be considered a
suspect. But the detective rejected the editor's theory about Loder,
since Novak had owed the saloonkeeper about two hundred thirty
dollars. In fact, Loder claimed he simply wanted his money back and
was quoted as saying that he would pay a hundred dollars to have
"the damned thief captured."[18]

After talking with Endicott, Hurst visited Ralph Van Vectern, a
cashier at the Cedar Rapids National Bank. Van Vectern said that
Novak had had financial problems for the past two years, and that
he had taken out six hundred dollars in cash between January 29
and February 2, and became upset when the bank refused to cash

any other checks that he presented. The withdrawals left him with a balance of sixty-two dollars in his account. In addition, Novak had borrowed about twenty-two hundred dollars from George Dostle, a Cedar Rapids butcher, as well as about twelve hundred dollars from a farmer named Farates. Hurst discovered that Novak had tried to obtain loans from just about everyone he knew, including friends, family members, and other residents of the town.[19]

Satisfied with the information he had gleaned in Walford and Cedar Rapids, Hurst attempted to pick up Novak's trail after the fire broke out on February 3. The detective took the train from Cedar Rapids to Williamsburg, Iowa, meeting with William E. Holmes, who, like Endicott, was one of the city editors for the *Gazette*. As the train rattled down the track, Holmes told the detective about an intriguing sideline to the case. Holmes had met a man named Hoadley, who told the editor that he had been in Novak's store a few days before February 2 and found Novak studying a map of the United States with a man named Young from Gardena, California. Novak had peppered the Californian with questions about two Arizona towns in particular—Flagstaff and Pinaveta—and also asked about living far away from any railroads, out in the high country.[20] The *Gazette* editor thought that this was highly suspicious, and so did the Thiel detective. He cautioned Holmes not to say anything about it, especially in Walford, where rumors spread as quickly as the wind ripples across a wheat field.

The mayor of Williamsburg, H. E. Hull, met Hurst and explained that a storeowner in nearby Holbrook named Dunn had seen someone fitting the description of Novak on the evening of February 3. Hurst traveled to Holbrook and interviewed the storeowner, who told him that on that evening, a stranger entered Dunn's store and asked if he could exchange some coins for folding money. Dunn assumed the amount was about ten dollars in change, but the man, who was carrying a double-barreled shotgun, took about fifty dollars in silver from the pockets of his hunting jacket. Dunn gave him the bills and the man took out a sack that looked like it might hold about seventy-five to one hundred dollars more in change. The stranger said that he had collected the coins from along a nearby creek and asked if the storekeeper would take more silver in exchange, but Dunn refused, as he had now become suspicious.[21]

According to Dunn, a wagon had then pulled up to the store, driven by John Bryson, a twenty-one-year-old farmer who lived outside of Williamsburg. The man with the shotgun talked to Bryson for a moment, then hopped up onto the seat, and the wagon left, headed east toward Iowa City. Then Hurst showed Dunn a photograph of Frank Novak. Dunn said that he could not be sure whether it was the man for whom he had changed money, since the stranger he saw appeared to be much heavier. However, his wife was positive that the photograph matched the man she saw, except that he appeared to be older and had gained some weight since the picture was taken.[22]

Now the detective had his first lead regarding the direction of Novak's flight. If this was in fact Novak, the fugitive had headed due south. Hurst's next move was to find Bryson and ask exactly where he had taken the man with the shotgun. The Thiel man returned to Williamsburg after first telephoning Mayor Hull to try to locate the young wagon driver. When he arrived, Bryson and Hull were in the mayor's office. Bryson told the detective that the man had paid him five dollars for the wagon trip to Iowa City, a distance of about twenty-one miles from Williamsburg. After studying the photograph of Novak, Bryson agreed that this was the same man he had picked up in the wagon. He signed an affidavit, swearing that that the person he had taken to Iowa City was indeed Frank Alfred Novak.

It seemed obvious to Hurst that Novak had one goal: to travel as far away from Iowa as quickly as possible. Since Iowa City was on the Rock Island line, it served as a major hub for that railroad. Once he reached the station, Novak could purchase a ticket and head for any destination he chose.

But before following this lead to Iowa City, Hurst decided to obtain a more recent photograph of the suspect, since the one he carried apparently was too out of date to be used for positive identification.

Hurst returned to Kansas City and filed his report, sending it to Gus Thiel in St. Louis. The operative had done an excellent job in gathering background material on Novak and tracking the suspect's flight from Walford.

Six days later, on February 24, Hurst sent one of his agents back to Iowa. Identified only by the initials "E.A.D.," this Thiel detective traveled to Williamsburg and attempted to gather more information on the fugitive. He presented a letter of introduction from Hurst to Mayor Hull, who gave the agent the names and addresses of several people who claimed to have seen Frank Novak on February 3. In order to make sure that the affidavits were properly validated, the agent found a man named Pugh, a notary who lived in Williamsburg, to accompany him on his visits to these witnesses. Hull also helped the Thiel detective engage two horses and a carriage for the next day's journey.[23]

The morning of February 26 was frigid, with the temperature hovering at seven degrees below zero. Not surprisingly, the notary refused to go as he didn't relish the idea of traipsing around the frozen countryside in an open buggy with only a few blankets for warmth. After some persuasion from the agent, Pugh changed his mind and they left at about 10:00 AM for Holbrook, the first town where Novak was allegedly seen, about nine miles from Williamsburg. There they met with R. H. Dunn and his wife, both of whom, when they viewed a more recent photograph of Novak, instantly identified him as the man with the shotgun who visited their store on February 3. The agent and notary then traveled about a mile east of Holbrook, where they met with Morris and Kate Fitzgibbons. Mrs. Fitzgibbons recognized the photograph as the man she saw walking along the road on February 3, the same day that the Dunns saw him.[24]

Since it was about 18 miles farther to their next destination, the two men decided to head back to Williamsburg. On February 27, they started out again, this time traveling to the Cressinger farm. A man matching Novak's description had stopped at the place for breakfast on the morning of February 3. Cressinger, his wife, and daughter all signed affidavits that the photograph was indeed that of the mysterious visitor.[25]

After a few more days of digging, "E.A.D." took the train from Williamsburg to Oxford. He could not find another notary to accompany him and decided to hire one in Iowa City, his next stop. Once in Iowa City, he walked to the hack barn on South Capitol Street and discovered that there were three men who may have seen Novak that night—Charles Merrifield, Thomas Jennings, and Robert Bell.[26] Of these three, only Merrifield was present. The hack driver, who didn't know Novak, instantly recognized the man in the photograph as the same man in the hack barn the night of February 3. Moreover, Merrifield claimed that the man, who was carrying a shotgun and had a hat pulled down over his eyes, asked him where the next train was headed. Which direction? Merrifield had asked. Either way, the man replied. The hack driver told him the next train was westbound, going toward Omaha and would leave at 12:15 AM.[27]

The Thiel operative went back to the hack barn the following day to meet with Bell and Jennings. Both men agreed that the photograph matched the man they had seen on the night of February 3, but the detective still could not be positive that this was the same man who may have taken the westbound train, as Merrifield had implied. The night operator at the railroad could not confirm that the man who boarded the train for Omaha was the man in the photograph. This was a vital link, and the agent realized that either he or some other Thiel man would have to pursue this lead further.[28]

"E.A.D." stopped off by the Amana Colonies and met with one more witness, a man named William Williams, who had given a ride to someone dressed in a hunting outfit at about 2:15 PM on the afternoon of February 3. Driving a horse-drawn sleigh, he had picked up the man and taken him to a nearby schoolhouse, about four miles from Williams's house. He identified that man as the same one in the photograph.[29]

Agent "E.A.D." had done everything he could in Iowa and returned to Kansas City on March 5, 1897. That same day, Bayard Holmes at

Thiel's New York office sent a letter to Dr. Lewis of Travelers in Hartford. The letter described another lead in the Novak chase, one from a man named Frank Shimek of Baltimore, who informed the agency that a man named Charles Kroulik from Iowa—the same man questioned about his identity back in February—had recently purchased a steamship ticket for Bohemia. According to Shimek, this man matched the description of Frank Novak. A Thiel agent took a train from New York to Baltimore and nosed around the dock area, trying to find Shimek. When he found him, he showed him a photograph of Frank Novak. At first, Shimek was convinced that this was the man he had seen buying the steamship ticket, but when the detective pressed him, Shimek admitted that the man he saw was not bow-legged and had a larger mustache than Novak. He finally confessed that he had heard about the two-hundred-dollar reward for Novak's capture and that he might have fingered the wrong man.

After talking with friends of Shimek, the Thiel agent believed that if not an outright liar, Shimek was what the agent called a "romancer," someone who likes to stretch the truth and a man "of rather excitable temperament."[30] Nevertheless, Gus Thiel, following the case from St. Louis, had to be sure. Thiel had the New York office telegraph the U.S. consul in Bremen, George Keenan, and alert him to the arrival of the steamer with Kroulik on board, sending along a detailed description of Frank Novak.[31] As soon as he disembarked, Kroulik was arrested. Shortly thereafter, however, Thiel received a telegram from Keenan, who had compared the physical description of Novak—complete with dental records—to the man standing in front of him. This man could not be Frank Novak, the consul wired back, because Kroulik was not only much taller than Novak, but also had much worse teeth than the Iowa suspect. Because of these two characteristics, the consul was positive that the man standing in front of him was not Frank Novak.[32]

FIVE

•————————————————————•

Following the Trail

The focus on the chase now returned to Iowa. It was time for someone else to pick up the trail. The next agent would board a westbound train from Iowa City to Omaha to follow the one remaining active lead. The new detective on the case was Dr. Charles E. Peterson, Gus Thiel's right-hand man and the assistant general manager of the St. Louis office. An extremely capable and savvy detective, Peterson traveled to Cedar Rapids on March 11, as he believed there was some unfinished business in that city.

His first stop was at the office of Louis Hasek, the young dental assistant who had determined that the corpse's teeth did not match those of Frank Novak. However, when pressed, Hasek could not recall the condition of Novak's other teeth, which caused the short-tempered Peterson to refer to him rather disgustedly as "a stupid thickheaded Bohemian and inclined to be reticent." Peterson's next stop was the *Gazette*'s newsroom to talk with Endicott and Holmes. Endicott had done some more investigating and discovered that Novak had received no insurance payout when Wencil Jilek fell off the train and died on the way to the Chicago World's Fair in 1893. Also, Endicott said, Jilek was conscious for a day after the accident and never once claimed that Novak or anyone else had pushed him off the train.[1]

Holmes showed Dr. Peterson a newspaper article from February 20 that detailed some of Novak's rather shady business dealings and also noted that he owed money to a number of people in Cedar Rapids and Walford. This information confirmed for Peterson that Novak had lost a great deal of cash through poor business decisions as well as mounting gambling losses. It was clear, the detective believed, that Novak had been desperate. The newspaper report also mentioned that Novak had unsuccessfully tried to lure a man named Morris Ferreter into spending the night with him in the store. In fact, on February 2, the day before the fire, Novak asked Ferreter's sister if her brother was coming to Walford.[2]

Peterson next met with Dr. Wencil Ruml, the physician and surgeon who had testified at the coroner's jury. Ruml described in detail how the top of the skull had been burned off, leaving the brain exposed. Under the intense heat, the brain had shriveled down to about the size of a large fist, Dr. Ruml explained, but, as he had told Tobin before, he was still unwilling to say whether the skull had been shattered with a blunt instrument. The physician would only confirm that in his opinion Murray had died as a result of the fire and that there was no concrete proof that a blow to the head resulted in the man's death.[3]

On March 12, Peterson decided to move on to the next stop along the suspect's trail. He assumed that Novak had taken the first train out of Iowa City and boarded a westbound Chicago, Rock Island, and Pacific night train from Iowa City to Council Bluffs, crossing the Missouri River into Omaha, Nebraska. There, the detective found a Union Pacific depot policeman named Flemming at the station office. When Peterson began speaking about the suspect's appearance, Flemming finished the description for him, taking the words "right out of the doctor's mouth."[4] The policeman had found it odd that a man dressed in hunting garb was traveling on the train without a game bag, shotgun case, or other luggage.

This confirmation that the suspect had arrived in Omaha was encouraging news. The Thiel man had an eyewitness who swore that the "Iowa Incendiary," as one paper later called him, had been there.[5]

Next, Peterson looked up Omaha's chief of police, Albert Sigwart. The two men may have known each other already, for when Peterson

asked Sigwart for help, the chief promised full cooperation and assigned two detectives to accompany the Thiel man in Omaha. Unfortunately, a check of the pawn shops in town and some promising
leads on a few transients turned up nothing. It appeared that Novak
had moved on, so the Thiel agent stopped by every railway ticket office in the Omaha area to see if someone matching Novak's description had purchased another ticket or a transfer, but he turned up no
further leads.

Then he arrived at the Union Pacific office. Its records showed
that someone had purchased a ticket through a local broker on February 4, from Omaha to Vancouver, British Columbia, an unusual
final destination for a traveler from Omaha. Peterson tracked down
the broker, a man named P. H. Philbin, who had not recorded the
name of the person who purchased the ticket. However, he gave a
detailed description of the man, and mentioned that the purchaser
was carrying a shotgun with no case. Peterson showed the broker a
photograph of Novak.

"That's the man," Philbin replied. "It was ticket number 2984, form
69, good over the Union Pacific and the Oregon railroad to Portland, Oregon, with an additional order for a ticket from Portland to
Vancouver."[6]

Now Peterson was sure that he had picked up Novak's trail again.
After visiting the Pullman offices to obtain the names of the porters
who had worked on the Omaha–Portland train during February 4,
he wrote to William St. M. Barnes of Thiel's Portland office, asking
him to obtain the signature on this particular ticket, take a photograph of it, and send the picture to St. Louis immediately. Peterson
also urged Barnes to search all the hotels, train stations, and other
transient places in Portland to determine whether Novak was still
there or had moved on. He included a photograph and a detailed
description of Novak, paying particular attention to the suspect's
hunting garb and shotgun. Finally, Peterson informed Barnes that
the Portland office could hold Novak under a fugitive warrant for the
murder of Edward Murray.[7]

On March 13, Peterson wrote to M. J. Tobin in Vinton, responding to the Benton county attorney's correspondence from a few days earlier. This was probably the first time that a Thiel agent had contacted Tobin. From this point forward, the Thiel agency and Tobin would work closely together. Tobin informed Peterson that he had previously received a letter from a man named MacConnoughay, stating that someone matching Frank Novak's description was staying at a ranch about 25 miles from Hay Springs, Nebraska. Peterson noted that this information was false, as he now had details confirming Novak's passing through Omaha on February 4.[8]

In addition, Peterson informed Tobin that he was handing off the case to another Thiel detective in Portland, and had asked the West Coast operative to leak some false information indicating that Frank Novak was seen heading east so that Novak's cousin and attorney, Jo Novak, would read or hear about it. Both Peterson and Tobin believed that Novak might be communicating with his lawyer. Finally, Peterson sent a letter to W. I. Endicott of the *Gazette* and asked him to run a story or two in the paper to give the impression that Novak had in fact gone east instead of west. Like Tobin, Peterson suspected that some of Novak's friends or relatives were involved in the fire and murder and he hoped to mislead them.[9]

Pleased that he had now done everything he could at this point, Peterson went back to St. Louis on the night of March 14. He was sure that the trail was heating up. Based on the clues that the Thiel agent uncovered along with the interviews he had conducted, Peterson was convinced that Novak had headed west, with about a six-week lead on the pursuers.

Because Gus Thiel had the United States cut into sections like a pie, with each piece served by a branch office, Dr. Peterson was out of his geographical area. As the doctor had explained to Tobin, he had now turned the search for Novak over to Thiel's Portland office, under William St. M. Barnes. But from the beginning, Gus Thiel had taken a personal interest in this case and had been actively involved in directing his operatives, corresponding with them by letters and telegrams while observing their next steps in the pursuit. In the meantime, Barnes had put one of his best detectives, a man named Werngren, on the hunt. Armed with new information that Novak had sold the portion of his ticket from Portland to Vancouver, Werngren began his search in Oregon and scoured the West Coast, checking hotels, flophouses, and bars for any sign of the Iowa fugitive.[10]

Then Werngren had a stroke of luck. He had found nothing in Portland and moved up the coast to Seattle. On March 31, while poking around that city's Skid Row area, checking the docks and the ticket offices, Werngren played a hunch and met a ship named the *Al-Ki*, which had just returned from a trip to Juneau. The detective showed a photograph of Frank Novak to all of the disembarking passengers as well as the ship's officers and crewmen. One passenger plus each member of the crew identified the photograph as that of a man who had taken the steamer *Kingston* to Port Townsend and then transferred to the *Al-Ki* on February 23, bound for Juneau.[11] The passenger who had recognized Novak from the photograph was a Chinese gambler named Lu Gong. He said that he had met Novak on the *Al-Ki* and had spent time with him on the voyage up through the Inside Passage to Juneau. Lu reported that Novak was drinking heavily while playing poker and another card game called pedro.[12]

The *Al-Ki* had landed in Juneau on March 4. According to Lu, Novak was wearing German socks—the same ones that he wore during his flight from Walford. The gambler also told Werngren that Novak was almost broke and was playing card games for low stakes as he didn't want to lose the rest of his money. Novak still wore a diamond ring at this point, although the Chinese man explained that Novak later sold the jewelry to another gambler in Juneau for sixty-five dollars. Werngren picked up an additional clue when another passenger on the *Al-Ki* recalled that the man traveling with Lu was an excellent violinist. This new information confirmed to the Thiel agent that the person who disembarked from the *Al-Ki* in Juneau was in fact Novak.[13]

The Portland office's coordinator, Captain D. D. Anthony, then received instructions from Thiel to return to the home office in St. Louis. The agency's owner had decided to use the captain as a courier for a special message.

On April 4, Thiel had sent a long letter to Tobin, summarizing what the agency had discovered to date and stating that his agents were hot on Novak's trail. In fact, the detective agency now had a copy of the Union Pacific ticket from Omaha to Vancouver that had been signed, "Frank Alfred"—Novak's real first and middle names. The agency also had obtained a copy of Novak's signature and Thiel himself compared the two, concluding that the two signatures were written by the same man. Later, Thiel agents found another sample of Novak's handwriting that perfectly matched some of the letters in the "Frank Alfred" signature, confirming that the man who signed this ticket was the missing man. Thiel also explained that he had sent Werngren on to Juneau, as "Novak [may be] uncertain in regard to whether he would remain in Alaska or not and may possibly ere this have retraced his steps."[14]

Because he suspected that Novak might head to Canada, Thiel knew that he had to obtain legal authority there and urged Tobin to provide the agency with a certified copy of the indictment. This could be used for any extradition papers from the Canadian government, which could be obtained later. Thiel also requested that the Vinton prosecutor have Iowa Governor Francis M. Drake name Werngren as an agent for the state.[15]

Considering the quick progress of his detectives, Gus Thiel should have been pleased with the way the pursuit was unfolding. He and his agents had tracked Frank Novak across the country from Iowa to Seattle and now Juneau. Since there was no way in or out of that Alaska city except by boat, Thiel knew that Novak had two choices: stay in Juneau or keep moving north. He doubted that the fugitive would double back down the West Coast, especially since it had taken so much effort to reach Juneau. Furthermore, Thiel suspected that

Novak was running out of money, based on Lu Gong's statements plus the knowledge that the fugitive had left Walford almost two months before. The Iowa man might not have had any other escape routes in mind, but Thiel could not be certain. Alaska was then as it still is today, a largely uninhabited wilderness and a place where a man can easily lose himself.

Nevertheless, Thiel wasn't quite satisfied with the way the chase was unfolding. Something was bothering him. He thought about his options and decided that Werngren, while apparently a competent detective, might not have the physical makeup or mental toughness needed for the pursuit, especially if Novak was merely using Juneau as a jumping-off point for uncharted territory. The next leg might be dangerous. It would require someone with a different constitution than Werngren. This would be a job for a man who was physically tough and persistent, someone who would stick to the fading trail like Mississippi mud.

Fortunately, Thiel already had someone in mind. There was only one man in the entire agency, he thought, who could handle the task, a man who could not only find Novak but bring him back to justice. Thiel was about to unleash one of the most relentless trackers in the annals of crime detection. The detective's name was Red Perrin.

᭡ ᭡ ᭡

For as long as he could remember, Cassius Claud Perrin had hated his name. As soon as he was old enough to write, he shortened it to C. C. Perrin, but everyone referred to him as either "Cash," a corruption of his first name, or more often, "Red," because of his thick auburn hair. A wiry man, he stood about five feet ten inches and weighed one hundred sixty-five pounds. Determined was perhaps the best word that described him, for he was a superb manhunter and an extraordinary tracker and, according to one report, "a man of force, energy, powers of endurance."[16]

If someone was able to create in flesh and blood the embodiment of a nineteenth-century dime-novel detective, he might have matched this man. Seeming half bloodhound and half rattlesnake, with a thick, droopy red mustache, large sun-baked nose, and piercing, bullet-hole eyes, Red Perrin appeared to see twenty miles past anyone he met.

His early days are obscure, either because of his own efforts or perhaps because of the rather primitive recordkeeping in the American Southwest. Perrin was born and raised in Tucson, in the Arizona Territory, in about 1857[17] and as a young man may have seen some action in the Apache Wars in the late 1870s, "with a number of scars to show his active participation in the stirring events of those days," according to one newspaper.[18]

Other papers noted that Perrin was once a U.S. marshal in Tucson, although records indicate that he was, less glamorously, a constable and later a deputy sheriff, so the report of his federal service may have been newspaper exaggeration or Perrin's own self-aggrandizement.[19] In any case, Perrin handled his rough-and-ready job efficiently. An article in the *Arizona Republic* stated that "Constable H. Arey received a letter from Deputy Sheriff Perrin at Tucson stating that Juan Castellain, [a] desperado caught at Gila Bend, who had been shot in the leg while being captured, will probably die from the wound."[20] Perrin also served as a constable in Pima County, and because of his duties often served as a debt collector. Occasionally, he employed strong-arm tactics to seize goods or property as compensation for debts that residents owed to businessmen. As a result, he was named as a defendant in a few civil suits filed in that county.[21]

In 1892, Red Perrin left Arizona and drifted around the western part of the country for several months, spending some time in Colorado. What he was doing in that time period is unknown, but he may have been involved in some of the campaigns to bust the frequent miners' strikes of that era. It also was possible that he met John Farley, the retired U.S. cavalry officer and veteran of the Apache Wars who was then head of Thiel's office in Denver.[22]

The next place Red Perrin surfaced was the Chicago World's Fair in 1893, where he was employed as superintendant of the night divi-

sion of detectives at the Midway Plaisance. This was the long bou-
levard lined with dozens of rides, exhibits, and popular attractions
such as the belly dancer known as "Little Egypt" and the 264-foot-
high Ferris wheel.[23]

Perhaps his undercover work in Chicago and possibly his connection with Farley in Denver led to Perrin's subsequent hiring by Gus
Thiel's Chicago office.[24] He handled a few cases for the agency and
quickly became comfortable with Chicago and its streetcars, mad
crush of people, and big-city crimes, all of which were quite different
from what he must have been accustomed to in the Arizona Territory.

Following a few years of work for Thiel, in 1895 Perrin was given
the task of finding an embezzler. This was not a common criminal
but one with patrician roots. Charles "Kit" Larrabee, the accused
man, was the blue-blooded nephew of former Iowa governor William
Larrabee. Kit had been employed as head cashier and accountant for
Boyd, Stickney & Co., a large Pennsylvania coal brokerage firm with
an office in Chicago. After about eight years with the company, Kit
Larrabee disappeared with about fifteen thousand dollars in cash.

With tactics similar to the Novak case, police and the American
Surety Company sent photographs of Larrabee to newspapers and
law enforcement agencies across the country as well as many port cities. The case received a great deal of publicity because the Chicago
papers were intrigued with the news story's lead: an Iowa governor's
nephew who became an embezzler. There also were rumors that a
woman was involved in the theft and was accompanying Larrabee.[25]

The American Surety Company paid off the brokerage's insurance
loss and engaged Thiel's Chicago office to find the embezzler. Using
his skills as a manhunter, Perrin followed Larrabee's twisting trail
from Chicago to Texas, and then crossed the border into Mexico
along with Bradbury Williams, an inspector for Boyd, Stickney & Co.
Some reports noted that they tracked Larrabee to Monterrey, Mexico, and arrested him at a fish market, while another story claimed
that Perrin lured Larrabee back into Texas and arrested him there.
In any event, in March 1896, a year after Larrabee had fled with the

money, he was captured and returned to Chicago, where he was tried, convicted, and sentenced to serve time at the Joliet Prison.[26]

Perrin's success in the hunt for Larrabee was remarkable, since he had picked up the embezzler's trail and followed it for more than 1,500 miles into Mexico. His success made a strong impression on Gus Thiel, who had kept track of the detective's actions from St. Louis. Based on this case, Thiel was confident that the rugged former Arizona lawman was the perfect choice to spearhead the search for Frank Novak. His instructions to the agent were simple: find Novak and bring him back to Iowa.

Novak's lengthy head start meant nothing to Red Perrin. As one paper succinctly put it, Perrin "was given a photograph and told to find the original."[27] That was the detective's sole objective and he attacked it with his customary single-mindedness.

Like a knight on a chessboard, Perrin had moved forward into position. Now it was time for him to follow the red tip of the compass needle. It was time for Red Perrin to head north.

PART TWO

HARDSHIPS

•——————————————————•

SIX

Klondike Madness

As Perrin made his preparations, hundreds of miles away, the Klondike gold rush was just beginning, for even though the discovery of gold on Bonanza Creek had occurred almost a year earlier, in 1896, the news had trickled slowly out through the Yukon Territory and down the Alaskan Panhandle. Now the once-sleepy little town of Juneau was a mad anthill of activity with a surging population of about two thousand people. Some Californians optimistically referred to Juneau as "the San Francisco of the North," which might have been a valid comparison if the famous City by the Bay was ringed by snow-covered mountain peaks and had an occasional black bear lumbering through downtown. Juneau's winding, muddy paths (one could hardly call them streets yet) were hard to navigate, not only due to the rough terrain but also because they were packed with prospectors and Indians, many of the latter doing a brisk business selling goods to the former. The town was the busiest supply port in Alaska and it was believed that anything that a man needed for the Klondike could be obtained there, from gum boots to chewing gum.

Juneau had grown to be the largest city in Alaska, which at the time was not saying very much. It was certainly bigger than Wrangell, another Panhandle town that a French geographer once called "the most tumble-down looking company of cabins I ever saw,"[1] but was nowhere near as civilized as Sitka, the staid old Russian capital. One visitor during the early part of the Klondike rush described Juneau as having "a courthouse, several hotels and lodging houses, theaters, churches, schools, newspapers, a hospital, fire brigade and a brass band, but more saloons and dance-houses than all the other institutions put together."[2] Juneau's location made it ideal for any trips from the Panhandle into the rest of Alaska or the Yukon.

❦ ❦ ❦

After the other Thiel detectives had briefed him about Novak, Perrin decided that there was no time to lose and elected not to wait for the requisition papers from Washington. Those documents, which order an individual to appear in court, would have to follow the quick-moving agent. Perrin booked passage on the first steamer north from Seattle, which happened to be the *Al-Ki*, the same boat that Novak had taken, and left for Juneau on April 4. Waiting for him in that city was D. L. Clouse, another Thiel agent—with a message from Gus Thiel himself. The company president urged Perrin to go immediately to Ottawa, the Canadian capital city, and obtain extradition papers in case Novak had left Alaska and fled into the Yukon Territory, at that time governed by Great Britain. Although Clouse had been digging around Juneau for about a month, he hadn't found any trace of Novak, nor was he able to recover the diamond ring that Novak had supposedly gambled away, despite searching all of the pawnshops.[3]

Before heading to Ottawa, Perrin instructed Clouse to take the first steamer bound for Unalaska, a remote island far out on the Aleutian archipelago. The island's port served as a refueling point for all ships traveling to and from Alaska via the long Bering Sea route. At that choke point, Perrin reasoned, Clouse would be able to check the passengers on all steamers traveling the region.[4]

A clever and methodical man, Perrin had had some time to think about the situation, and now devised a trap for Novak. Like a salmon fisherman, Clouse would hold one end of the net and draw it in a large circle, trapping the fish inside. It was up to Perrin to secure the other end, making sure that Novak could not escape. Then, he reasoned, it was simply a matter of reeling in the net with the fugitive trapped somewhere in it. Because Perrin knew that Novak was no longer in Juneau but was not certain where he might be, the next step was to eliminate any other routes that Novak might take once he left that city. Perrin guessed that Novak had only one real direction to go—north to Dawson City and the Klondike gold fields.

Before he could proceed, Perrin had to be certain that he had all of the legal documents he needed, as Gus Thiel insisted. Already armed with a warrant of extradition from the governor of Iowa to the governor of Alaska, the detective also now possessed a warrant of *recipias*—legal authority to receive the prisoner—that was signed by President William McKinley and Secretary of State John Sherman. But if Novak in fact was headed to Canada, Perrin needed more legal documentation.[5]

The agent returned to Victoria in British Columbia and boarded a train from Vancouver to Ottawa. There, Perrin received the written approval and documents from the Canadian government allowing him to extradite Frank Novak, in case he apprehended the Bohemian on Canadian soil.

Perrin didn't get back to the West Coast until May 20, and the trail was growing cold. So far, Clouse had come up empty in Unalaska. Because of the time lost during his long train trip to Ottawa and back, the detective was now far behind Novak. Undaunted, on May 24, Perrin returned to Juneau on the steamer *Mexico*. After a few days, he traveled to Sitka, where he met with Governor James Sheakley, obtaining the necessary legal paperwork needed to arrest Novak in Alaskan territory. While in Sitka, Perrin realized that he couldn't chase after Novak alone. There was simply no way that he could transport all of his supplies into the wild Yukon country, let alone make the grueling trip to Dawson City by himself. After talking with some veteran prospectors in Sitka, Perrin decided that he needed a man who could build a watertight boat that would be strong enough to navigate the treacherous Yukon River.

Fortunately, Perrin had met an experienced Norwegian woodsman and carpenter named Knudson in Washington, D.C., when the man had been a guard responsible for transporting prisoners from Alaska to the nation's capital. By a stroke of luck, Knudson happened to be back in Alaska. Perrin found him and promptly hired him as an assistant.[6]

Then Perrin returned to Juneau and began amassing roughly fifteen hundred pounds of supplies for the journey that lay ahead of him.[7] Perhaps he was inspired by some diaries from other agents or was aware of several crime-solving detective books that Allan Pinkerton had written, but in any case, Perrin had decided to keep a journal of his trip. His partner Knudson joined him in Juneau on June 6. The next day, both men loaded their supplies on board the rickety steam launch *Taku* and headed up the choppy, slate-gray Lynn Canal on the one-hundred-eighteen-mile voyage to the village of Dyea.

While the detective guessed that the fugitive was ahead of him, Perrin also knew that the chances of locating his prey were slim, as there were hundreds of miles of territory where Novak could easily lose himself. Moreover, his head start over any pursuers had increased substantially since the Walford fire some four months earlier. Perhaps there was only one man in a million who would not be discouraged by the thought of such a journey, someone who could travel deep into Alaska and the Yukon while searching for a fugitive he was unlikely to find.

SEVEN

Inside, Hell Begins

Perrin and Knudson's journey had a rough start as soon as the *Taku* left Juneau. Lynn Canal, a long fjord that is a thousand feet deep in some places and lined with the gloomy Coast Mountains, can turn from placid to stormy in a matter of minutes. That was exactly what happened on their trip: a howling wind attacked the ship shortly after it left the docks.

By 1:00 AM, about eight hours after its departure, the boat had made only a few miles when the fire died in the steam boiler. The *Taku* began taking on water. The waves shoved the boat onto the rocks, and as the crew desperately tried to restart the engine, the captain contemplated abandoning ship. After hours of pumping out the water and fiddling with the boiler, the harried crew managed to start the fire again and floated the battered vessel off the rocks, heading north once more. But by now the storm had increased in strength, almost as if there was a bottled-up hurricane blasting around the channel, and the captain decided to drop anchor in Bruner Bay to ride out the powerful winds in safety. After several more hours, the *Taku* started again for Dyea, only to stop at Seward Harbor for wood and other supplies. Perrin also noted in his diary that "a Siwash buck and three squaws" climbed on board.[1]

Finally, at 9:00 AM on June 9, the little steamer chugged up Taiya Inlet and reached Dyea. The voyage, which normally took only hours, had lasted two days. It was a harbinger for the perils that lay in store for Perrin and Knudson.

The small settlement of Dyea (pronounced "Dy-EE") was, like many other Alaskan names, an Anglicized corruption of an Indian word, in this case *Taiya*. This word means "pack" or "load," which is certainly appropriate, since Dyea was the terminus for the Chilkoot Trail, which leads into the Yukon River valley.[2] Although there were many ways to enter the Yukon country, the two most popular routes began at Dyea and Skagway. Each place was then little more than a cluster of cabins, separated by about four miles of trail. Skagway, another bastardized English version of an Indian word—*Skagua*, or "windy place"—was the gateway to the White Pass, little more than a footpath through the mountains, and about 600 feet lower than the Chilkoot.[3] But the White Pass itself was not an easy trail, and had its own dangers.

A seasoned prospector summed up the two routes best: "There ain't no choice. One's hell. The other's damnation."[4]

Dyea sat on a flat piece of land and was no more than "an Indian village of 250, a white town of four." A forlorn, muddy little patch of squalid tents and cabins that had sprouted up around John Healy's trading post, the village was located at the end of a long inlet and possessed no harbor or unloading dock. Any vessel that wished to land passengers or goods had to bring the cargo to the shore by way of rowboats or barges. The teamsters running the small boats generally dumped the goods wherever they chose, right onto the rocky beach. What made it especially frustrating for travelers was that the packers typically charged twenty dollars an hour when the tide was out and then fifty dollars an hour when the water came barreling up Taiya Inlet.[5]

Perrin and Knudson's steamer anchored about two miles from shore, about as close as the ship could go without running aground. A rowboat took their provisions off the *Taku* and brought them to within about three hundred yards of shore. From that point on, the two men had to carry the entire load on their backs, making several trips through the thigh-high icy water as they ferried their goods to dry land. After two hours, with all their provisions safe, the half-frozen and exhausted men barely had enough strength to draw them-selves up onto the shore. They hired a teamster with a wagon and moved their goods about a mile inland over a rough road to John Healy's trading post.

The two men sat down to dinner at Healy's—the first meal they had eaten all day. Then Perrin began negotiations with some Chilkoot Indians for the transport of his supplies up the twenty-six-mile-long trail over the steep Chilkoot Pass to Lake Lindeman. The Chil-koot were a whipcord-tough group of men and women. The men were stocky and powerfully built with tremendous strength and en-durance, each one capable of carrying up to two hundred pounds of provisions on his back over the rugged terrain. These Indians had served as the informal guardians of this route for many years and owned the pass leading to the Yukon. Anyone who wished to have goods packed over the mountains had to negotiate a price with them, a price that often seemed as capricious as the winds that frequently raked the trail. The packing costs could fluctuate wildly and might even change during the course of the trip. It was not unusual for a Chilkoot man to drop his pack right in the middle of the trail and demand a higher fee. If his employer disagreed, the Chilkoot would simply walk ahead and try to do business with another prospector.[6]

Perrin was worried that others in Dyea were bargaining with the Chilkoot packers and he didn't want to lose any more time. The de-tective devised a clever strategy. "I influenced [seven] Indians into transporting our outfit ahead of all others by exhibiting the large red and gold seals on my extradition papers and explaining . . . by a liberal use of sign language and Chinook, that I was a 'High Mogul' from Washington, D.C., representing the Great Father, all of which the chief explained to his subordinates with the desired result." Once they had agreed on a price of twenty-five cents per pound, or about four hundred dollars for the entire load, Perrin turned in. Worn out from transporting the goods ashore, the detective knew he would need every ounce of strength over the next twenty-four hours.[7]

The Chilkoot Trail began innocuously enough. In fact, for the first several miles, someone who had never traveled on the trail might feel optimistic regarding any hardships ahead. The beginning of the trail was fairly flat with little undergrowth and could be traversed either by wagon or by canoe up the Taiya River, which flowed parallel to the pathway and was at that point merely a stream. But nothing was easy for travelers on the Chilkoot Trail. The devilish little river cut back and forth across the trail in many places, and although it was shallow—as little as eighteen inches in some spots—the men still had to wade through the cold water.

About five miles from Dyea, according to one account, "hell begins."[8] The terrain began to change, from relatively open country to dense underbrush and moraine, alternating between slippery footing on slick rocks and the omnipresent boot-sucking muck, so prevalent on many Alaska Panhandle trails. It became a small victory just to keep one's balance while moving forward through the woods. Even in good weather, a rarity in that part of Alaska, one could not make decent time, and Perrin noted in his diary that this climb was especially difficult since they battled a hard, cold rain.

Completing a long, uphill slog through this challenging terrain, Perrin's group made it to a place called Sheep Camp, located roughly twelve miles from Dyea and about one thousand feet above sea level.[9] It was now 7:30 PM and it had taken them nine-and-a-half hours to go twelve miles. But the real work was just beginning, for Perrin was learning that while the Chilkoot Pass could kill in a moment—the seventy people who died in an avalanche near the spot the following April would be mute witnesses to this—it also could torment a man to death.

After a short rest, at 1:00 AM, they shouldered their packs again and began the final push toward the pass. The Indian packers explained to Perrin that it was best to go as early as possible, preferably in the dark, since the snow would still be frozen and the footing more solid. Once the sun came up, the Chilkoot said, the snow would become slippery, making the climb much more difficult. Perrin and his men trudged on past the tree line and headed toward Stone House, an enormous boulder that most likely received its name because it bore a rough resemblance to a house.[10] Although Stone House was just a mile from Sheep Camp, the altitude had already jumped about six hundred feet.

Next, the climbers passed the Scales, about three thousand feet above sea level and six hundred feet beneath the summit. The Scales were where goods sometimes were reweighed and the Chilkoot might increase their packing fees, but Perrin made no mention of any such occurrence in his diary. All of the party's efforts were now focused on the final forty-degree push up to the forbidding pass itself, which loomed in front of them in the semidarkness like a granite gatekeeper from hell, protecting the entrance to the Yukon. For Perrin's group, and for many thousands of others who were to follow, the last portion of the climb must have appeared to be nearly vertical.[11]

At 4:30 AM, on June 11, just around sunrise, the group reached the summit, about thirty-seven hundred feet above sea level. Perrin mentions nothing in his journal about the spectacular panoramic view—Crater and Morrow Lakes to the north; the Coast Mountains, some of them capped with a few brilliant white glaciers; and south, back down the threadlike path to Dyea. It is possible that he may not have seen anything, because weather conditions often were poor on the pass, but Perrin's omission of any details probably was due to the detective's preoccupation with his mission. He had only one objective in mind: the capture of Frank Alfred Novak. To Perrin, everything else on the trip was a distraction. In fact, throughout his diary, he wrote little about the singular beauty of Alaska and the Yukon.

After a brief rest at the summit, Perrin's party discovered a few abandoned sledges and loaded their goods. For the next two to three hours the men slid down the north side of the mountain until the sun heated up the trail and it was impossible to use the sleds any longer. The Chilkoot removed the packs and everyone slogged through three miles of "very rough portage" until they finally arrived at the head of Lake Lindeman. This point was as far as the Indians were contracted to go, so Perrin paid them and the Chilkoot immediately headed back to Dyea. Even though it was only 9:30 AM, the detective and Knudson were "totally exhausted," and after a quick meal, both men lay down and immediately fell asleep. Overall, Perrin was extremely pleased by the speed of their trip and noted that the average hike over the pass with a similar load took anywhere from three to six days. Perrin and his group had accomplished the trek from Dyea to Lake Lindeman in about twenty-three hours.[12]

The two men were still about six hundred miles from Dawson City, and since there were no roads to the Klondike, traveling over land through such territory was out of the question. The only way to make the trip was to build a boat to navigate down the Yukon. This was the primary reason that Perrin had hired Knudson, as he was an expert carpenter, a man whose woodworking skills would soon be put to the test.

After resting for a few hours, Perrin walked around the lake, visiting with each of the hundred and fifty or so other prospectors who were camped there, all of them building boats for the next stage of their journey. He had previously learned, possibly in Juneau, that Novak was traveling with a group of gold-seekers led by a man named Swift, and that he had changed his name again, and was no longer "Frank Alfred" but was now going under the alias of "J. A. Smith." No one whom Perrin spoke with at Lake Lindeman had heard of either Swift or J. A. Smith. The detective must have felt that he was wasting his time, since he believed that Novak was in Dawson City by now. Nevertheless, he continued working his way around the shore, checking each man to see if he resembled his prey. The men barely had time to speak to him as each of them was just as obsessed as he was in making it to the Klondike as soon as possible.

Every person struggling on the shore was part of a vanguard of thousands more who would be arriving at Lake Lindeman or Lake Bennett within the next several months.[13] As busy as paper wasps building nests, all of the would-be prospectors were engaged in finding suitable trees, cutting them down and floating the logs back to camp, whipsawing the lumber, nailing the boards together, sealing the cracks, loading their goods, and preparing for the roller-coaster ride down the swift-moving, dangerous Yukon River to Dawson City.[14]

If Perrin was disappointed in not finding Novak at Lake Linde-man, he did not mention it in his diary. But he was crestfallen to discover that there was no good timber nearby, since the banks of the lake were covered mostly with scrub evergreen trees much too small for building a raft or scow. In fact, he discovered that the closest us-able trees were about five miles from the lake, up a small tributary. So on June 14, right after breakfast, he and Knudson set off for this loca-tion. From the abundance of fir and pine trees, Knudson selected the former, probably because he knew that although fir was an inferior wood, it was much softer than pine and thus would be easier to saw into planks.[15]

They cut down three trees, each about twenty-two-feet long and more than a foot in diameter, lashed them together to form a crude raft and headed back down the fast-moving river to the lake. As a harbinger of their upcoming Dawson City journey, the unstable raft slammed into some rocks, knocking Perrin overboard into the cold water and forcing him to swim after the logs, "with nothing to keep me up but my pike pole."[16]

The men finally reached their camp at Lake Lindeman about 8:30 PM. Even though the sun was still high in the sky and wouldn't set for about two more hours, they collapsed into their tent, spent from another long, fatiguing day.

Their real work began the next morning, as they began whipsaw-ing the rough green timber into planks. They stripped the logs of all limbs and bark, erected a sawpit, and hoisted the wood on top. Knud-son ran chalk lines down each log, marking where the saw blade would follow when they cut the long planks. Then one man stood on top of the slippery logs about ten feet off the ground and grasped the two wooden pegs at one end of the long saw. He pushed down with all his strength, the sharp teeth biting into the wood, while his partner on the bottom pulled down on the other end of the blade, looking up into a blizzard of sawdust. Then it was the turn of the man on the bottom to push the saw up as the top man pulled at the same time.

The process of sawing these boards was tedious and caused more fights among the men at Lake Lindeman than any other task. Of all the work done in traveling from tidewater to Dawson City, whipsawing was by far the most despised job. "It should be suppressed," said one prospector later. "No character is strong enough to withstand it. Two angels could not saw their first log with one of these things without getting into a fight. It is more trying," he concluded, "than the Chilkoot Pass."[17]

Once the planks were cut, Perrin and Knudson nailed the wood into place, constructing a boat that was twenty-one-and-a-half-feet long, with a beam of roughly four feet and a depth of about twenty-two inches. Knudson had the presence of mind to make sure that the hull had a nine-inch flair, which he believed would give the craft more stability in the rapids. After the boat was nailed together, the two men used oakum[18] and pitch to seal the seams and then carved out oars, a mast for a canvas sail, and a long sweeper for steering. Because there was so much sunlight during this time of year, the two men worked up until the point of exhaustion every day during the five days it took to complete the boat. Perrin noted that both his and Knudson's hands were now covered with blisters.[19]

During this time, a mail carrier from Circle City named Hayes arrived in camp. He had left that settlement on April 7, about ten weeks earlier, and was headed for the outside world with more news of the Klondike gold strike.[20] He rested for awhile, asking the men about any news from "Outside" while they questioned him about the conditions at Dawson City. There is no mention in Perrin's diary of whether he asked Hayes about Frank Novak, but knowing the thoroughness of the detective, it was likely that he did.

Despite their sore hands, Perrin and Knudson finished the boat on the next day. They christened it the *Viking*, in honor of Knudson's Norwegian heritage, set the main sail and jib, and pointed the heavily laden vessel down the placid lake. Now, for the next six hundred miles or so, the two men would battle at least a dozen hardships. The first one appeared just an hour and a half into their voyage as the craft approached One-Mile Rapids. Other travelers urged Perrin to unload his boat and let the craft go through by itself, but Perrin was, as usual, resolute. It might have been because someone told him that no one ever had run these particular rapids before, but after walking along the swift, rock-strewn water and examining the passage, Perrin decided to chance it. In retrospect, his decision was both arrogant and foolish, as just one-third of the way into the rapids, the *Viking* slammed into a wrecked raft and nearly capsized. Only through great effort were the two men able to salvage their goods, offloading the sacks and boxes while they righted the boat in the shallows and bailed out the foundering *Viking* before continuing through the rest of the rapids. But they and almost all of their provisions were thoroughly soaked. The two men spent a "dismal night," wet and shivering from their tumble into the cold, choppy waves.[21]

The country was teaching them a lesson in humility. They still had hundreds of miles to go to Dawson City and already they had had a small taste of what an untamed river could do in just one-third of a mile. It promised to be a lot worse in the days ahead, and at times both men wished they were dead. For them, and for so many others in 1897 and 1898 who traveled down the Yukon to the Klondike, the release that death provided seemed preferable to continuing the journey.

Some men took matters into their own hands and committed suicide, but for Red Perrin, this was not an option. The obsessive detective had no choice.

EIGHT

•────────────────────────•

Down the Yukon

After their ride through One-Mile Rapids, Perrin and Knudson beached their boat on the shores of Lake Bennett. The *Viking* was no longer seaworthy, so the two men resealed the seams and hammered in the loose nails. While they worked, one of them realized that they had left some provisions behind so they hired a few Indians to walk upstream to retrieve them, and then they reloaded the *Viking* and relaunched her at the point where One-Mile Rapids joined Lake Bennett. The lake is one of several bodies of water that feed the mighty Yukon River as it makes its two-thousand-mile trip to the Bering Sea. About twenty-eight miles long and surrounded by jagged mountains, Bennett can be an unpredictable body of water, but Perrin and Knudson's trip across was relatively smooth. The *Viking* bounced over the gentle rollers for about three hours until they reached a spot called Caribou Crossing. This Indian settlement was at the junction of Lake Bennett and Lake Tagish, named for the Tagish Indians who lived there. Adapting to the territory, Perrin wrote that as they rowed through the crossing into Lake Tagish, they caught a few fish by trolling off the *Viking's* stern. They also shot and cooked a duck, a most welcome change from their monotonous diet of jerked meat, bacon, and beans. Perrin noted that this was the first game they had in the Yukon.[1]

Earlier, while working their way across Lake Bennett, the men passed a scow that also was headed for Dawson City. This was a large craft, carrying nine prospectors and their provisions, and as the *Viking* passed by, both parties shouted greetings across the water:

"That scow wasn't built for a racer, was she?" hollered the detective.

"She's slow, but sure," was the reply.

"Well, good-bye," said Perrin, as they left the slower vessel behind.

"So long," said a man in the scow. "Save a little of the gold for us."

"Of course."[2]

Perrin wouldn't find out about it until much later, but his pursuit of the Iowa fugitive could have ended right there on Lake Bennett.

Frank Novak was on that scow.

Ironically, despite Novak having had a long head start, the detective had closed the gap through speed, doggedness, and sheer will. But Perrin didn't know that at the time. He was under the impression that Novak was already in Dawson City, possibly playing a violin in one of the dance halls. This missed opportunity would cost Perrin dearly for during the next two weeks, he and Knudson came close to losing their lives many times.

Lake Tagish was well known for the fierce winds that frequently tore across its surface. That first day they made little progress and, after another long, fatiguing effort, decided to beach their boat and wait for the rough water to die down. While ashore, Perrin found an abandoned Indian village and carefully studied the different names carved into the trees and on a few log cabins; he was looking for either the name Swift, as this was the party that Novak was supposed to be traveling with, or J. A. Smith, the alias that Novak had been using since he left Seattle. But finding neither, he and Knudson shoved off again and made the shore of Lake Marsh at about 9:00 PM on June 22.

By this time, Perrin had realized that he was in for an adventure of a lifetime. For him, nothing else would be as dangerous as this pursuit. Just as their boat tacked across the lake, the two men seemed to sail from one incident to the next, some just small annoyances, while others turned out to be much more perilous. Some days they

would make as much as twenty or thirty miles; other days, only three
or four. But that was the nature of the Yukon—an untamed land of
nameless hills and mountains framing the swirling cold gray-green
waters; a river that could kill without pity or remorse in a place that
could drive a man to the brink of insanity and then haul him back to
the shores of reason again.

Throughout his diary, Perrin frequently complained about one
persistent pest—the Yukon mosquito. Sixteen years earlier, an ex-
plorer named Johan Adrian Jacobson called the annoying insect a
"plague" and wrote that "against the relentless pursuit during waking or sleeping carried on by mosquitoes which are constantly replaced by millions of new ones, there is no defense."[3]

It was not unusual to see large animals such as caribou and bears
driven to madness by the incessant insects.[4] The mosquitoes attacked
in serried squadrons, thick clouds of them, and there was no relief,
save for a rainstorm or a smoky fire. Having seen some Indians at
a fish camp build one of these fires, Perrin and Knudson tried the
same trick, sleeping for about six hours among the smoky moss and
burning trees. On another night, a spark from their campfire jumped
to some deadwood and nearly caused a forest fire.

As the miles played out, the trip turned into sheer torture. The
sun was now up for about twenty hours each day; working the oars
had become an endless, mind-numbing chore. Sleep was scarce, for
even when they tried to nap during the day, things went awry. In one
instance, with both men asleep, the *Viking* floated down the Lewis
River and drifted onto a sandbar, stranding them until Perrin woke
up, slipped on his rubber boots, jumped in the water, and shoved the
boat back into the current. After that incident, they decided that one
man would sleep while the other worked the sweeper oar. By now,
they were in a constant state of sleep deprivation, which could be
fatal as the boat swept through rapids and banged on past bear-sized
boulders. They ate in the same fashion that they slept, in fits and
spurts, shooting some ducks or geese when they could and having
a little luck with their fishing line. And every night, when the spent

men drifted into the riverbank to set up camp, Perrin and Knudson had to deal with the intolerable mosquitoes, which, the detective noted, were "so thick as to nearly obscure the sun."[5]

On June 24, Perrin was napping while Knudson was on watch, manning the oar and floating down a part of the river that "twists and turns like a huge serpent in distress."[6] Suddenly the Norwegian's frantic shouts awakened the detective, who saw that the boat was now in fast current, sweeping past a ragged patch of red cloth fixed to a stick on the east bank. It took considerable effort for the two men to beach the *Viking* and work their way back upstream to the marker.

At the bottom of the stick was a board that read: "Cañon one mile ahead. Beware!"[7]

The men had reached Miles Canyon, a dangerous section of the Yukon and a real test for any boatman. They would need all of the skill and luck they possessed to run the *Viking* safely through the churning water. "If a man is a skilful navigator, he can run his boat through the Canyon, a distance of three-fourths of a mile, and land on the right-hand side," claimed a popular guidebook that was carried by hundreds of prospectors a few months later, including a twenty-one-year-old former oyster pirate named Jack London. "If not," the guidebook added crisply, "he had better make a portage."[8]

Carved out of reddish-brown volcanic rock, with hundred-foot cliffs on each side, the canyon compressed the Yukon from about five hundred feet into a narrow seventy-five-foot-wide funnel. The whitewater made a deafening roar as it tore through the canyon like a wounded animal. The scene was unforgettable to anyone who saw it. One prospector wrote, "The water was boiling through [the canyon] at such terrible speed that it ridged up in the center, while along the perpendicular banks it whirled in huge eddies which had a very threatening look." It was, he thought, as if "all the waters in creation seemed to have fallen into a space seventy-five feet wide."[9]

Upon reaching Miles Canyon, many travelers paused and wondered if the trip downstream to Dawson City was really worth it. At the peak of the gold rush, this spot would claim a number of lives and would destroy dozens of vessels. In fact, when asked about taking a boat through the canyon, one guide wrote succinctly, "My advice is—don't!"[10]

Portaging was obviously safer, but it usually took a few backbreaking days to carry all of one's goods along the path overlooking the canyon. Each traveler had to consider the choices: spend several long days moving the gear, food, and the boat itself on the pathway, or wager one's life in exchange for about thirty seconds of sheer terror as the craft battled through the rapids. And even if the boat made it past the first portion of the canyon, an enormous whirlpool lay just ahead, waiting to devour any vessel and its unlucky passengers.

Perrin and Knudson weighed their chances. They spent considerable time studying the rushing water, which the detective clocked at about thirty-two miles per hour. After discussing the best route through the narrow canyon, they gathered their courage, launched the *Viking* into the raging current, and tore downstream, with the rocky basalt walls "dashing by like twin lightning express trains," as Jack London wrote later.[11]

The two men were lucky. Their boat, despite being heavily laden with very little freeboard, "shot into the head of the canyon as though propelled from the mouth of a mortar . . . riding the crests of the huge wall of water that was thrown up by the terrific torrent."[12]

They slipped past the whirlpool and in a little less than a minute had passed through the canyon. The men worked the *Viking* toward shore, where they beached it and examined the hull for any damage. Having found no leaks, a relieved Perrin wrote in his diary that "each of us set up several kinds of high resolves that we would not make this passage again for all the gold in the Yukon country." Once their goods were secured, Knudson went back to the first landing point above the canyon and retrieved his dog. It was the first instance that Perrin's diary mentioned that an animal had accompanied them on the trip from Juneau. Perhaps fittingly, the dog was a bloodhound. When Knudson reached the dog, however, he saw that the poor animal was battling clouds of the ubiquitous mosquitoes.[13]

As frightening as it was, Miles Canyon was a precursor to what lay ahead about a mile or so downstream. After the two men picked their way through Squaw Rapids, a nasty little stretch of the Yukon with menacing rocks strewn just above and below the water's surface, they spotted more red flags planted on the bank, along with a large sign: "Stop."

They rowed out of the current to contemplate their next move—a wise choice as both men were now just upstream from the infamous White Horse Rapids, so named because the frothy water resembled a pack of stampeding white horses. The rapids were about seven-eighths of a mile long, with the last one thousand feet including many waterfalls. During the gold rush that followed, about one hundred fifty boats were destroyed in "the mane of the Horse" and at least ten men drowned in the turbulent waters.[14]

Tappan Adney, a newspaper reporter from *Harper's Weekly* who was traveling in the thick of the Klondike stampede a few months later, described the last portion of the rapids, stating that the river "lashe[d] itself into a perfect fury, and then, with a jumping and tossing, it bursts through a gorge a span wide with banks level with the water, and then spreads out serene, once more the wide, generous river."[15]

Many who had previously contemplated running White Horse had learned a valuable lesson from Miles Canyon, where they had either lost most of their goods or had come close to drowning, and opted to portage five miles around the rapids. Some of them, acutely aware of their boats' lack of freeboard, removed the heaviest cargo—sacks of flour and other provisions—deposited them on the shore and then pushed off into the whitewater. Once they made it through, the prospectors returned for their supplies. Later, during the peak of the Klondike rush, Samuel Steele, the tall, imposing superintendant of the North West Mounted Police and a man who set down rules in his wilderness empire like a benevolent despot, decreed that no women or children could travel through the rapids and only experienced boatmen were allowed to pilot the different vessels.[16]

Perrin and Knudson joined the other men on the riverbanks, watching the water as it exploded over the rocks. It was now 10:00 PM and although the sun was still up, there was no relief from the dozens of mosquitoes that circled each man. Here appeared to be the ultimate litmus test of how far a man was willing to go. It was as if some omnipotent being had devised a series of dangerous tasks for the men, testing the limits of human endurance. At several junctures—the Chilkoot Pass, building a boat on Lake Lindeman or Bennett, navigating down the Yukon to this point—travelers faced a test of will. Now, at White Horse, some men looked at the rapids, stopped, laid down their packs and either sold all of their goods for a few cents on the dollar or just turned around and began the long upriver trip back to Dyea. But as Perrin contemplated his next move, he never considered turning back. As far as he was concerned, quitting was out of the question. The only way to go was forward, continuing downriver to Dawson City.

Perrin inspected the rapids again the following day. Studying "the inspiring effect of a large number of scows and boats wrecked and hanging on boulders in midstream and along the shore" was indeed sobering. After some consideration, he decided to play it safe with a portion of their goods, since he realized that although they could obtain new provisions, the extradition papers were irreplaceable. Perrin removed ten days' worth of food from the boat, along with a satchel containing all of his important documents, and left them in a pile on the shore. The two men then shoved off in the *Viking*, caught the current, and shot downstream, "whirling through the roaring rapids with possible destruction staring us in the face."[17]

After "riding the Horse" successfully, they rowed the *Viking* into a shallow area and beached it for another inspection. Again, luck was with them. A number of nails had backed out of the wood and the pitch had cracked in part of the hull, but otherwise the boat was in decent shape. Knudson's skills as a carpenter had paid off and they were now through the toughest parts of the river. They recaulked the hull, walked back through the portage area, and retrieved the items

left on the riverbank, pausing to see if any other boats were passing by. When they returned to the *Viking*, they loaded everything on
board, pushed off, and at about 11:00 PM had a late dinner on the river.

During the next few days, a thick fog blanketed the Yukon, making it difficult to see much farther than the bow. This was more of an
aggravation than a real hazard, since the current was slow and their
job consisted of keeping the *Viking* in the main channel, away from
the many sandbars that dotted this particular stretch of the Yukon.

After drifting through Lake Laberge and running safely through
two more sets of rapids—Five Fingers, which the Indians called "*Tthi
Cho Nadezhe*" or "Big Rocks Standing Up,"[18] and Rink Rapids—Perrin
and Knudson tied up at the junction of the Yukon and Pelly rivers.
This was the site of an old military station, Fort Selkirk, as well as
the ruins of a nearby Hudson's Bay trading post. Perrin spoke with
a large group of Indians living nearby and met with a party of Canadian surveyors who also had camped there. As always, he showed his
photograph of Novak to everyone he saw, but no one had seen him.

The Canadian party was led by a man named William Ogilvie, who
later would become famous throughout the territory. He, along with
Charles Constantine and Samuel Steele of the North West Mounted
Police, emerged as a symbol of honesty and incorruptibility during
the fledgling gold rush. Built like a fireplug, with black hair and a
full salt-and-pepper beard, Ogilvie was responsible for surveying and
determining ownership of the patchwork quilt of gold claims that
lined both sides of the rivers and creeks in the area—an enormous
task, especially considering the rough terrain and numerous legal
disputes regarding the different parcels of land. Like his mounted
police counterparts, Ogilvie could probably have made a fortune
staking Klondike claims, but the surveyor was not interested in gold.
He realized the vital nature of his job in the Klondike and was a
hard-working, fair-minded man who earned the trust and respect of
all the prospectors.[19]

This was the first meeting between Perrin and Ogilvie. The two
men would see each again in Dawson City and once more on the

Yukon, and the Canadian surveyor was to play an important part in the Novak case later on.[20]

🌿 🌿 🌿

After speaking with the Indians and Ogilvie, Perrin met with a trader, a feisty man named J. J. Pitts who had kept a log of about twelve hundred people who had passed through, traveling either up or down the Yukon.[21] Perrin scrutinized the list of visitors' names carefully, looking for either "J. A. Smith" or "Swift," the party with which Novak was reported to be traveling. The detective studied the travelers' signatures as well, but came up with nothing. He said good-bye to Ogilvie and the *Viking* drifted on, with Perrin and Knudson eating as they traveled instead of putting in to shore and facing the hated mosquitoes. From this point on, they resigned themselves to catching whatever rest they could as the boat moved downriver. Trying to sleep was hopeless, Perrin acknowledged in his diary, noting that "one more night was added to the season of torture."[22]

After gliding past the White and Stewart Rivers, the latter the site of an earlier gold strike, Perrin checked his map and saw that they were approaching the confluence of another tributary. He determined they were now opposite the mouth of the Klondike River, where two towns were located. The first settlement took its formal name of Klondike City from the river, but was known among the miners as Louse Town. The two men kept going, floating past Louse Town to the second settlement, where they tied up the *Viking*.

They had made it to Dawson City. It was July 1, 1897, and Red Perrin had his first glimpse of the largest city in the Yukon. Dawson City was a town of about three thousand people "living mostly in tents or rude shacks, and stretched along the Yukon River for a distance of two and one-half miles and probably one and one-half miles along the Klondike River."[23] As he stared at the scene before him, Perrin finally grasped the seeming impossibility of his task—finding one man in a sea of others. As William Ogilvie put it so aptly later, Dawson City's "myriad of tents and their ever-flitting occupants seemed like the proverbial haystack in which [Perrin] had to search for his needle."[24]

Only seven months earlier, the site of Dawson City was a dismal mud flat with a population of fewer than one hundred people. The town was located at the base of an old mountain slide area that locals called the "moosehide" because of its light brown color. But now Dawson, like everything else around it, was growing in front of everyone's eyes. It was as if some nameless ragtag army had descended upon the land. Wooden false-fronted buildings popped up like mushrooms all along Broadway and Front Street; the air rang with a bedlam of hammering, shouts, sawmills, and dog howls while tinkling piano music drifted out of the bars. Within a year, there would be thousands more people in Dawson City, claims would already be staked for miles in virtually every direction, and there was little left for the arriving horde except to work for wages in the mines or perform some other menial jobs. Since everything in Dawson City was either packed in from Dyea or Skagway or transported by steamer—the latter of which took much longer and cost much more—the price of goods was astronomical, roughly seven to ten times what anything would cost in the continental United States.[25]

☙ ☙ ☙

As he and Knudson beached their boat and began walking through Dawson City, Perrin reflected on what was happening around him. In his life so far, the red-haired detective had captured a Mexican bandit in Arizona Territory; lived near hostile Indians and was allegedly a veteran of the Apache Wars; and had tracked and captured a Chicago embezzler in Mexico and brought him back to trial after thousands of miles of detective work. But none of his previous experiences had prepared him for the wild carnival wheel that was spinning unabated in Dawson City. Perrin noted that "saloons were found running by the score, and a number of dance halls and gambling hells wide open and running without cessation."[26]

To Perrin, it must have seemed like hell on earth, a Bosch triptych

come to life, with every aspect of purgatory in full view. The carnival
never stopped, as it was now summer in the Yukon and the sun was
up for close to twenty-four hours a day.

The gold nuggets and dust in Dawson City seemed to be alive,
like capricious spirits, moving around the town, never staying in one
place very long, slipping from one person to the next. The yellow
metal seemed almost hot as it jumped from the prospector's poke to
the bar owner, then to the dance hall girl, to the gambler, over to the
dry goods store, and on and on, around and around. And since there
was little paper money and few coins, almost everything was paid for
in nuggets or gold dust. Miners made money by panning the sawdust
on the floor of the bars; bartenders kept their fingernails long in
order to scrape off some gold dust for themselves, while all around
them, the whole mad tea party whirled faster and faster.[27]

The inexorable detective had no time for any of it. He was only
interested in the pursuit. He began by watching the waterfront and
the main streets, remaining as unobtrusive as possible.[28] With his
characteristic tenacity, he walked through the area immediately surrounding Dawson City, expanding his search, checking every tent,
and showing his now-tattered photograph of Novak to everyone
he met.

After trudging through town for days, he developed one lead—
a waitress at the Star Restaurant with the lilting Irish name of Sadie
O'Hara, who had worked at Juneau's Circle City Hotel in March.
O'Hara was said to have information on Novak and Jack Swift, supposedly one of Novak's traveling companions, but when Perrin asked
her about these two men, she replied that she had not seen either one
in Dawson City. Disappointed, Perrin spent the next two days hiking
around the claims on El Dorado and Bonanza Creeks, searching the
tents and cabins that lined these two tributaries. Later, he claimed
to have walked seventy-five miles in forty-eight hours, arriving back
in town "footsore and weary."[29]

On the next day, July 8, Perrin checked the waterfront area and saw that the steamer *J. J. Healy* had arrived from Circle City. On the boat with about two hundred other passengers were Inspector Charles Constantine of the North West Mounted Police and Jack Swift's wife. Perrin began tailing Mrs. Swift, hoping that she would meet up with her husband, but after speaking with her, he concluded that she could not help him. During that time, he introduced himself to Inspector Constantine and presented his documents to the NWMP officer. After a few questions, Constantine accepted the detective's mission and promised him the Mounties' full cooperation. Satisfied with the meeting, Perrin continued patrolling the banks of the Yukon, checking any new boats coming from upriver.[30]

On July 10, Perrin recognized a couple of familiar faces—two men he had met on the Yukon who had just arrived in Dawson City. They told him that the Swift party was behind them because their members had stopped to prospect at a few Yukon streams before continuing to Dawson City. The men also said that they had passed the same scow around Five Finger Rapids. Perrin must have cursed his luck, for if he had only passed closer to the Swift scow back at Lake Bennett, he might have recognized the fugitive on board and thus would have avoided the rest of the journey to Dawson City. Still, the news from the two men was encouraging, for if they were right, Novak was perhaps only a few days away. After this discussion, Perrin decided to interrogate Mrs. Swift again. He went to her quarters and demanded if she knew where her husband was. She told him that she thought Jack Swift had landed at Dawson City, but because of the crush of people in the town, she had not seen him just yet.[31]

Now Novak was close and Perrin could feel it. He walked the town again and took up his post at the riverbank, searching for any new boats and inspecting the faces of the men.

Then on Monday, July 12, as he was stalking the waterfront, Perrin spotted a scow that apparently had just arrived. Sitting in the craft was a man in ragged clothing, about five feet nine inches tall and one hundred eighty pounds, with a high forehead and a full beard of

reddish-brown whiskers. Based on the photograph he had carried for
three months, Perrin believed that this man sitting placidly in front
of him was Frank Alfred Novak.[32]

Perrin walked over to the scow.

"Hello, Novak," he said calmly. "I have followed you a long time but
I caught up with you."[33]

The bearded man paused for a moment before he answered:

"You are mistaken. My name is J. A. Smith."

"It is, is it? Well, you are accused of killing a man by the name of
Ed Murray in Walford, Iowa, and that is why I have had you arrested
and am holding you under arrest now, but if you can identify yourself
as being J. A. Smith, why, we will turn you loose."[34]

The man in the scow denied everything and said that Perrin was
making a big mistake. He insisted that he had never been in Iowa
but was born in Cincinnati, Ohio, and had more recently lived in
Chicago. But when Perrin grilled him about the latter city, the suspect had little knowledge about Chicago and could only tell him the
names of two streets there—Clark and State.[35]

Nevertheless, the ragged-looking man with the reddish-brown
beard was confident that it was just a case of mistaken identity and
was ready to stand up and walk away. "He seemed to think I was a bit
discouraged then, and looked steady and cool," Perrin said later.[36]

But Perrin, who needed to be sure he was right, was undeterred.
He took out an envelope and said, "You claim to be J. A. Smith.
Please write it down." The man scrawled "J. A. Smith" on a piece of
paper. Perrin then produced a letter that Novak had written to someone in Iowa, compared the two writing samples and found them to be
practically identical. He was convinced that this was Novak.[37]

Despite the bearded man's protests, Perrin quickly frisked him,
taking from him a small-caliber revolver, and marched the suspect
through the dusty Dawson City streets to Inspector Constantine. The
detective explained to the Mountie post commander that he believed
this was Frank Novak, the alleged murderer whom Perrin had sought
for the past four months, and he was prepared to prove it. In addition

to the handwriting samples, the detective had brought the alleged murderer's dental records. Constantine called in the assistant post surgeon, Dr. Alfred E. Wills, who scrutinized the dental charts and compared them with the suspect's teeth.[38]

After the examination, both Dr. Wills and Constantine were positive that the teeth of the man standing in front of them matched those described in Novak's dental records.[39] But Constantine wanted additional proof. He had learned that there was someone in Dawson City who had once been in Walford and had done some business in the area. The inspector had him brought to Mounties' headquarters. Without any prompting, the man looked at the suspect and exclaimed, "That is Frank Novak of Walford," and then turned and said, "Why Frank, you know me; we were in the same lodge together."[40]

The accused man had no reply.

Now Constantine was convinced. He placed Novak under armed guard and discussed the next steps with Perrin. They decided it was best to have a Mountie accompany Perrin and Novak for a portion of the long trip down the Yukon, at least as far as the Bering Sea, since Constantine felt that part of the journey would offer the prisoner the greatest chance for escape. Fortunately, a constable named Mathew Gowler was retiring from the Mounties and had planned to leave the country at the same time. Constantine immediately ordered Gowler to assist Perrin during the journey back to the United States.[41]

First, Perrin, Gowler, and Novak traveled downriver to Fort Cudahy, a distance of roughly forty miles, where the prisoner was deposited in a rough log stockade. He would be kept there, in the custody of Inspector W. H. Scarth, until a steamer could pick him up for the seventeen-hundred-mile trip down the Yukon to the Bering Sea. Scarth was a friend of Constantine's from their days at the NWMP camp at Regina, Saskatchewan, in 1895. He made sure that Novak, who was now wearing leg shackles, was watched twenty-four hours a day.

Perrin returned to Dawson City and treated himself to one last look at all the chaos swirling around the burgeoning gold rush town.

By the time Perrin was ready to leave, word of his extraordinary pursuit and arrest of Novak had spread around town, and many of Dawson City's citizens considered him a hero. They threw him a lavish party headed by a man named C. A. Bowman, a leader of a mining syndicate that was poised to move into Dawson City to supply the largely untapped gold fields with more manpower and funding.[42]

The laconic detective said goodbye to Knudson, who had taken a job as a miner for fifteen dollars a day.[43] He thanked the Norwegian for all of his help, which had proved so invaluable on the trip from Dyea to Dawson City. Then Perrin reflected on what he had seen in the Klondike, writing an entry in his diary dated July 14:

> Boarded the steamer *J. J. Healy* for St. Michael's, bidding goodbye to Dawson City with its long and promiscuous array of boats, scows, tents, flimsy shacks, saloons, dance halls, gambling hells, and two lonely mercantile establishments, also bidding good-bye to its fatal epidemic of typhoid fever, from which no stricken patient ever recovers; bid a cheerful good-by to the 1,500 Eskimo dogs, roaming, fighting, and snarling over the tundra which passes for streets in this arctic habitat, and headed down the Yukon bound for civilization.[44]

When Perrin returned to Fort Cudahy, he found a pleasant surprise waiting for him. William Ogilvie, the quiet Canadian surveyor whom Perrin first met at the Fort Selkirk trading post, also was headed out of the country through St. Michael and would accompany the detective on the voyage.

The *Healy* picked up Novak and Constable Gowler and then, once its crew had loaded the vessel with ample wood for the boiler, began the trip downriver. Perrin and the Mountie split their time watching Novak, who so far had said very little. They had reserved two staterooms on the boat, one for Novak, who was under round-the-clock watch, and the other for Perrin and Gowler. As the *Healy* passed by Circle City, Perrin noticed that the former mining town was practically deserted. Virtually every able-bodied man in the territory had gone to stake claims at the Klondike gold fields. Perrin finally took the time to admire the country, which he called the "grandest" on the Yukon, whose beauty he compared to that of the Hudson River in New York.[45]

On the next day, Perrin was fortunate to see a midnight sun—the only one he had witnessed on his trip, visible because they were now inside the Arctic Circle. His prisoner had begun to "thaw out," as Perrin wrote later in his diary, talking at length with the detective and Constable Gowler. For the first time, Novak admitted that he was the man Perrin had been searching for during the past four months. In contrast to his journey to Dawson City, Perrin had a good time floating down the Yukon. "We had many enjoyable hours; our chief amusement being poker and pedro. Novak indulged in both games, playing in hard luck. The miners had great stores of whisky on board and they treated my prisoner as though he was not under arrest. I might add that I never saw the man refuse a drink and his capacity for tobacco was amazing."[46]

Most of the trip was uneventful, except when the steamer struggled in shallow water. One time the boat ran aground onto a sandbar at the Yukon River delta, a maze of tidal flats, false leads, and blind channels. The *Healy* captain was an experienced pilot, however, and when the tide lifted the steamer, he located the Aphoon Passage, which served as a shortcut to St. Michael. But the steamer soon encountered more difficulties. Even though she only drew two feet, near Norton Sound, the vessel labored in water so shallow that its hull constantly scraped the thick mud. Meanwhile, strong winds slammed into the little ship, so much so that the crew was afraid the flimsy cabins would be blown off into the water. Although it was mid-July, the temperature was so cold and the winds so unceasing that the passengers spent most of the day huddled around an inefficient stove in the combination salon and dining room, trying to keep warm.[47]

On the morning of July 21, after traveling about seventeen hundred miles, they reached St. Michael, a dreary little port town that was founded in about 1833 and lay roughly one hundred twenty-five

miles southeast of Nome. Like many other Alaskan coastal settlements, St. Michael was part of the chain of old Russian forts and fur-
trading posts that stretched from the Aleutians to the Alaskan Panhandle. Perhaps because it was the last place that any long-suffering
voyagers stopped in before leaving the country, it was later referred
to as "Fort Get-There."[48]

At St. Michael, Perrin linked up again with D. L. Clouse, the Thiel
detective who had earlier traveled from Juneau to Dutch Harbor,
guarding Alaska's "back door" in case Novak had tried to leave
through that route. Clouse had been checking all the steamers as
they passed through Dutch Harbor, but had no success and moved
up to St. Michael after a few weeks so he could be closer to the mouth
of the Yukon.[49]

While there, Clouse and Perrin discovered that there were no out-
bound steamers in port, so the two detectives joined about two dozen
prospectors waiting for the next ship. Perrin asked Ogilvie—who was
an amateur photographer and had a supply of photographic paper
and chemicals with him—to take two separate photographs, one
showing Novak with his full beard and another after the whiskers
were shaved off. Ogilvie had the detective sit next to Novak; he also
wrote the date and his own initials in soft pencil, along with Perrin's,
on the photographic plate holder. That way, there would be no question about when the photographs were taken and who took them. In
addition, the pictures would serve as evidence that Novak had indeed
been captured, in case the prisoner escaped or committed suicide
during the long ocean voyage.[50]

Interestingly, one of these snapshots provided Ogilvie with a
source of amusement for many years afterwards. The Canadian, who
had a sly sense of humor, liked to play a parlor game with some of his
acquaintances. He explained later in his memoirs, "I have hundreds
of times shown the picture [of Novak and Perrin] to people, remark-
ing as I did so, 'Here is a picture of a cruel murderer and the detective who followed him nine thousand miles to arrest him. Now, which
is the murderer?' Very seldom is the right one chosen."[51]

Perrin's group spent more than two weeks at desolate St. Michael, with little to do except constantly check the horizon for any inbound steamers. The detective wiled away the time talking to the post traders and slogging around the island, which he described as a large peat bog surrounding an extinct volcano. He allowed Novak to take walks around St. Michael as well, always making sure that his captive was under guard.

Finally, after they had spent fifteen days at this drab little outpost, a steamer anchored about a mile offshore, since the water was too shallow for docking. Along with Ogilvie and the prospectors, Perrin, Clouse, Constable Gowler, and their prisoner were headed back to civilization, but instead of sacks jammed with gold dust or nuggets like most of their fellow passengers, they had a much greater treasure.

They were returning with an accused murderer.

NINE

The Long Journey Home

The vessel that finally arrived was the SS *Portland*, an aging twelve-year-old steamship that had helped kick off the gold rush only a few weeks before. Although news of the Klondike strike had been trickling out of the Yukon since about February, it took the arrival of the two now-famous treasure ships—the *Excelsior* in San Francisco on July 15 and the *Portland* two days later in Seattle—to jump-start the last major gold rush of the nineteenth century. Now, less than a month later, the *Portland* was completing her first trip back to the Yukon, crammed from bow to stern with gold seekers.

Since St. Michael had no docks, the crew spent the next four days unloading the vessel's passengers and their cargo into smaller boats that could reach the shore. The excited would-be prospectors were first off, streaming down the gangplanks and onto Alaskan soil, each one trying to book passage on the handful of small steamers heading back upriver to Dawson City. But after the *Portland* was unloaded, the southbound travelers still had to wait several more days, as the water was extremely rough and no boat could venture out to the ship. Finally, on August 16, the little *Hamilton*, a river steamer that had just been launched, ferried Perrin, Novak, and the other passengers onto the *Portland*, which began its long voyage back to Seattle.[1]

The trip was uneventful, with the ship stopping to refuel at Dutch Harbor. A wild rumor about supposed Chinese pirates lurking just offshore had prompted a Coast Guard cutter to escort the *Portland* down the Canadian coast, safeguarding the steamer and her gold cargo.[2]

After a few more days, the *Portland* reached Port Townsend, Washington, and Perrin was able to send a telegram to Gus Thiel announcing the arrest of Novak. An alert Associated Press reporter saw the message and broke the story, which was picked up by dozens of newspapers throughout the country. With typical understatement, Perrin's diary mentions nothing about the scene at Seattle, where the dock was crammed with hundreds of people clamoring to go to the Yukon.

The phlegmatic detective seemed oblivious to the bedlam that was now his nearly constant companion. While reporters, relatives of the prospectors on board, and a large crowd surged toward the *Portland*, Perrin and Novak slipped through the mass of people and holed up in the Seattle Hotel for a few hours until the detective could purchase train tickets to Iowa. Later that same day, Perrin, Novak, and D. L. Clouse boarded the Northern Pacific Railway train with a destination of St. Paul, Minnesota, where they arrived at about 4:40 PM on Wednesday, September 1. They had several hours between trains, so Perrin and Clouse brought Novak to the Thiel offices, killing time by chatting with other detectives. Then they returned to the station and headed down the "Albert Lea Route," the final leg of the trip that had begun in Dawson City about five weeks earlier.[3]

Their now-famous prisoner was initially panic-stricken, convinced that he would be dragged from the train and lynched. Perrin assured him that this would not happen, but as the train clattered through the Iowa towns, drawing closer and closer to Vinton, Novak was still worried. He peeked out through the blinds and saw clusters of people watching the train pass, each one trying to catch a glimpse of the alleged Walford murderer. "The Kodak fiends," as one paper called them, were out in force, as photography had become more popular with the invention of more compact (even pocket-sized) cameras and commercial film developing. Some even were sold as "detective cameras"[4] and were meant to be used discreetly.

Once again, photography was playing its own small but important part in the many twists of the Novak case, bookending the beginning and end of the chase. In February, the Thiel detectives had covered the route across Iowa and Nebraska, armed with a photograph of Novak; Perrin had carried one with him as he traveled from Juneau to Dawson City; Ogilvie had taken photos to document the prisoner's arrest and appearance both with and without a beard; and now Novak was afraid that if he wouldn't be hung on the spot when he stepped back onto Iowa soil, the Hawkeyes armed with cameras would be ready to attack him. Now well aware of the power of photography, Novak was certain that his ignominious return would be documented by hundreds of Iowans bearing the little Kodak box cameras.[5]

Despite his concerns, Novak consented to an interview with a reporter from the *Cedar Rapids Evening Gazette* who had boarded the train in St. Paul. More than any other paper in Iowa, the *Gazette* had been plugged into the case from its beginning and in fact had been in close communication with Tobin as well as Red Perrin.

After speaking about his experiences in Juneau and the Klondike, Novak was asked about his upcoming arraignment and trial. He protested his innocence: "I have nothing to say regarding my defense, except that it will be sufficient to acquit me. I am not going to say a word to anyone until I go before the grand jury. If they believe my story, all right. If not, I'll have to take my medicine." He continued after a moment: "I wish you would make it just as easy on me as possible. You know that under the law a man is presumed to be innocent until he is proven guilty, and I want and am entitled to the benefit of the doubt. Where I made my mistake was in leaving Walford but my friends will all understand in due time. There are circumstances which they do not understand and which I cannot explain now." Novak then asked about his wife and children but, according to the

Gazette, "never once did he betray the slightest emotion at the mention of a name or circumstance."[6]

Novak was permitted to send a wire to La Porte City, asking for a meeting with Cato Sells, a celebrated attorney from that town. Sells was one of the most well-respected lawyers in Iowa, a man dubbed "The Boy Orator" at the age of nineteen for his elaborate speeches. A former mayor of La Porte City, Sells had moved to Vinton years later and twice had been elected Benton County attorney, once in 1891 and again in 1893, immediately prior to M. J. Tobin's term in 1896. A formidable opponent in any courtroom, Sells had made his mark in statewide legal and political circles.[7]

Frank Novak was pleased to learn that Cato Sells had received his message and agreed to meet and discuss the case. While it's doubtful that the two men had known each other previously, Novak welcomed the famous attorney warmly when Sells boarded the train in La Porte City. The two men had a long discussion around midnight as the train steamed toward Vinton.

At precisely 2:30 AM on the morning of September 2, the train pulled into the Vinton train station. About one hundred people were gathered in the darkness, straining to catch a glimpse of the fugitive, but Novak, Perrin, and Clouse stepped directly from the train into an enclosed wagon. Among those waiting was M. J. Tobin, the dynamic Benton County prosecutor. He and Perrin shook hands; though the two men had exchanged telegrams through the Thiel Agency, they had never met before. As he stepped down from the train, Perrin did a brief interview with reporters, casually mentioning that what he had feared most about the trip was Novak's suicide, since he believed that the suspect would "welcome a chance to get off the earth and out of the world."[8]

Within a few minutes, Novak was taken through the town to the old Benton County jail, where county Sheriff Sam Metcalf unlocked the cell door. Novak entered; the sheriff clanged the big iron door shut, turned the key in the lock, and shuffled back to bed.

At last, after six months and roughly twenty-five-thousand miles, in a chase that ranged across North America to Europe, over the Chilkoot Trail and down the Yukon River, through rolling tundra that brushed the Arctic Circle, and then across the Bering Sea and the North Pacific, the long pursuit was over.

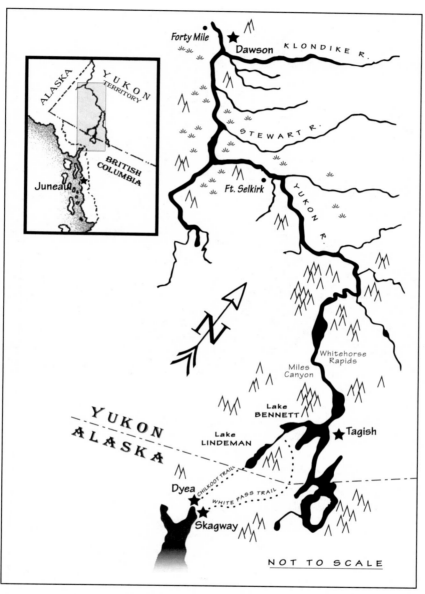

Map of Alaska and the Yukon.
Created by Charles M. Biscay, © Peter Kaufman.

The burned-out ruins from Novak and Jilek's store, taken a day or so
after the fire. The remains of Novak's bank vault can be seen on the left.
Lucy Dosh Tobin Scrapbook, courtesy of the family of Lucy Dosh Tobin.

LOOKING UP THE ONE MILE RIVER BETWEEN LINDEMAN AND BENNETT   COPYRIGHT 1898

One-Mile Rapids. Perrin and Knudson capsized and had to repair their boat after running these rapids. One can see the wreckage from some earlier mishaps. Courtesy University of Washington Libraries, Special Collections, Hegg 3147.

Miles Canyon. According to Perrin, the current was just more than thirty miles per hour. A large whirlpool lay just behind the outcropping to the left. Courtesy University of Washington Libraries, Special Collections, Hegg 449.

"In the mane of the Horse" at Whitehorse Rapids. Many boats were lost here, while other gold seekers viewed the ferocious rapids, gave up, and turned around. Courtesy University of Washington Libraries, Special Collections, Hegg 2164.

Dawson City in 1898. One year after Perrin and Novak left, the population had soared from about three thousand to thirty thousand—a tenfold increase. Photograph by Eric A. Hegg, P277-001-080, courtesy Alaska State Library, Wickersham State Historic Sites Photograph Collection.

Novak (right) and Perrin, taken at St. Michael. Novak had had his beard shaved off, but insisted on keeping his handlebar mustache. The photographer, Canadian surveyor William Ogilvie, used this picture as part of a parlor game for years afterward. Courtesy Library and Archives Canada/William Ogilvie fonds/PA-205054.

G. W. BURNHAM
Judge

M. J. TOBIN
County Attorney
Prosecution

EDWARD MURRAY

C. L. BOIES
Prosecution

TOM MILNER
Defense

J. J. NEY
Defense

The principal lawyers in the case, as well as an artist's sketch of Edward Murray.
Courtesy State Historical Society of Iowa, Iowa City.

M. J. TOBIN,
County Attorney of Benton County.

"The bulldog—" M. J. Tobin. © 2013, reprinted with permission of SourceMedia Group, Cedar Rapids, Iowa.

Inside the stone-cutting shed, Anamosa State Penitentiary. Courtesy Anamosa State Penitentiary Museum.

View of Anamosa prison yard. Note the limestone slabs and the guard tower.
Courtesy Anamosa State Penitentiary Museum.

First violinist Novak is seated at left in this photograph of the Anamosa Prison Orchestra, circa 1900. Two of the three grades of prison classes are shown here. First class wore gray, while second class wore checked uniforms. Third class (not pictured) wore stripes. Courtesy Anamosa State Penitentiary Museum.

Old view of Fort Madison.
Courtesy State Historical Society of Iowa, Iowa City.

Three different classes of prisoners. The inmates were promoted or demoted depending on their behavior. This system, a fixture for many years at Anamosa State Penitentiary, was instituted at Fort Madison shortly after Novak's arrival.
Courtesy State Historical Society of Iowa, Iowa City.

Cellblock at Fort Madison.
Courtesy State Historical Society of Iowa, Iowa City.

PART THREE

THE TRIAL

TEN

•————————————————•

Setting the Stage

For the past seven months—from the blustery winter winds in early February through the stifling summer heat of the corn-growing season—Frank Novak had been the talk of Iowa. Stories flew around the farms and dusty crossroad towns, at county fairs and downtown courthouses, in the large cities and small villages, from Keokuk to Decorah, from What Cheer to Elkader and out west to the Missouri River valley. Most people believed that Novak had fled the state and had been gone for some time, although some were convinced that his family was hiding him right under the nose of the Benton County sheriff.[1] Others thought that Novak and Murray were both still alive and had worked on the insurance scheme together.[2] A small number of people were sure that, despite the news reports, Novak had died in the fire along with Edward Murray.

The leader of this last group was Jo Novak, Frank Novak's cousin from Iowa City. Now representing the Novak family's claims against the insurance companies, Jo was still positive that his cousin was dead and the insurance companies were liable for the amount owed to Frank's wife and two young boys. The stories that Frank was deeply in debt were all lies, Jo argued; the whole concept of his cousin's financial distress was a complete fabrication constructed by an imaginative reporter.[3] Furthermore, he pointed out, Frank's life insurance policies amounted to about seventeen thousand dollars—not the twenty-seven thousand that the newspapers claimed—and were not taken out in the past eighteen months or so but dated back to about

1882. Jo Novak also pointed out to reporters that there was no motive for his cousin to commit this crime and that all of the charges would eventually be dismissed. Finally, he believed not only that Edward Murray had perished in the fire along with Frank Novak, but also that the farmer's body was completely consumed by the flames. To Jo Novak, a man who appeared to file lawsuits as often as he changed his socks, the legal system was the only way to clear his cousin's name, and Jo spent most of the summer gathering evidence to present his case against the Travelers company.

In fact, by the end of August 1897, Jo Novak's lawsuit had already begun. At Iowa City, M. J. Tobin served as the defense attorney for the insurance agencies and had so far refused to bring any of the exhibits, including Edward Murray's skull, to the court as evidence. Based on the letters that he had received from Gus Thiel, Tobin was sure that Novak was still very much alive and did not wish to do anything that might compromise the evidence that he possessed. Moreover, Tobin had filed a countersuit against Frank Novak for the amount of twenty-six dollars and fifty-three cents, the money that Novak had earned as a part-time agent for Travelers but had never turned over to that company.

On August 27, the court was debating this issue, with Tobin himself on the witness stand, when a messenger burst into the courtroom and handed him a telegram from the *Cedar Rapids Evening Gazette*.

The Benton County prosecutor immediately read the newspaper's message to the courtroom: "Novak has been captured. Will print story tonight."[4]

Upon hearing the news, Jo Novak became pale and left the courtroom for a few minutes to regain his composure. When he returned, he informed the court that he had nothing further to say except that he did not believe the news report. Further, Jo Novak was adamant that Frank was dead and would not be convinced otherwise unless he actually saw his cousin alive.

At Tobin's request, the judge granted a continuance in the case and the courtroom emptied. Tobin later confessed to a reporter that he could scarcely believe that, after all these months, Novak's flight was over and the fugitive had actually been apprehended.[5] Tobin returned to Vinton and began making plans for what he was sure would be an extremely difficult prosecution. He knew that the real work in the case was just beginning.

❧ ❧ ❧

The news of Frank Novak's capture spread quickly through the state, rolling across Iowa like ball lightning. It was difficult to pick up any newspaper without seeing some bold, sensational headline announcing his return. "Novak is captured. Escaped Walford Murderer Taken At Dawson City, in the Klondike Region, Where He Was Playing the Violin in a Dance Hall,"[6] cried the front-page story from the *Cedar Rapids Evening Gazette*, while its arch-rival, the *Daily Republican*, initially slow to cover the news, had the story on page five the day after the *Gazette*: "Caught in the Klondike Country. . . . One of the most startling tragedies in the history of the state of Iowa about to be cleared up by the capture of the central figure."[7]

Never forgetting his roots in Oswego, New York, and showing an adroit hand in dealing with the newspapers, Tobin made sure the journal of record in his hometown received the news. A newspaper there carried an article that was headlined: "A Western Criminal Brought to Justice by a Former Oswego Boy."[8]

The state of Iowa buzzed with the news, as avid readers absorbed each twist and turn of the story of Novak's flight and capture. "Nine out of 10 people in Cedar Rapids are talking about his arrest," the *Gazette* reported, while other papers dug deeply into the case's history, recapping all of the details, beginning with the Walford fire and the death of Edward Murray.[9] At a county fair not far from Solon, where Novak was born, the news filtered through the crowd and was discussed by everyone within a few minutes of its announcement.[10] And as usual, since it was the largest city close to Walford, the Cedar Rapids newspapers ran with the details, including artwork of Frank Novak, Red Perrin, and Edward Murray (as photography was still somewhat limited in most dailies), while other papers carried in-depth articles about the chase as well as sidebars on Jo Novak and the pending grand jury investigation.

Reporters searched for comparisons between Novak and other no-torious figures of the recent past. "Cunning Villainy Would Seem the Principal Characteristic of Frank Novak, the Iowa Criminal," a head-line proclaimed in the *Waterloo Daily Courier*, which added, "If half of the charges against him are true, he is worthy of a place alongside of Holmes, Hayward, and other arch fiends in the annals of crime."[11] H. H. Holmes was one of the first serial killers in the country and may have been involved in dozens of murders, while Harry Hayward had achieved notoriety by contracting for the murder of Catherine "Kitty" Ging in 1894, his motive fueled by some insurance policies that she had recently signed over to him.

Editors and reporters pored over their dictionaries, searching for the right words to describe the Novak case. They revived the stories printed earlier on Novak's past failed business dealings; the suspi-cious death of his partner and brother-in-law Wencil Jilek, who fell to his death from a train in 1893; the alleged robbery of Novak's safe and the fire that ravaged his place in 1895; and finally the burning of the Walford store and death of Edward Murray, ending with Novak's flight across the continent to Alaska and the Klondike.

Despite the news of Novak's arrest, many people still doubted the story and greeted these articles with a healthy dollop of Hawkeye skepticism. In fact, a blurb in the *Cedar Rapids Daily Times* said that some were betting on whether Novak had in fact been captured. The paper stated that odds posted were five-to-three that the "Iowa Incen-diary" was still at large.[12]

But most other papers accepted the story of Novak's capture as fact. "There was absolutely no doubt that the man arrested in the Klondike country is Frank Novak of Walford," an Iowa City paper announced,[13] while the *Waterloo Daily Courier* summarized the story with its own headline: "It Is Novak."[14]

Many of Novak's family and friends still refused to accept the news of his capture. Tillie Novak, another cousin of Frank's, who along with other family members believed that he had died in the fire, was employed as a stenographer in the Cedar Rapids city solicitor's office. When a man came into the room and broke the news, according to one paper, she cried out and fainted.[15] John Novak, Frank's father and the patriarch of the family, still harbored questions about the identity of the arrested man, and left Walford for Vinton as soon as the news story broke.

Once the train carrying Perrin and his captive rumbled into the Vinton station early in the morning of September 2, however, all doubts instantly vanished. Most of the one hundred or so people at the station had only a brief glimpse of the man who was loaded into the wagon and moved across town to the jail, but it was enough to prove to John and Jo Novak that the prisoner was in fact Frank Novak. Next to Novak was Red Perrin, the detective who had, in the parlance of the era, "got his man." To the newspapers, just as every story has a villain, it must also have a corresponding hero, and the Thiel detective was the man of the hour. As far as the newspapers were concerned, Perrin was perfect, the almost stereotypical "Pinkerton man," with his dark red handlebar mustache, large, sunburned nose (for sniffing out clues), and implacable demeanor that underscored his resolve to finish the job. To the reporters and onlookers, he was the embodiment of a dime-novel "dick," a former Arizona deputy sheriff who had achieved the impossible. According to the *Gazette*, "C. C. Perrin is [now] known among detectives and police officials the world over."[16]

Other Iowa papers searched for their own hyperbolic descriptions. "The Greatest Piece of Detective Work on Record," declared a headline in the *Dubuque Herald*,[17] while the *Vinton Eagle* flatly stated that "the part taken by Detective Perrin will be recorded in the records of detective work as the greatest of recent times."[18] The accolades for Perrin poured in, with one reporter insisting that the Thiel man was "one of the shrewdest detectives in America."[19]

Perrin's arrival in Vinton with his celebrated prisoner coincided with a shift in the public's perception of detectives. Prior to this time, many people regarded detectives negatively, considering them spotters, spies, strikebreakers, and thugs. But during the latter part of the 1890s, this view was changing. Increasingly, the detective was a "conquering hero," a phrase that one of Novak's attorneys sarcastically mentioned during the trial.[20]

This shift was due to a number of factors—the growing popularity of dime novels, police magazines, newspaper coverage of murder cases, and even a few melodramas. In many of these works, the detective was portrayed as an avenger, a righteous figure seeking retribution, using whatever means necessary to apprehend criminals. In particular, the detective books of the late 1800s underscored this change in perception. From the early works by Harlan Page Halsey, whose "Old Sleuth" character was based on Allan Pinkerton, to other short stories and novels, the triumphs of both real and fictional detectives made exciting reading for thousands of Americans.[21]

      🌿 🌿 🌿

In Iowa, much of the state was primed for the upcoming Novak case, which promised to be a battle royal. The newspapers were salivating at the pending trial coverage. "Few counties in the state escape having a sensational murder trial," commented the *Butler County News*, a small paper from Shell Rock. "Last year, Chicasaw County was all excited over a poison case. The year before that Floyd County was the scene of a trial for the murder of a woman at Marble Rock. Franklin County had a father and stepmother on trial for the killing of a daughter. The grand jury is now investigating the facts in the Kehrn murder case in Bremer County." It was now, the *News* suggested, Benton County's turn.[22]

This was Tobin's first case as county attorney and the young lawyer was anxious to prove himself. Tobin knew that he would have a hard uphill fight, since the lawsuit would be built entirely on circumstantial evidence, often the most difficult means to obtain a conviction, especially in a murder case. Circumstantial evidence required building the case one thread at a time, like weaving a tapestry until, by the end of the trial, the woven piece is finished and the pattern of guilt is clear. The prosecutor who is forced to use this type of evidence must convince the jury that the small, seemingly insignificant pieces of scrap material fit together into one complete fabric.

Usually, but not always, a murder case has a mixture of direct evidence—a jimmied lock, a knife with fingerprints, or a bloody shoe —combined with circumstantial evidence. Some of the latter can be instantly suspicious, "like finding a trout in the milk," as Henry David Thoreau once explained, but most circumstantial evidence is hidden in the shadows, waiting for someone to turn on a light and illuminate each fact, one by one. And while prosecuting a defendant in a conventional murder case is challenging enough, obtaining a conviction based solely on circumstantial evidence was and is extremely difficult.[23]

The Benton County attorney had been careful to preserve the evidence over the past ten months. After the coroner's jury had ruled that the body was that of Edward Murray, Tobin had the corpse exhumed and had taken the scorched and fractured skull along with the stomach. The badly burned organ was sent to a laboratory for chemical analysis. Tobin may have hoped to present the findings as evidence that Murray may also have been poisoned, but no trace of any drug was found in the stomach.[24]

Tobin lined up all of his other facts to present in the case. He had the testimony of Murray's sister, Nellie Murray Shea, who swore that the corpse was wearing a stars-and-moons blue patterned shirt. In addition, Mrs. Shea mentioned during the coroner's inquest that the corpse had the remnants of a St. Joseph's cord, an item Murray had worn around his waist. During the inquest, Louis Hasek had testified that the teeth of the corpse did not match Novak's. In addition, four of the fugitive's personal items—the dental bridge, pocket scissors, folding knife, and identification check—had been left under the cot, apparently in an attempt to disguise the true identity of the corpse. Finally, Tobin gathered the evidence from the chase itself—

eyewitnesses who had spotted Novak in Iowa, the similarity of the handwriting samples on the signed railroad ticket with Novak's signature, and the pseudonym of "Frank Alfred" that Novak had used when he purchased the ticket from Omaha to Portland.

Tobin had been in constant communication with Travelers insurance company almost from the beginning and, due to the work of the Thiel agents, knew about Novak's gambling woes and mounting debt problems. To the county attorney, this knowledge added up to a powerful motive for murder. But despite his extensive work in preparing for this case, Tobin understood that once he stepped into the courtroom, the defense would quickly exploit his own lack of courtroom experience. Moreover, he was positive that the defense would include one or more of the best lawyers in the state, handpicked by Novak and his family. Tobin astutely realized that the upcoming case was far too complicated for him to handle by himself so he began talks with several other attorneys, hoping to enlist one who would offer the most experience in prosecuting this case.

He found just such a man in Earl Louis Boies, a seasoned lawyer from nearby Waterloo. Four years older than Tobin, Boies was a perfect complement to the young county attorney, as he had extensive courtroom experience. He also possessed deep roots, not only in Iowa but in America as well. His father, Horace Boies, was governor of Iowa from 1890 to 1894, and could trace the family's origins back to a Revolutionary War soldier. The older Boies had a sterling reputation as an excellent lawyer himself and was a man who also knew something about beating the odds, as he had served as the only Democratic governor in the state from 1855 to 1933.[25] He was "sound, clear-minded and well-trained," and was regarded both as a fine lawyer and statesman.[26] His son had many of the same attributes, including an enviable track record as an accomplished trial attorney.

It's quite likely that Boies and Tobin were already acquainted, as they had both been members of the same literary club at Cornell, most likely in separate years. But besides that association, the two men couldn't have been more different. Boies was an Iowa blueblood, while Tobin was an ambitious descendant of hardscrabble Irish immigrants. Boies had years of legal practice under his belt at a prestigious firm headed by his father, while Tobin was still untested as Benton County attorney. Boies's deliberate and unflappable personality perfectly offset Tobin's feistiness. The older attorney sculpted his cases slowly and methodically, working the courtroom as if it were a block of Carrera marble and employing each word as a chisel, chipping away at the defense's case piece by piece. Moreover, Boies possessed a sharp legal mind, able to adapt instantly to any changes in courtroom tactics by the defense. "In intellect he was a Titan," an opposing trial lawyer once remarked.[27]

❧ ❧ ❧

Meantime, Frank Novak looked forward to meeting Cato Sells again, and if Sells consented to take the case, the accused man was optimistic that the LaPorte City lawyer could prove to a jury that the evidence was not strong enough for a murder conviction. Now ensconced in the Vinton jail under the watchful eye of the Benton County sheriff, Novak had little to do besides read, think about his defense strategy, and consume three home-cooked meals a day, prepared by Sheriff Metcalf's wife. As he awaited trial and put on weight, Novak became anxious to talk over his theories with Sells.

On September 8, newspapers ran articles stating that a grand jury would soon be empanelled in Vinton and that Frank Novak would finally offer his version of the events that occurred in Walford on the night of February 2, 1897. A story circulated around Benton County that some of Edward Murray's friends planned to ride into Vinton, storm the jail, and hang Novak themselves. Rattled by this rumor, Sheriff Metcalf had guards placed around the jail twenty-four hours a day. Company G of the Iowa National Guard was on alert and one paper claimed that the whistle atop the Vinton Water Works would summon everyone in town to the jail if needed. However, no vigilante group ever appeared.[28]

The grand jury convened as planned. But there was a surprise in

store, and it came from Frank Novak himself. Ever since July 12, when
he had been captured in Dawson City, Novak had told everyone that
he would only tell his version of the story to the grand jury, but now he
had changed his mind and refused to talk. His statement that he
had nothing to say caused a wave of murmurs through the gallery,
which was packed with witnesses ready to testify, Novak's friends and
relatives, and curious residents of Benton County. Outside the old
courthouse, Novak's decision to remain silent had reporters scurry-
ing to file their stories while a disappointed crowd left the grounds.
Despite their frustrations, one journalist wrote, "the people [in Vin-
ton] are on the *qui vive*, anxious to learn anything they can about
what is going on."[29]

Another twist to the story occurred when Cato Sells decided
against representing Novak. It is easy to speculate why he refused to
take on the case. Perhaps he felt that Novak's defense was beneath
him, since Sells was a prestigious lawyer who had nothing to gain at
this stage of his career by serving as lead attorney for the plaintiff in
a high-profile murder trial, especially one as controversial as Novak.
Or perhaps, based on his previous discussion with Novak, Sells may
have decided that the case was a lost cause and not worth the effort
involved. This seems most plausible, since he had mentioned from
the beginning that he would take the case only if he thought there
was reasonable doubt as to Novak's guilt.[30]

Novak was frustrated when Sells withdrew but his disappointment
was short-lived, as he had several other promising attorneys in mind.
Four other lawyers traveled to Vinton, each seeking to meet with
the alleged murderer, but he sent them all away. Novak had already
selected his defense attorney. It turned out that he had an ace up his
sleeve—a redheaded ace as it turned out, and not Red Perrin.

Novak's choice as lead defense attorney was Thomas Hale Milner,
a fiery, ebullient, and downright cocky lawyer from Belle Plaine, a
small town about 40 miles west of Cedar Rapids. The son of a Meth-
odist minister, Tom Milner's red hair perfectly matched his hot-

blooded personality. He was well known in eastern Iowa, especially among the many Bohemians who lived in the area.

Milner was one of a handful of lawyers in that region who ran advertisements in the local newspapers. Like his personality, his ads were brash and boastful: "Am . . . red-headed, smooth-faced . . . and always in the stirrups. . . . Quick as a hippopotamus and gentle as a sunstroke." One ad also contained the bracing slogan that Milner later had printed on his stationery: "Fees are the sinews of war."[31]

Referring to himself as "The Napoleon of the Slope," he also ran advertisements in county fair flyers, minstrel show programs, and his hometown *Belle Plaine Union*, with each ad brimming with his supreme self-confidence. Another Milner advertisement underscored his bellicose nature: "Practice under the sign of Mars, god of war. Seldom licked, never surrender."[32]

As flamboyant as the other lawyers in the state were conservative, the eccentric Milner was as colorful as a cloud-strewn sunset. Known for possessing one of the most extensive collections of curse words in the state and never afraid to employ any of them, Milner carefully chose every word to provoke a specific reaction.[33] A habitual cigar smoker and loquacious to a fault, he would much rather speak than write words, since he had such poor penmanship that a judge once ordered him to provide documents written legibly. But whenever he entered a courtroom, he was all business—smart, focused, and deadly serious. As an admirer wrote years later, "He was one of the keenest and [most] versatile lawyers at the bar in eastern Iowa . . . his fame as a lawyer rest[ed] largely on his reputation as a jury lawyer. His many masterful pleas in this part of Iowa are well-known."[34] One other paper described him as "a genial fellow, quick to see a point and fearless to make it."[35]

Milner excelled as a defense attorney and was noted for taking cases that were too hot for other trial lawyers, a sort of St. Jude—the patron saint of lost causes—for any defendant. His advice never varied for his clients, whether they were petty thieves or, as in the case of

Frank Novak, an accused murderer and arsonist: "It is best always to
deny everything and ask for proof."[36] A ferocious questioner, Milner
was well known for his constant sniping at the Achilles heel of any
prosecution witness, and there was no doubt that he would be at his
best in this facet of the upcoming trial.

As competent as he was, Milner believed that he needed someone
else on the defense team to augment his own legal knowledge, especially in a complex case of this nature. This would be the defense's
cleanup hitter, someone thoroughly respectable and armed with an
excellent legal background. Milner approached John Joseph Ney of
Iowa City, a stolid former judge who had spent ten years in the state's
Tenth Judicial District until 1894, when he left that position and became a resident professor at The State University of Iowa (the current
University of Iowa) in Iowa City. A graduate of Notre Dame who had
compiled a peerless legal record—he experienced few reversals of
any judgments while serving on the bench—Judge Ney lent a *gravitas*
to the defense that Tom Milner lacked. The retired judge was deliberate, as slow-moving as a tortoise; but Ney also possessed an encyclo-
pedic knowledge of the law. With his outstanding reputation on the
Iowa bench and low-key demeanor, Ney made a perfect counterpart
to the incandescent Milner.[37]

❧ ❧ ❧

Immediately after Novak had selected Milner, an odd story appeared
in the *Cedar Rapids Evening Gazette*. A local tavern owner named Billy
Smith told a reporter about a trip that the defendant had made to
Cedar Rapids a few days before the Walford fire. As was his custom,
Novak would arrive in town, either by train or wagon, do some business at the Cedar Rapids National Bank, gamble a little bit in a back
room at one of the city's taverns, and treat some of his friends to a
few drinks. On this day, which Smith described as a frigid January afternoon, Novak entered the tavern and asked for something to drink.
He spotted two friends, Ed Wilhelm and J. H. Crosby, and bought
several rounds. Novak spoke about problems with his business, and

how he was having trouble collecting on some outstanding debts. Then he reached into a vest pocket and pulled out a small envelope, the kind that druggists used for storing poison or drugs like morphine. He told Wilhelm that it contained "something that will put me out of trouble when I can't stand it anymore."[38]

Someone asked him what he meant by that cryptic remark. Novak explained that he was going to mix the powder with some whiskey and place the bottle in his safe. Both times that his bank had been burglarized, the thieves had drunk some of his whiskey. If they came again, the contents of the envelope would take care of them. When asked about the possibility that one of his employees might drink from the bottle, Novak said that he would tell everyone who worked with him about the spiked liquor, so that there would be no chance that any accident would occur.

The tainted-whiskey story was an intriguing new aspect of the case. The druggist's envelope—if it ever existed—was gone, as Perrin made no mention of it when he searched Novak in Dawson City. But if this was true, and if Novak did carry out his plan, perhaps the whiskey bottle had been in either the bank or the store on the night of February 2, when Edward Murray was there. Murray, whose fondness for any type of alcohol was well known, probably was not aware of Novak's plans for revenge on the alleged burglars and may have taken a few drinks when the store owner was either out of the building or had his back turned. This theory was speculative, as the coroner's report did not mention anything about any drugs, and no useful evidence surfaced when the corpse's stomach was removed and analyzed at a laboratory.[39] Besides, after examining the corpse, Dr. Ruml said nothing about morphine or poison when he stated to the coroner that Murray might have died from a blow to the back of the head, probably from an axe. Still, some people had always believed that there might be another explanation as to the cause of Murray's death, and Billy Smith's comments added a new theory to the mystery.

Two men must have read the *Gazette* article with great interest. They were M. J. Tobin and Tom Milner. The spiked-whiskey anec-

dote, which had never been told before, injected more doubt in the
prosecution's case and would play a key part in the upcoming trial.

❦ ❦ ❦

During the first part of September, many key witnesses in the case
arrived in Vinton and testified before the grand jury. These included
several men who had seen Novak during his flight from Walford in
early February, among them John Bryson of Holbrook, the young
farmer who had given Novak a ride to Iowa City, where the suspect
caught a westbound train to Omaha. After meeting with the grand
jury, Bryson found Sheriff Metcalf and asked to see Novak. The sheriff led the man to Novak's cell, where Novak instantly recognized
Bryson and said, "You are the man who hauled me to Iowa City." Metcalf witnessed the two men speaking briefly for a few minutes, and
then Bryson left. The day before, Metcalf had traveled to Walford to
subpoena other residents there, including Mary Novak, Frank's wife.
The sheriff was under instructions to obtain the insurance policies,
which Mrs. Novak still had in her possession.[40]

Jo Novak, Frank's cousin, also was called to testify. After speaking with the grand jury, the Iowa City lawyer met with Frank under
the watchful eye of Sheriff Metcalf. It was the first time that the two
cousins had spoken to each other since Frank's return to Iowa. They
had much to discuss because as recently as two weeks ago, Jo Novak
had believed that his cousin had died in the fire. Jo was one of many
family members and friends who were allowed to visit with the prisoner in the Vinton jail during early September, bringing him tobacco
as well as books and a few Cedar Rapids newspapers. During that
time, Novak once again spoke to reporters about his experiences in
Alaska and traveling back to Iowa. But when the newsmen pressed
him about the grand jury, he refused to talk about the case.

One reporter expressed disbelief at what he perceived to be Novak's strange behavior. "Novak knows . . . that night's awful history
and how he can keep it within his own breast and yet enjoy good
sleep and appetite and meet his friends in a jovial mood is one of the
things that passes the comprehension of the human mind."[41]

Besides family members and journalists, a special visitor had traveled to Vinton to meet with Novak. This was William Murray, the father of the late Edward Murray. The retired farmer, now eighty-four, had suffered a great deal in the past two years, having lost two sons in the span of five months. This would have been a nightmare for any parent, but William Murray also had to endure the testimony at the coroner's inquest. He had sat with the body and arranged for the funeral that weekend, and then a few days later was forced to return to the cemetery to watch the corpse's exhumation at Tobin's request. Murray had had to watch as the coroner severed his dead son's head from its spine.

Ever since Novak's return to Iowa, Murray said that he wanted to meet with him and hear him admit that it was in fact Edward Murray who had died that night in Walford. Now William Murray would have his chance.

The old man tottered into the jail, leaning on the arm of his nephew, A. J. Murray, as Sheriff Metcalf escorted them to Novak's cell. The prisoner seemed eager to talk with his visitor. In fact, Murray was the only person Novak expressed a desire to meet with, acknowledging that the elderly man "has had more trouble than any man in Walford except myself."[42]

The aged farmer stared through the bars at the man whom he was sure had murdered his son. In a trembling voice, he said that he was an old man and probably wasn't going to live much longer. Then he asked Novak directly if it was Edward who died that night.

"I believe it was your son in the fire," Novak answered, and then said after a pause, "There are some things I cannot explain—things I do not understand."

"But," William Murray persisted, "we knew that Ed was in the store with you that night."

"Yes," Novak said, "he was in the store, but there are circumstances which I do not understand and cannot explain." After that, both Murrays left the jail. The nephew spoke briefly with a reporter later: "Novak had admitted that the body found in the ruins was that of Edward Murray, which settles the case as far as the *corpus delicti* [foundation of a crime] is concerned. What defense he can offer now is hard to tell."[43]

For the past seven months, many people were sure that Edward Murray had not perished in the fire. In fact, there were reports through the spring and summer of 1897 that Murray had been spotted in different parts of Iowa. But now, here in his cell in Vinton, Novak made what appeared to be a partial admission, agreeing that it was Edward Murray who had died.

At first glance, this admission was a special gift for the prosecutors. From the very beginning, M. J. Tobin had been interviewing witnesses and obtaining testimony, analyzing the coroner's inquest plus requesting independent forensic reports, all contributing to the goal of a positive identification of the burned torso. Novak's admission that he believed that the body was Murray's was a serious mistake, according to some observers, since once a jury was armed with that information, it might be considerably easier to obtain a conviction of first-degree murder.

But seen from another angle, Novak's statement really added little to the prosecution's case. Because no one contested the fact that a burned body was found in the ruins, Novak's belief that it was Edward Murray may have been a deliberate attempt to swing the focus from the defendant back to the prosecution. Tobin and Boies would have to prove beyond reasonable doubt that Novak murdered Murray and that the young farmer did not die in any other way. It was exceedingly difficult to obtain a first-degree murder conviction based on circumstantial evidence alone, and this was all Tobin had. It was far more likely that if the jury found Frank Novak guilty, it would convict him of the lesser charge of manslaughter. For a habitual gambler and risk-taker who had lost a fortune on the turn of a card, this defense was by far the biggest gamble he had ever taken. At this point, Novak's story of the whiskey laced with a lethal amount of morphine or poison might come into play. For if Murray had happened to see the spiked liquor bottle and had taken a few drinks before Novak could stop him, the death could be termed accidental.

On the other hand, it was well known that Murray and Novak did not get along, so it was possible that the two of them had a fight. Then Novak, acting strictly in self-defense, might have struck Murray with an axe or blunt instrument. Either of these theories, if advanced in court, would make it very hard for the prosecution to obtain a first-degree murder conviction.

In short, the remarks Novak made to William Murray were the equivalent of castling in chess, a move made to shore up the defense while simultaneously freeing up another piece to attack. When Tom Milner, head of Novak's defense team, was asked about the prisoner's exchange with William Murray, and specifically what tactics would be used in the case, the firebrand lawyer was his usual cocky self.

"Defense? Oh, I dreamed of one," he remarked idly to one reporter.[44] Milner never lacked confidence going into court but at this point he was not about to tip his hand about two possible strategies he might use. He could cast doubt on the identity of the corpse or, if he admitted that the dead man was Edward Murray, the defense attorney could argue that Murray had died as a result of drinking the tainted whiskey. Milner would certainly draw out the trial and would employ every type of stalling tactic in his arsenal. Ultimately, Milner knew that these delays would test the strength of the prosecution's case by putting the focus on what the defense team believed was meager circumstantial evidence. If he wasn't apprehensive enough already, Benton County Attorney Tobin knew from these tactical pre-trial moves that he would have to be careful of the traps that Tom Milner and Judge Ney were bound to set for him.

※ ※ ※

On September 23, the grand jury handed up its verdict. Novak was indicted for the murder of Edward Murray, along with two lesser charges of arson and conspiracy.[45] One newspaper speculated that the latter charges were not made public because Novak would never be tried for them unless he was acquitted of the first indictment.[46] A bench warrant was issued for his arrest, and Sheriff Metcalf, who

had spent much of the past three weeks smoking and chatting ami-
ably with his prisoner, formally arrested Novak in the courtroom,
as Judge Obed Caswell instructed. Metcalf and Novak then headed
back to the jail, where a large crowd had gathered, straining for a
glimpse of Novak. Only a high window above his cell was visible from
the street.

The next day, Novak returned for his arraignment along with two
other prisoners, Charles Miller and Henry M. Marshall. As big as
the crowd had been around the jail previously, an even larger group
appeared outside the courthouse. When the doors opened, people
shoved each other, fighting for seats inside. Everyone wanted to hear
Novak's response to the charges. They also were interested in seeing
him in person, since so far the only portraits of Novak had been a
few sketches by newspaper artists like Cy Fosmire of the *Gazette*. The
papers had described the prisoner as looking somewhat tattered but
toughened up by his trip to the Klondike and back, and now Iowans
wished to gauge what three weeks in prison had done to him. One
paper described Novak as looking somewhat "bleached out" from
being inside for so long but that the three home-cooked meals a day
from Mrs. Metcalf were agreeing with him, especially after his beans-
and-bacon diet in the Yukon.[47]

At 3:00 PM, Sheriff Metcalf led Novak, Marshall, and Miller into the
courtroom. The most famous of the three prisoners briefly nodded
to Judge Caswell and some friends, then sat down and began speaking with defense attorney Tom Milner. It was not until hearing the
murder indictment that Novak became visibly nervous, turning pale
as he stood before the judge. But the defendant was not the only un-
easy man in the courtroom. Another was seated across the aisle, and
his name was M. J. Tobin. The impending trial had occupied virtually
all of his thoughts since February, and it weighed heavily on him. As
Tobin began reading the long indictment that he had prepared, the
paper in his hand shook slightly. But the longer he spoke, the stronger and clearer his voice became, until he reached the meat of the
charges, where the torrent of words fell like sledge-hammers in the

now-silent courtroom: "burn . . . poison . . . asphyxiate . . . mutilate," and then, "kill and murder."[48]

Novak frowned as the words tumbled out of the prosecutor's mouth. When Tobin finished reading the indictment, he handed the document to Novak, who hastily put it in his own pocket.

The grand jury indicted Novak on two specific counts: assaulting Edward Murray with a weapon and beating him with the intent of murder. Curiously, the second count also included the use of poison and "other means and instrumentalities, unknown to the grand jury" as part of Novak's effort to kill Murray. This last clause would be a key point in the trial.

Now came the moment that everyone had been waiting for. When asked how he would plead, Novak simply said, "*NOT* guilty," emphasizing the word "not."[49] Then he took his seat again. He was overheard commenting to one of his attorneys, "That was a pretty strong indictment."[50]

After Novak's plea, Tobin and Milner argued about the schedule for trying the case. Milner mentioned that he had not had a chance to consult with his associate defense counsel, Judge Ney, who had not yet arrived in Vinton. The defense attorney had also mentioned beforehand that he might push for a change of venue, as he believed that Novak would not receive a fair trial in Benton County. But after some discussion, Milner agreed to drop his request for a change of venue in exchange for a continuance until November, when the Benton County district court would convene. Most likely, because of the complexities it presented, the Novak case would be moved up to the first spot on the November docket for Judge George W. Burnham.

Judge Caswell then banged down the gavel and closed the proceedings. The crowd filed out of the courtroom somewhat disappointed by the lack of histrionics. Anyone wishing to see fireworks between the prosecution and Novak's defense team would have to wait for another six weeks.

ELEVEN

•————————————————————•

Orange Pumpkins and
Yellow Journalism

By late 1897, the two competing Cedar Rapids newspapers had
given extensive coverage to the Novak case. Now that Novak's
arraignment had taken place, the papers' respective city editors, William Holmes of the *Gazette* and William Ashford of the *Republican*,
tried to outdo the other with hyperbolic articles matched with outrageous headlines. Holmes worked closely with W. I. Endicott, the
latter pacing the newsroom like some linotype Zeus, hurling his hot-type thunderbolts throughout eastern Iowa, hoping to shine any new
light on the Novak case while keeping his readers' interest until the
trial began.

One weapon Endicott frequently used in the circulation war was
an artist named Cy Fosmire. A wonderful illustrator with a knack for
capturing someone's personality in a few short strokes of his pen,
"Fos"—the three-letter name he used for his work—had drawn several
portraits of Novak, Edward Murray, and the scene of the Walford
fire, and now illustrated the articles with a few sketches of Alaska
as well as the Vinton jail and courthouse. The *Gazette* trumpeted its
prowess in covering the case and promised to increase the amount of
newsprint in weeks to come: "If your friends want a full and complete
report of the Novak trial they better see that The *Gazette* [subscription] list contains their names. We shall also have some illustrated
features impossible to be secured in any other way."[1]

Meantime, as M. J. Tobin and Tom Milner prepared their arguments and plotted strategies for the upcoming trial date, the Benton County attorney was eagerly following the Adolph Luetgert murder trial, which was wrapping up in Chicago. This case had some remarkable similarities to the Novak trial, probably the most important one being that the prosecution's efforts revolved largely around a few pieces of circumstantial evidence.

A German immigrant, Adolph Luetgert had come to America with nothing in his pockets and worked at various trades before saving enough money to build a large sausage factory. He lived in the adjoining house with his second wife, Louisa, two children, Louis and Elmer, and Mary Siemering, his wife's cousin, who served as a maid in the household. Like Novak, beneath the veneer of success, Luetgert was in serious financial trouble, having lost about twenty-five thousand dollars to an English con man and being forced to close the sausage factory in March 1897. The due date for a chattel mortgage—a note that uses personal property rather than real estate as security—was coming up; the sheriff was preparing to seize what remained of his assets, and Luetgert was virtually staring down the barrel of a cocked shotgun.[2]

On the evening of May 1, Louis Luetgert had returned home from attending the circus and excitedly told his mother and father about what he had seen there. This was the last time anyone would admit to having seen Louisa Luetgert. Three days later, on May 4, her brother, Diedrich Bicknese, came to the Luetgert house and asked to speak to her. Adolph Luetgert asked, "Ain't she at your place?" Concerned that something had happened to Louisa, Bicknese asked friends, relatives, and other acquaintances if they had seen his sister but no one had any information on her whereabouts. And strangely, Adolph remained indifferent to his wife's disappearance.[3]

Bicknese contacted the police, who searched the area for her body. Finally, two weeks after she vanished, they turned their attention to the factory itself, draining a steam vat with gunnysacks over the outflow to catch any solid items trapped in the smelly refuse.[4]

Their hunch paid off. Picking through the disgusting mess and clambering into the vat, the police found a few fragments of bone, a hairpin, part of a false tooth, and perhaps most importantly, an eighteen-carat gold ring engraved with the initials "L. L." Based on this evidence, plus other bone fragments and materials they found later, they arrested Adolph Luetgert and charged him with first-degree murder. At the trial, the prosecution used this circumstantial evidence to hammer home its interpretation of events: Luetgert and his wife had had constant arguments and in fact no longer slept together; he was in financial trouble; he may have had an affair; and at this point was looking to start a new life without her. To get on with it, he had killed her and disposed of her body in the steam vat.[5]

Lacking a strong counterargument, Luetgert's defense team focused on challenging practically every single statement by the other side, attacking each prosecution theory, and objecting to every piece of evidence, no matter how small. To many people's surprise, on October 23, the jury declared that it could not reach a verdict on Luetgert's guilt or innocence. The case had to be retried. In the second trial, which began in January 1898, the prosecution placed much more emphasis on forensic science and brought in an expert witness to testify that the bones found in the steam vat were indeed Mrs. Luetgert's. His testimony was the linchpin that resulted in a unanimous vote by the jury to convict. But even then, the jurors voted for life imprisonment, not the death penalty. To the second jury, the circumstantial evidence was still not strong enough for a first-degree murder conviction.[6]

The Luetgert story ended somewhat anticlimactically. After serving only a year of his sentence, Luetgert died in prison in 1899. But the legal repercussions of the case, in particular regarding the prosecution's use of circumstantial evidence, reverberated for many years afterward.

Certainly, both Tobin and Milner were well aware of the arguments presented in the Luetgert case, as the Cedar Rapids papers carried the story in detail. It was one of Chicago's most publicized cases for some time and was discussed for years in journals and books, with many authors arguing over Luetgert's innocence or guilt.[7]

🌿 🌿 🌿

As he prepared his case, Tobin felt apprehensive. After reading the accounts of the Luetgert case, he knew what could happen when a clever defense team attacked a prosecution based largely on circumstantial evidence. Moreover, Tobin had good reason to be worried, since Tom Milner was exactly the type of attorney who relished a difficult case, especially one that a lawyer as distinguished as Cato Sells had turned down. Milner had all the characteristics of a successful defense attorney: he was tough, unpredictable, and a brilliant strategist who would stop at nothing to vindicate his client. Also, Milner was adroit at shaping public opinion in a case and had spent years cultivating reporters in eastern Iowa, most of whom looked upon him as a veritable quote machine, always ready with a good quip. Tobin lacked Milner's public relations experience and was anxious about how the story would play in the newspapers, particularly the *Gazette* and the *Daily Republican*. The young prosecutor would need every bit of legal knowledge and fortitude to deal with the charismatic attorney from Belle Plaine.

Moreover, it appeared for a short period of time that Tobin would not have the assistance of E. L. Boies. The Benton County Board of Supervisors, which oversaw the county attorney's office, refused to pay for additional legal counsel, and it appeared for awhile that Tobin would be on his own against Tom Milner. However, a few weeks before the case was to begin, the state of Iowa agreed to pay Boies for his services.[8]

Gratified at having Boies on board, Tobin pushed forward in gathering evidence. He wrote to Travelers for information on Novak's policy, explaining that that "this will be a desperately fought case, as all the evidence is of a circumstantial nature. . . . Novak's case is one of the most heinous in the history of crime in Iowa and the state

proposes to convict him of murder if it is possible to do so, because
we believe him guilty."[9]

On the other side, Tom Milner spent much of October preparing
his list of witnesses. Like Tobin, he had followed the Luetgert case
and had paid particular attention to the defense team's tactics. He
granted several interviews with the newspapermen, assuring each reporter that he would be more than ready to meet any challenge from
the prosecution. One paper noted, "The Novak trial will certainly be
one of the foremost in the history of crime . . . and it will be a fight
which has never before been equaled in the state."[10]

At about the same time, someone—probably Milner—finessed a
critical leak to the press, one that proved to be vitally important during the trial. It turned out that when Novak and Perrin were floating
down the Yukon to St. Michael, Novak had confessed that he had
some role in Edward Murray's death. According to Novak, after he
realized that Murray had drunk some of the whiskey the shop owner
had drugged to trap burglars, he carried the unconscious man upstairs and laid him down on the cot. Then Novak read for a while
before falling asleep, awakening only after the fire had broken out.
Apparently, Novak grew more comfortable with Perrin as the long
trip unwound, because while they were at St. Michael waiting for the
steamer to Seattle, he repeated this confession, and asked the detective what its impact might be when the case came to trial later. Perrin
was characteristically noncommittal on this point, but Novak made
him promise not to mention the confession until the grand jury convened. Perrin agreed to keep Novak's statements in confidence.[11]

Despite this assurance, Perrin had written about this conversation
in his diary, which was published in several papers, including many
in Iowa. The journal spelled out all the details of the detective's trip,
from Seattle to Dawson City, down the Yukon River to St. Michael,
and then back to Vinton by way of Seattle and St. Paul, Minnesota.
His exploits, told in a straightforward style reminiscent of a military
historian, fascinated newspaper readers, but it was Novak's alleged
confession that had people talking. One paper summed it up:

"Here is a man who says that when he found the visitor to his store had taken a dose of poisoned whiskey which had been fixed up for burglars, and was stretched out under its influence, he carefully carried him upstairs and put him to bed. Then [Novak] coolly stretched himself out on the counter and read . . . until he was wooed to sleep, only to be aroused by the fire that burned the store and the helpless victim of poison. If he is accused of murder, how can he escape either from the [in]criminating character of the circumstances surrounding the case on the one hand or this confession on the other? Would a man without murder in his heart have nonchalantly stretched himself out to read while the victim of a deadly draught was in a death agony? Is it entirely rational to credit such a character with a normal heart? He may be innocent of murder, but he cannot win the public over to the belief that his story is worthy of credence."[12]

❦ ❦ ❦

Why would Milner leak such potentially damaging information about his client? By emphasizing the spiked-whiskey part of Novak's confession, the defense attorney was attempting to sow doubt about his client's guilt for Murray's death. If the farmer had drunk the whiskey of his own accord, how could Novak be held responsible? Milner also informed reporters that Novak had never told William Murray that Edward had died in the fire, as one newspaper article had reported. Lastly, Milner made sure that the papers published both the confession and Perrin's promise not to reveal it until the grand jury convened in Iowa in September.

In addition to preparing the ground for his defense through the press, Milner gathered several witnesses and had them ready to testify that Novak had spoken about thwarting any would-be burglars with the spiked bottle of whiskey. Their statements would support the theory that Edward Murray had drunk some of the allegedly tainted liquor.

Due to Milner's work, public opinion regarding Novak's guilt now seemed more mixed. "Novak has a defense, notwithstanding the reports which have appeared in the papers and it will be a fight which has never before been equaled in the state," Milner told a reporter.[13] Stories of the alleged doctored whiskey and Novak's confession to Perrin popped up in papers in Iowa and other parts of the country. Earlier in the year, Tobin had flitted about the eastern part of the state like a man possessed. Now it was Tom Milner's turn to be the busiest lawyer in Iowa, popping up in Vinton and Cedar Rapids, while traveling back and forth to Belle Plaine; chatting with reporters in these towns; and above all, keeping everyone guessing what kind of a defense he would offer in the case. Milner was proving to be a shrewd poker player and he assured everyone that he would take Tobin to the woodshed in November. He anticipated the chance to attack what he believed to be a very weak case and looked forward to the upcoming court date, which was now fixed for November 9 in Vinton.

TWELVE

•—————————————————————•

Inside the Courthouse

The old courthouse in Vinton was a mystery to anyone who saw it. Of course, the mystery was why the forty-one-year-old dilapidated structure hadn't collapsed or been razed years ago. The county was one of the more prosperous in the state and served as the home of many wealthy farmers as well as a number of growing businesses. Vinton's location on the Burlington, Cedar Rapids & Northern Railway and the Illinois Central Railroad, plus the town's proximity to Cedar Rapids, made it most desirable for any budding Babbitt seeking to advance in the business world. The arrival of the Iowa Canning Company in 1892 made it easy for farmers to deliver their corn, soybeans, and other produce right to the factory, which had built spur lines to the rail station. As Vinton grew, many of the old buildings were torn down and new ones erected, but somehow the aged courthouse survived.[1]

The reporters who arrived in town to cover the upcoming Novak trial were united in their hatred of the dilapidated structure. One account called it "far inferior to the needs and wealth of the county"[2] and another described the old building as "a ramshackle old ruin, and is the laughing stock of [Benton County]."[3] A third reporter described the discomforts of what he referred to as "picturesque ruins," adding, "The offices are small, dingy and poorly ventilated and miserably lighted affairs; the halls are fair representations of the 'chamber of horrors' in the Mammoth cave," an enormous cavern in western

Kentucky. He expressed a particular distain for the courtroom itself, calling it "a decided curiosity. It will seat about two hundred people. The seats are arranged on an incline, like the dress circle seats in a opera houses [sic], and steps lead up to the level of the seats from the wide aisle which runs down the center of the room. There is plenty of room inside the railing for counsel, jury, reporters and witnesses, but the low ceiling and lack of ventilation make a day's confinement in the place anything but pleasant." The ceiling in the courtroom was so badly cracked, gouged, and marked that the reporter thought the space would be best used as a map of Benton County, rather than a bulwark against the sun and rain. Two thick ropes dropped through holes in the ceiling, leading the reporter to suspect that they might have once been used for a "lynching bee."[4]

In this dilapidated building, at precisely 10:00 AM on Tuesday, November 9, a blustery cold day, the presiding judge of the seventeenth district court of the state of Iowa took his seat. Burnham banged down his gavel and instructed the bailiff to call for order, beginning what one account called "the most remarkable trial ever held in the state of Iowa."[5] From this point forward, it would be referred to in both law textbooks and legal briefs as *State of Iowa* vs. *Frank A. Novak*.

If there was one judge who understood the letter of the law, it was the man who sat in front of the prosecutorial and defense teams in the poorly ventilated courtroom—Judge George W. Burnham. Patient, knowledgeable, and a no-nonsense jurist, he appeared to be well suited for the task ahead. Forty-seven years old, he had been practicing law since 1873. The fourth of nine children, his father R. T. Burnham had built the first saw- and grist-mill in Hardin County and had been a keen observer of local and state politics. He always made sure that he backed the right candidate in any political race and became a close friend of Governor William Larrabee, campaigning for his election and second-term campaigns. Young George Burnham took courses at Upper Iowa University in 1867 and stayed there for two years, then transferred to the Agricultural College at Ames (now

Iowa State University) for two more years of education. By then, he had decided to become a lawyer, so after he finished college, he traveled to Ohio and apprenticed with Colonel J. C. McCloud, who had a reputation as one of the best criminal lawyers in that state.[6]

Ever since he had begun studying law, Burnham had been convinced that one of the primary roles of a judge was to maintain absolute control in the courtroom. In a speech before the Iowa State Bar Association in July 1897, just four months before the Novak trial, he had declared: "There never was a country where judicial authority was so strong and supreme, and so respected and acquiesced as in this country . . . [especially] the power, the influence, and the wisdom and honor of the judicial decision."[7] It was very clear that Judge Burnham would have little tolerance for any legal tricks or histrionics from either side in the upcoming trial.

❦ ❦ ❦

On November 9, the dank courtroom was packed with reporters and the curious, with everyone trying to gauge Novak's reactions as the prosecution and defense teams questioned each potential juror in a pool of fifty-eight men, as women were not allowed to serve as jurors.[8] Both Tobin and Milner were especially interested in each man's opinions regarding a first-degree murder conviction, especially one based solely on circumstantial evidence.

Meanwhile, the famous prisoner must have been pleased to be released from the cell where he had been living for more than two months, although his was by no means a spartan existence. Novak possessed a small library of magazines, newspapers, and books and had recently been reading Harper's *New History of the Civil War,* two plays by Shakespeare, *The Personal Memoirs of U. S. Grant,* and several other books.[9] He enjoyed smoking cigars with Sheriff Metcalf and engaged in occasional card games through the bars with some of his friends, while continuing to feast on home-cooked meals prepared by the sheriff's wife.

🌿 🌿 🌿

The next day, on Wednesday, November 10, a cold fall day which one paper described as "cloudy, chilly and disagreeable," the jury selection was completed. The jurors comprised an interesting cross-section of Benton County men. While some of them were from Vinton, others came from Polk Township, LeRoy, Cedar, Union, Garrison, and Keystone. They ranged from age twenty-seven, a farmer named Harry Miller, to S. T. Saunders, another farmer, who was sixty-three. Of the twelve men, ten of them described themselves as either farmers or retired farmers. The eleventh man was a cooper and the twelfth man, a German immigrant with the rather strange-sounding name of Nels Degn, was a former farmer who at first described himself as a horse trader, a somewhat unsavory line of employment. When pressed, he said that he was currently out of work. Interestingly, all but one of the twelve stated that they were in favor of the death penalty based on circumstantial evidence alone, provided that the evidence was strong enough to show conclusively that Novak was guilty of first-degree murder.[10]

The twelve men selected were:
William Reicke, 29, a farmer from Van Horne
Jacob Schoelerman, 60, the mayor of Keystone
Nels Degn, 43, unemployed, Vinton
B. Forrester, 59, a cooper, Vinton
Charles Wahl, 47, a farmer living near Urbana
Grant Henkle, 33, a farmer, Garrison
Carl Struve, 44, a farmer, Mt. Auburn
John Auman, 31, a farmer from Polk Township near Urbana
Harry Miller, 27, a farmer, Vinton
James Fry, 43, a farmer from Van Horne
J. T. Heath, 57, a farmer, from Polk Township near Urbana
S. T. Saunders, 63, a farmer, also from Polk Township[11]

After these jurors were designated, the other potential jurors were excused from the room and the jury was sworn in and seated in the

box. Judge Burnham urged the jurors to complete any business before they returned on the next day. They would be placed under the
care of the bailiff, Captain J. W. Barr, a man who was initially in the
pool of potential jurors but was excused because of his new duties as
court officer. Burnham forbade the jurors to discuss the case among
themselves or with anyone else. He said sternly that disobeying any
of these rules would not only result in the juror being disqualified
but would also subject him to contempt of court and possible imprisonment. There was little doubt among any of the jurors that the
judge meant business and would carry out his threat.[12]

Furthermore, Judge Burnham declared that cots would be brought
into the jury room. From this point on, with the exception of their
meals, the men would be spending virtually all their time inside the
dimly lit old courthouse. This was a sobering prospect indeed for the
new jurors.[13]

At 3:30 PM on November 10, M. J. Tobin stood up and began speaking to the court. First, he read the indictment, which accused Frank
Novak of murder in the death of Edward Murray and arson in the
burning of the Walford general store and bank. As the county attorney read, almost everyone in the courtroom watched the prisoner for
any reaction to the charges. Novak sat with studied indifference, his
chair tipped back on its hind legs; he casually chewed on a toothpick,
his face devoid of any emotion, as if he were attending someone else's
trial instead of his own. Only his eyes showed any flicker of interest,
and they were riveted on the young Benton County attorney, absorb-
ing each of Tobin's words and gestures.[14]

Tobin finished reading the indictment and began his opening
argument:

"The State expects to prove beyond a reasonable doubt the guilt
of the defendant, Frank A. Novak, of the crime of murder in the first
degree, as is charged in the indictment." Noting that the state would
make its case mainly through circumstantial evidence, the prosecutor defined this term as "evidence which shows certain acts and certain circumstances which, when linked together, will lead you to find

another fact—that is the guilt of the defendant in this case." He added that "it will not be necessary for the State to prove every fact or every circumstance in itself beyond a reasonable doubt, but it will be necessary, and the State expects to prove the crime itself beyond a reasonable doubt."[15]

Speaking for about an hour, Tobin carefully laid out the basic physical evidence: that the burned body found in the smoldering wreckage was indeed that of Edward Murray; that it could be positively identified by the missing incisors on the upper left part of the young farmer's mouth, the few remnants of a patterned shirt that his sister had given him, and the scorched pieces of a St. Joseph's cord that Murray was known to wear around his waist. Then Tobin began reconstructing the timeline on the night of February 2, 1897.

The chronology began in Walford on a cold, windy night. The sun had set long ago and had taken the temperature down with it. A light snow fell, gently dropping a white blanket over the town. At a little before 9:00 PM, three men—Charley Zabokrtsky, Ed Murray, and Frank Novak—entered Martin Loder's saloon. Loder testified that the men each had three glasses of beer, with Novak buying one round for the house. They made small talk, and after they had finished their beers, all three stood up to leave. Charley Zeb went home to his pregnant wife, while Murray and Novak left together. After the men departed, Loder locked up the saloon, walked the few hundred yards to his house, and went to bed.

At 10:30 PM, someone rattled Loder's front door, waking him. Outside he saw two farm boys, seventeen-year-old Mike Houser and eighteen-year-old Jake Haage. They wanted him to open the saloon so that they could buy some beer for a party. Loder dressed, put on his coat, and walked with the boys back to the saloon. They wanted some cigars, too, but Loder didn't sell them and suggested that before they bought the beer, the boys should first go over to Novak and Jilek's, where he could still see a few lights shining in the store and adjoining bank.

Loder and the two boys walked up the street through the soft snow to the bank, where the saloonkeeper was surprised to see Ed Murray standing outside the building. Novak was inside, behind the wire screen, looking at some business papers.

The two farm boys asked Novak if he would reopen the store to sell them some cigars. Novak agreed, closed the bank, and unlocked the general store. Haage and Houser followed Novak, while Murray hung around just inside the door, as if he was waiting for something.

After Novak rang up some cigars and candy, the two boys walked back to Loder's saloon, bought three pony kegs of beer, and drove off into the Iowa night, their horses' hooves muffled by the snow. Martin Loder locked up his saloon for the second time that night, and went back home to bed.[16]

It was now just past 11:30 PM.

At about 1:30 AM, a fire broke out in the store and the townspeople rushed to extinguish the flames. The next morning, Loder and several others saw some bones sticking out of the ashes. They worked their way through the wreckage and pulled a corpse from the gutted store's cellar. The body's legs had been burned off, as had most of the flesh on the torso. The skull was completely exposed, revealing a fracture on its lower left side and a shriveled mass of clotted brain tissue.[17]

Tobin stated that he had testimony from the coroner's inquest in February that the teeth in the skull did not match Frank Novak's. He now added that the evidence would show that someone had struck the skull, possibly with a blunt instrument.[18]

Having outlined the physical evidence and the facts of the fire, Tobin began to lay out the circumstantial evidence suggesting that Frank Novak was responsible for Murray's death and the razing of the store. He started by describing Novak's financial problems, his frustrations in his business dealings, and his growing desperation in the few months leading up to the night of the fire. Turning back to the burned-out basement, Tobin brought up the four clues that were left at the scene: the pocket-knife, dental bridgework, folding scissors, and identification badge, all of which, he declared, were deliberately planted there by Novak to imply that he himself had died in the fire, so that the insurance companies would pay large sums to his family.

Finally, Tobin traced Novak's flight, mile by mile, first from Walford to Iowa City, then across the continent to the Northwest, and finally to Alaska and Dawson City, Yukon Territory, mentioning the fugitive's use of two aliases—"Frank Alfred" and "J. A. Smith." Of Novak's "confession" to Red Perrin on the boat down the Yukon, he noted simply that Novak's version of the events of February 2 would be proven false.

The county prosecutor concluded his opening remarks with a number: twenty-seven-thousand dollars. That was, Tobin said, the figure that Novak's estate would have received from the five life insurance companies after his alleged death. "With these things in mind," Tobin told the jurors, "we ask you, gentlemen, to scrutinize the testimony as it comes, the testimony for the State—for it will be [built] link by link until it arrives at the point where you are to form by your verdict the last fact, and we know that you will listen to the evidence carefully, both in behalf of the State and in behalf of the defendant, to the end that full and impartial justice be done."[19]

After he spoke, Tobin sat down, spent from his effort. The Vinton paper called his remarks "excellent in every particular." During his partner's opening remarks, E. L. Boies had whispered to a nearby reporter that "Mr. Tobin is making a splendid statement."[20]

Then it was the other side's turn, and Tom Milner had selected Judge John J. Ney to make the defense team's opening remarks. Balding and bespectacled, with a thick, drooping mustache, deep-set beady eyes, and pince-nez eyeglasses, the portly Ney resembled a small walrus stuffed into a dark business suit.

Ney drew a deep breath and began:

"May it please the court, Gentlemen of the jury:

"You have heard the links of testimony as claimed here on the part of the State, under which they pretend to say that you will be satisfied beyond a reasonable doubt of the charge in this indictment; that is the thing that we are to try in this action, the truth or falsity of that charge." The evidence that the prosecution presented, Judge Ney emphasized, "must satisfy you of the guilt of the defendant beyond a reasonable doubt, not only of the matter and means by which he took the life of Edward Murray—as stated in the indictment—but of his intention deliberately and premeditatedly formed to take that life."[21]

Ney then drew on Novak's early days in business, to paint a somewhat different portrait of the defendant than had the prosecutor. Novak was, Ney said, a "young farmer's boy with an education obtained through some commercial school" who with some help from his wealthy father had become a highly successful businessman in Walford. Unfortunately, Ney said, Novak was the target of petty jealousies of his Walford neighbors as well as some lies and innuendos about his business methods. His appointment as postmaster by President Harrison, Ney believed, increased the resentment of some people in town. Pointing out that Novak's businesses continued to thrive until the 1895 fire that burned down the first Novak & Jilek store, Ney remarked that there was "no question about the good faith of that fire; there will be no doubt furnished about the fire as to its being a loss, for the stock was valuable." Novak, he concluded, was a responsible businessman who tried to pay off his creditors.[22]

After the fire in 1895, Novak fell on hard times, but he owed less than thirty-five-hundred dollars to people in the Walford area. That alone was no reason for him to murder Edward Murray. Obviously, Ney said, there must be a motive when there is a murder, and he insisted that there was no motive for Novak to murder Edward Murray. And when the fire broke out and Novak fled, Ney emphasized, he did nothing to disguise his identity as he walked away from the conflagration. As a general rule, the defense attorney claimed, Novak was not a schemer or a planner of anything that was evil; he was merely a victim of a run of bad luck. To make this case, Ney had to downplay the insurance policy issue, which he did by mentioning that Novak himself was a part-time insurance salesman who surely had no intention of concocting such an elaborate plan to defraud five agencies.

If he was guilty of anything, it was the guilt of carrying too much insurance, Ney said.[23]

About the bottle of spiked whiskey, Ney argued that Novak had kept the drink in the bank as "a means of defense" and that his goal was "not to poison or kill anybody" but "for the purpose of detecting anybody that undertook to rob that store, or set it on fire, as had previously occurred."[24]

Finally, like his counterpart Tobin, Ney urged the jury to consider the evidence impartially. "The defendant is entitled to a fair trial at your hands, gentlemen. When the evidence is in in this case and it is all summed up and weighed by you as impartial jurors . . . I have confidence that there will be no conclusion adverse to the defendant in this case, in your mind."[25]

Ney sat down, satisfied that he had introduced some doubt regarding any motive Novak might have for murdering Edward Murray. In addition, he felt that he had successfully characterized Novak as merely a victim of bad luck and not a man who had made a series of poor business decisions. All in all, Ney probably believed that he had done a capable job in laying the groundwork for challenging each aspect of the State's case.

Even though it was now late in the afternoon, Tobin had time to call his first three witnesses—Martin Loder, Mike Houser, and Charles Zabokrtsky. Along with Houser's friend, Jake Haage, they were the last people to see Edward Murray alive on the night of February 2, 1897. In fact, there was only one other man who had been in the store that night, whom Tobin did not call to the stand. That man was Frank Novak.

Tobin used the first set of witnesses to help forge the links of circumstantial evidence. Their testimony confirmed the chronology of events on the night of the fire that the prosecutor had outlined in his opening statement. It also described the movements of both Novak and Murray in Walford on February 2.

From the beginning, almost as soon as Judge Burnham lowered his gavel, it was clear that the defense was going to take a page from the recent Luetgert trial's defense team. Tom Milner was quick to contest, delay, and in general wage a campaign of obfuscation against the state's witnesses and their testimony. When Tobin asked Loder if Novak and Murray were in the habit of drinking together, Milner objected to the question as being immaterial and incompetent.[26] Later, when Loder was questioned about the piles of coal in the basement where the body was found, Milner objected and called the question leading.[27] This effort, Milner most likely thought, would have two results. It would plant the seeds of doubt about Novak's guilt in the jurors' minds by underscoring a rather small hill of circumstantial evidence upon which the prosecution's case rested. Also, the barrage of objections could shake up Tobin, whom Milner probably sized up as bright and determined but as green as a cornfield in August. The defense attorney also knew that Tobin needed to build momentum in the case to link the facts together and push the trial constantly forward, much the same as a train gathered speed as it moved down the tracks from one station to the next, until it reaches its final destination. Milner's plan was to throw objects across the rails, slowing down, stalling, or derailing Tobin's train.

But Tobin was ready. He possessed two special characteristics that would help him resist Milner's tactics: a deep well of tenacity and a steady disposition. He would need an abundance of both for this trial.

THIRTEEN

•————————————————•

Point and Counterpoint

As the trial unfolded, it seemed clear that Tobin had done a masterful job in organizing the prosecution's effort. The county attorney had lined up thirty-two witnesses, from townspeople who had last seen Novak and Murray on the night of February 2 to forensic medical experts. Among the early witnesses were Hugh Humphrey, a Walford justice of the peace, who testified that the body had been secured in a locked shed; Alice Murray and Nellie Murray Shea, who confirmed that their brother always wore the St. Joseph's cord around his waist; and William Murray, who gave testimony about the missing teeth in his son's upper jaw.

Humphrey compared the signatures of Frank Alfred Novak to that of "Frank Alfred," the name scrawled on the Union Pacific railroad ticket, and concluded that they were written by the same man. In addition, the justice of the peace testified that Novak needed cash badly and at one point months before the fire had asked him, "Ain't you got any money for me?"[1]

The defense questioned Humphrey if Novak might have simply meant that he would have liked Humphrey to deposit funds in the shopkeeper's bank vault, and the man said no, he thought that Novak was soliciting a loan. Despite a rather rigorous cross-examination, Humphrey stood behind his original testimony. He was convinced that Novak owed money to many people and was in bad shape financially.

In response, Ney insisted that Novak was not insolvent and had simply asked if Humphrey wanted to deposit any money in the bank. As to Humphrey's testimony that the handwriting on the railroad ticket was Frank Novak's, Ney conceded the point. However, he argued, Novak had simply been confused and absentmindedly omitted his last name from the signature. Furthermore, the defense pointed out that Novak had traveled from Walford to Iowa City mostly in broad daylight, never trying to disguise himself, despite the fact that he was fairly well known in Iowa City and could have been identified at any time. This was not, they said, the behavior of a fugitive fleeing a murder scene.[2]

After Humphrey finished testifying and stepped down from the witness stand, he passed by Novak, who said: "I did not think, Humphrey, that you would go back on me."

"I didn't 'go back on you,'" Humphrey replied curtly. "I simply told what I saw after you left Walford and of course you were not interested in that."[3]

Following the testimony of his daughter about Edward's shirt and St. Joseph's cord, William Murray was called to the stand. The musty courtroom, which had been half-empty during the jury selection, was now packed with people jammed together "like sardines in a box."[4] Quite a few women were in attendance, watching Novak's every move, and more would come each day for the duration of the trial. Frank Novak's reputation as a ladies' man had preceded him; the prisoner would receive gifts of candies, cakes, and flowers from women throughout the proceedings.[5]

William Murray began by speaking about his son's background, especially his bad luck as a farmer and how he had lost everything in Portsmouth, Iowa. Edward had then "gone on the road," his father said, trying to make a living, before returning home to Walford to help husk all of the corn on the Murray farm in the winter of 1896. Edward had lost two teeth on the upper left side of his mouth some time ago, his father reported, so he had wanted his son to have them replaced as Edward "looked bad."[6] But Edward had never purchased a dental bridge, instead growing a mustache to cover up the ragged opening in his mouth. Tobin, knowing that the old man had wavered on the exact location of the missing teeth during the coroner's hearing, carefully helped Murray to describe the precise location of these teeth.

Tom Milner couldn't wait to begin cross-examination of William Murray. The feisty "Napoleon of the Slope" tried to cast doubt on Murray's recollections. If the defense attorney could show that the old man's memory was faulty, the jury might not accept his testimony. Milner exemplified his approach to the case—doggedly focusing on small issues as a way to break the links of Tobin's chain of evidence.

"Let me ask you if you didn't state to the coroner's jury . . . that your name was William Murray, that your age was 83 years," Milner began.

"Eighty-three?" Murray asked.

"Yes," Milner said. "You have unquestionably turned your [84] years since; now I am asking you if you didn't so testify before the coroner's jury."

"Yes," Murray replied testily. "I was there. I made inquiries and find that I am 84 last spring."[7]

Then Milner attacked Murray's testimony about the location of Edward's missing teeth, making the most of the old man's uncertainty during the coroner's hearing. Murray now told Milner emphatically that the teeth were gone from the upper left side.

"You now feel confident it was on the left-hand side?"

"Yes," Murray said. "I am confident it was on the left-hand side, certainly."

Milner pressed.

"Whereas at that time [of the inquiry] you were not quite positive?"

The tone in Milner's voice made Murray lose his temper.

"If it is written so, all right, but I don't recollect."

"All I want is your recollection," Milner said.

"You can have mine honestly," Murray answered, regaining his composure, "and you won't have it any other way."[8]

Milner then tried to get William Murray to admit that the body was left alone for a period of time before the burial—in an attempt to inject some doubt regarding the corpse's identity—but Murray insisted that someone was always watching the remains, either himself or some of his neighbors.

After a few more questions, Murray left the stand and returned to his courtroom seat, where he would remain for the duration of the trial. Despite Milner's efforts, Murray's account at the trial was consistent with his previous testimony at the coroner's inquest.

Tobin was on his feet again. To delve into the forensics in the case, he called Dr. Ruml, who testified about the skull fracture and the mass of clotted blood. The physician also identified the skull as the same one he examined in Walford on February 4.

"That is the skull," Ruml said, and added, "The brain was in the skull at that time and also a blood clot."[9]

The defense objected, stating that there was no real proof that this was in fact Ed Murray's skull, as the body had been left unguarded for some time, despite Murray's testimony to the contrary. Milner and Ney argued that the corpse had first been moved to a shed, then kept in William Murray's farmhouse, and finally buried, only to be exhumed a few days later. This skull, the defense asserted, had never been positively identified. But despite these protests, Milner declined to cross-examine Dr. Ruml.

The prosecution also called two other Benton County physicians to the witness stand—Drs. Griffin and Whitney. Both testified regarding the damaged skull and charred stomach of Edward Murray, with each man spending considerable time on two aspects of the head—the fracture and the baked brain tissue. The fracture, Griffin said, was not caused by heat but by a blunt instrument. He also noted that the hemorrhage that produced the blood clot occurred prior to death, which also convinced him that the man was struck in the head before the store caught fire. The latter was a conclusion that Dr. Ruml had not been willing to reach at the coroner's inquest.[10]

The defense challenged Griffin, asking him how this skull fracture had occurred.

"Doctor," Ney asked, "have you now an opinion . . . as to whether the injury in this skull occurred from a wound inflicted by a human hand, or by other means, such as falling, as the body falling head foremost on some object, or some object falling upon the body?" Griffin answered that he did not know how the fracture occurred. This point was a minor victory for the defense, enabling it to argue that the body had fallen from the second floor and might have sustained the head injury in that fall. Griffin also admitted that although he had examined the stomach, he had not done any chemical tests for the presence of morphine. He believed that such test would be inconclusive, as the stomach was so badly burned that no trace of any chemical would have remained in the organ.[11]

Trying to shed light on Novak's alleged financial problems, the prosecution called several witnesses. One of them, Morris Ferreter, testified that Novak had tried to borrow one thousand dollars from him, but he had refused, worried about whether Novak had the collateral to back up the proposed loan. A teller from the Cedar Rapids National Bank, John Playter, swore that Novak only had sixty-two dollars in his account and that Novak & Jilek owed the bank about eight hundred dollars. On the day of the fire, Novak had sent Playter an express envelope, allegedly with five hundred dollars inside, but there was no cash in the envelope when Playter opened it. Playter confirmed that Novak's handwriting appeared on the envelope, as the teller had seen it on many deposit slips.[12]

The defense countered that the express envelope incident revealed little about Novak's alleged financial difficulties, as he might have simply forgotten to place the cash in the package. The only issue was whether the store owed money to the bank and, in any case, Novak was not personally liable for any money not found in the express envelope.[13]

❦ ❦ ❦

In the early stages of the trial, the general perception was that Tobin had done well. "A Noose for Novak," one newspaper predicted, while another report claimed that the state was "weaving a chain of evidence, link by link, to show that Murray must have been in the basement when the fire started."[14] The paper called the amount of evidence presented "overwhelming" and waited expectantly for Milner to reveal his defense strategy, as he had done in so many previous cases. But so far Milner was not being clear in his tactics, which led another reporter to write that Novak's lawyers were "apparently at sea."[15]

The most widely held theory was that the defense would attempt to prove that Ed Murray died from drinking the tainted whiskey. Tobin had already made an effort to discount this premise, but many people were sure that it would be an integral part of Milner's defense plan, no doubt because Milner had most likely arranged for Novak's supposed confession to be leaked before the trial. One unnamed local lawyer attending the trial was confident that Novak would soon take the stand and place a great deal of emphasis on the spiked-liquor bottle.

"Did it ever occur to you that Novak may claim that Edward Murray was dead before the store caught fire, and that he died not at the hands of the defendant but from the effects of the poisoned whiskey?" the anonymous lawyer asked rhetorically, and continued, "[Novak] may say that after Murray died after accidental poisoning, the store caught fire by accident, the fire originating by spontaneous combustion or any other uncommon causes." Confused and disoriented in the aftermath of the disaster, Novak could claim that he simply wanted to leave Walford and start a new life.[16]

❦ ❦ ❦

Each day, five hundred people shoehorned themselves into the "wretched little building," as one account called it, making the poorly ventilated courtroom even more cramped. With the stoves going full bore in such crowded quarters, what happened next was probably inevitable. During the testimony of Tom Jennings, one of the hack drivers in Iowa City who claimed to have taken Novak to the train station on February 3, one juror, sixty-year-old S. T. Saunders, halted the proceedings by announcing that he was sick, and he appeared to be on the brink of collapse.[17] After a brief discussion, with Tobin pressing for one more witness and Ney arguing for a recess until the next morning, Burnham ruled that Saunders could go home and recuperate for the night. The judge knew that Saunders's health was critical as there were no alternate jurors selected. If the retired farmer could not return, Burnham would have to declare a mistrial and start over.

Meanwhile, unnoticed, a powerfully built man, slightly less than six feet tall with dark red hair and a prominent sun-baked nose, slipped into Vinton on November 11. No one recognized him as he stepped from the train and quietly made his way to a downtown hotel, but the stranger would soon be the most talked-about man in town. He walked briskly into the hotel lobby and carefully studied the guest registry before he signed his name and address: "C. C. Perrin, Denver."

Novak's pursuer was in town and with his arrival the overall tenor of the trial was about to change, for Red Perrin was the star witness for the prosecution. The defendant would have another chance to gaze into the implacable face of the detective who had chased him for thousands of miles and would, in the next few days, help determine his fate.

At this juncture in the trial, Tobin chose to rely on his partner E. L. Boies, who called the Thiel detective to the stand. This was one of the moments those following the case had been waiting for, since Red Perrin had become a hero. His journal detailing the arduous trip from Juneau to Dawson City had been carried in a number of newspapers in October and his name was forever linked to one of the longest pursuits of the century. Unlike the detectives in the popular crime stories and novels, Perrin was real, and here he was in Vinton. The spectators who had muscled their way into the courtroom strained for a good look at the now well-known operative.

Perrin began by discussing his background as a detective. Under questioning by Boies, he said that he had been with the Thiel Detective Agency for about four years and now lived in Colorado, working out of the agency's Denver office. He recounted the details of following Novak's trail, from Juneau through the Chilkoot Pass and down the Yukon for six hundred miles to Dawson City. Then Perrin summed up his arrest of Novak and the trip to St. Michael, where his friend, Canadian surveyor William Ogilvie, had taken several photographs of the suspect.

Milner and Ney repeatedly objected during his testimony, claiming that the detective's statements were immaterial, irrelevant, or incompetent. But they failed to derail the prosecution's star witness. Digging into the meat of his testimony, Perrin began describing Novak's poisoned-whiskey confession.[18]

As Perrin continued his narrative, the barrage of defense objections intensified until Milner finally exploded. In addition to his usual litany that Perrin's testimony was immaterial, irrelevant, and incompetent, he argued that Novak's confession had been made under duress, that the prisoner had been shackled with heavy leg irons and treated inhumanely for the long trip back to Iowa. For example, Milner said, for the entire time, Perrin was armed with a revolver and was watching over the prisoner. It was, Milner said, a form of cruel treatment that could best be described as "brutal."[19]

Unimpressed, Judge Burnham overruled Milner's vehement objections and Boies proceeded with questioning Perrin. At last, Milner had showed his hand. The defense attorney was going to mount an attack on Perrin and go after the detective with everything he had. When his turn came, Milner planned to tear Perrin apart, and would use everything in his considerable arsenal to try to rattle the unflappable detective.

After Perrin finished his account of Novak's poisoned-whiskey confession, Milner jumped up. His blood was on the boil and he was ready for the fight. The defense attorney began by asking if Perrin received a fee whether or not he returned with the suspect. Perrin answered that he was paid in either instance, and that the arrest was inconsequential in that regard.

"Then you play—in these cases, Mr. Perrin—you play the role fully of a detective, notwithstanding your principal duty is to apprehend the different defendants, is that true?"

Perrin answered, "In many cases it is not a case to apprehend at all; it is to get the evidence; apprehend is not in it; it is all evidence there."[20]

Milner was not satisfied with this response.

"Then in this case you had the double duty to perform of procuring evidence for the Travelers Insurance Company and also to apprehend the defendant if possible."

"I didn't have it to perform," Perrin said.

"Well, you did try to perform it, didn't you?" Milner shot back.

"One part of it," Perrin answered placidly. "The apprehend and return, that is all."

Milner ratcheted up his attack. He asked whether Perrin had all of the legal paperwork needed for Novak's arrest and extradition, and grilled the detective on this point. Perrin was prepared for this, responding that he had carried warrants from Iowa and British Columbia, a requisition signed by President William McKinley, and extradition papers from the Canadian government in Ottawa. Further, Perrin stated that he had been sworn as a constable of British Columbia and the North West Territories with the authority to arrest Frank Novak.[21]

As Milner tried to put more heat on the witness, Perrin countered by becoming calmer. The only sign that the defense attorney had bothered him a little was a few caustic comments Perrin allowed himself. But the detective's tone changed when Milner turned to the details of Novak's confession and asked whether the detective had told Novak that he would keep it a secret until the grand jury convened in Vinton.

Perrin said that he had made this promise, but admitted that he had informed Tobin and Sheriff Metcalf about Novak's confession soon after the train reached Vinton on September 2. The detective said he considered the agreement void since Novak had given the same confession to D. L. Clouse, the other Thiel agent, on the trip from Alaska to Seattle.

This was the moment that Milner was waiting for. By impugning Perrin's honesty, he hoped to disrupt much of Tobin's case or at least focus attention on the prosecution's star witness rather than Frank Novak. It was a classic stratagem of courtroom misdirection.

When Perrin said that he advised Novak not to tell any reporters about this confession, Milner said, "You wanted to tell that yourself?"

"Yes," Perrin said. "That is right."

"You wanted to come in the form of a conquering hero and publish that yourself, didn't you, Perrin?"

"Yes," Perrin snapped, "I was looking for all kinds of notoriety. That is right."

Before his next question, the lead defense attorney paused briefly and checked the time. It was almost six o'clock on Saturday evening and there were just a few minutes remaining before Judge Burnham ended that day's testimony. At this time, most lawyers would be winding down their questioning until the next session.

But blood was in the water and Milner knew it. The defense attorney could not resist getting in a few more licks.

"You didn't say to him that you would keep it until after he went to the grand jury, did you, Perrin?"

"I told him that I would give him a chance to make the statement before the grand jury himself."

"You didn't lie to him, did you, Perrin?"

"Do you mean that for a question or for an insult?"

The two men stared at each other.

"You can take it any way you like," Milner answered.

"We will see about that," Perrin retorted.[22]

"Yes," Milner shouted back, "we will see on Monday whether you are telling the truth."

The courtroom was bedlam. One journalist later wrote that "both men were as white as sheets and shaking with passion."[23]

Tobin stood up and asked for a recess and Judge Burnham quickly agreed, banging the gavel and ending that day's session. In that one moment, Burnham had lost control of his courtroom, and for a man who had spent most of his adult life in the legal profession, including the last half dozen years as a district judge, he found this situation unacceptable.

The judge ordered the bailiff to clear the room and in a few minutes the stuffy old courtroom was empty.[24] Released from the building, a group of reporters spread out into Vinton, looking for other angles to the story. One journalist found three of Edward Murray's family members standing outside the courthouse—Edward's father William, the dead man's sister Alice, and his cousin Frank Guinan. Alice and Frank had traveled from Portsmouth, Iowa, to testify.

When asked about his health, William Murray said he had been sick but was now feeling better. "I'm so glad I was able to come today," the old man said.

When the interviews were finished, and after a few more questions, the reporter wrote, "The three figures drew closer around . . . [and] poured out their pitiful tale of murder and outrage."

"'Don't you think he's bold?' they said, referring again to Novak. 'Oh, he's bad! And to think he'd pick out Edward, an innocent boy, to kill.'"[25]

Alice Murray's eyes filled with tears as she thought about her brother. "You know they think he choked Edward to death with gas," she said. "'And to think that Edward and me stood there together and watched while that [gas boiler] was put into Novak's store."

"I went down to the jail," said the old man. "[Novak] wanted me to. He told me he was sorry for me. I said to him, 'I'm an old man and likely to die at any time. I would like to know if my son was in that fire.' And he said to me, 'I think he was. I cannot tell.' Do I feel sure he did it? God knows," the old man said, and paused for a moment. Then he added, "I wouldn't be afraid to swear on a stack of any number of bibles that he did it!"[26]

𝄪 𝄪 𝄪

On Monday, November 15, Perrin was recalled to the stand. However, before Tom Milner continued his cross-examination, Judge Burnham cleared his throat and addressed the jury:

"An incident occurred just at the adjournment of court Saturday night, all of which the court did not hear. I have had it read since, and I think what is in the record following the question is improper. This witness is entitled to courteous, gentlemanly treatment, and I do not think that counsel should issue a challenge when he is upon the stand. What follows the question will be stricken from the record."

Defense attorney John Ney stood up.

"Your honor, the question is one that belongs to his [Perrin's] profession and was proper in that relation, and it was he that issued the challenge and wanted to know if it was an insult."

Persuaded by this argument, Judge Burnham allowed the question to stand and told Tom Milner that he could proceed with the cross.[27]

"Now, what was the answer to that question, Mr. Perrin?"

This time it was Tobin's turn to complain and he did so vociferously, firing a volley of objections—that the question was incompetent, immaterial, and improper, since Perrin had already recounted his conversations with Novak and that it was up to the jury to evaluate the facts in the case and not whether Perrin told the truth in this instance or not. Judge Burnham sustained Tobin's objection, and Milner was forced to alter his tactics slightly. Nevertheless, he continued to press Perrin on what had happened between the detective and Novak.

When Judge Burnham stopped Milner a few minutes later, he asked the defense attorney, "What is the object, Mr. Milner, to impeach the witness?"

"Yes, sir," Milner replied.

"I think you should lay a foundation."[28]

Milner responded, "That is probably true," and went over Perrin's recollections again, challenging the detective's memory concerning each individual fact of Novak's confession. But there was no chance that Milner would upset the Thiel man again and Perrin kept his composure for the remainder of the session.

He even allowed himself a little levity. When Milner asked about the alleged tainted bottle of whiskey, and that Novak's goal was to "put the burglars to sleep," the two men discussed the meaning of that phrase.

"Putting them to sleep or knocking them out is the same in detective —means the same in detective language that it does in the prize ring, does it?" Milner asked.

"We use practically the same language in the detective [business] as you do it the legal profession," Perrin observed.[29]

After several more hours of questioning, Perrin was dismissed. The veteran detective had proven to be as tough as a hobnail boot, having absorbed all of Milner's punches and left with his own integrity intact. More importantly, Milner had been unable to generate much doubt despite his constant attacks on the detective's memory and probity. The long hours of Perrin's cross-examination had to have been a reassuring moment for Tobin. The case had absorbed Milner's hardest hits and had come through in fairly good condition.

On November 15, the state rested its case. The general consensus among the reporters was that the prosecution had done an excellent job. But the defense had one last chance, and with the clever Tom Milner at the helm, everyone who had been following the case anticipated several days of surprises and fireworks.

❧ ❧ ❧

So far, the defense team of Milner and Ney had successfully tossed a web of obfuscation over their plans. No one knew exactly what tack they would take next, and followers of the trial sifted through comments from the two attorneys concerning their strategy. The two lawyers had adhered to Milner's principle and the hallmark of most defense attorneys—objecting to every single prosecution point, no matter how small. Because the prosecution's case rested solely on circumstantial evidence, casting doubt on every shred of this was vital to Novak's defense.

One theory still held that the defense would use the spiked-whiskey premise as the linchpin in the case. In this view, Milner and Ney would contend that Edward Murray drank from the bottle without Novak being present and that the pharmacist had given Novak too large an amount of morphine merely to put a person asleep. They might further insist that a gas jet in the basement had triggered the fire. Most importantly, the defense could emphasize that this unlit gas swirling around the store had caused Novak to behave strangely once he woke up during the early morning hours of February 3.[30]

The defense of Frank Novak began slowly, as some of the witnesses Milner and Ney had summoned arrived late. The courtroom itself was now barely half-filled, with most of the attendees being women. It was clear that Novak was still a favorite of the ladies, and he continued to receive a steady stream of flowers in his jail cell. But those who attended the defense's first day of argument generally found it to be boring, mainly due to the delays in obtaining witnesses. The spectators talked softly while both the prosecution and defense killed time at their respective tables.

Outside, the faint strains of a hand organ wafted into the room. Popular songs such as "Money Musk," "There's a Land That Is Fairer Than Day," the German and French national airs, and "Sweet Rosie O'Grady" drifted in and mixed with the foul courtroom air.[31] But in all, it was a very inauspicious day for the defense, and those who expected a session full of lightning and thunder from Tom Milner were sorely disappointed.

At this point it seemed that Frank Novak's best chance was to take the stand and testify on his own behalf. In an interview with the *Gazette*, one of the defense lawyers spoke anonymously to a reporter on this topic. The interview was clearly an effort to influence public opinion.

"I am frank to admit," the unnamed lawyer said, "that when I was first asked to take up Frank Novak's case I was prejudiced against

him. . . . Since I have talked with him and heard his story I am positively and absolutely convinced of his innocence. I cannot and do
not believe that he committed the crime with which he was charged.
Moreover, there has been absolutely no evidence to show any motive,
and still less than he had at any time planned any step that was not
in accord with his course of conduct in everyday life." Once Novak
takes the stand, the attorney claimed, "he will tell a story that will
admit of no contradictions and will explain many things which are
not now understood by those who have not heard his side of the
case. There are some things that are strange and a few which he may
not be able to explain, things which the defendant himself does not
understand."[32]

At last, on the morning of November 18, the defense's witnesses
arrived and began to testify. The defense's efforts concentrated, as
so many had thought they would, on the mysterious bottle of spiked
whiskey. Some witnesses swore that they saw a bottle in the bank
adjoining the store and one man, W. H. McDonald, said that Novak
had warned him about the contents of the bottle.[33]

Tobin pounced on this witness, pointing out that he had just con-
tradicted himself, since in testimony before the grand jury in September, McDonald claimed that he had not seen any poisoned whiskey in
the store or bank.[34] Tobin also worked to impeach another witness,
Frank Novak's brother-in-law, Joseph Shunka, who also had given two
different versions of what he knew about the whiskey bottle. In both
instances, Tobin was able to show that McDonald and Shunka had
in fact altered their stories, and he threatened both witnesses with
perjury charges.

Then Milner called two expert witnesses from Iowa State University
—Dr. L. H. Andrews, a professor of chemistry, and Dr. Frank Carroll,
a physician and surgeon. Their theories regarding what occurred on
the night of February 2 and early morning of February 3 centered on
the gases, mainly from a mixture of wood and coal smoke, present
in the store. Both experts contended that when Frank Novak had

woken up, he had suffered from what Dr. Carroll referred to as "a sort of anesthesia" or "a state of intoxication."[35]

Then it was E. L. Boies's chance to attack the defense's witnesses, and he did so by summarizing the evidence the prosecution had presented thus far.

"Supposing a man 32 years of age . . . was in a building that was consumed by fire, that another man was in that building; that the first man that I had spoken of had twenty-seven-thousand dollars of life and accident insurance on his life; that the condition of every policy . . . would be fulfilled by death, by burning in a building; that the first man I spoke of runs out of that building and leaves the other man in the building; that the man who is left in the building is afterward found, his body burned and charred, in the basement, and there being a fracture of his skull going through both the bone and *dura mater*, and there being eleven ounces of blood in his skull which must have gone there before his death, and the man who ran away goes under assumed names, walks the first day some fourteen or fifteen miles, rides from that place to Iowa City, a distance of some twenty-three miles from there, takes a train in the night time, after saying that he don't care which way he goes, goes to Council Bluffs and there signs his name—a wrong name—to a railway ticket for Portland, Oregon, and then goes to the Klondike, reaches Dawson City, and months afterwards when he is apprehended and told that he is charged with murdering of Murray, denies that he is Novak at all and says that he never lived in Walford where the fire occurred, and that they have got the wrong man, that there he is, going under an assumed name—a name other than his own."[36]

Now Boies paused and looked at the physician on the stand.

"I want you to tell this jury, doctor, whether you will say to them that in your judgment the conduct of that man is explained by the breathing of poisoned gases?"

"I do not attempt to explain his conduct," Dr. Carroll answered quietly.

"Will that gas crack a skull, doctor?"

"No, sir."

"Will it cause the brain tissue to be forced out through the *dura mater* to the point of rupture?"[37]

"No, sir," Dr. Carroll replied.

Boies turned and addressed the defense team. "You may ask the witness."

Ney stood up. He was clearly rankled at Boies.

"I don't think we want to ask the witness," he sputtered. "If you think you can run this case on that sort of buncombe, I have never seen a case tried that way, not a case where a man is on trial for his life, not the county attorney nor the prosecuting attorney, but . . . "

M. J. Tobin angrily cut Ney off. "I now ask that the statement of Ney be embodied in the record."

"I suppose it is there, sir," Judge Burnham replied mildly.

"In my own defense I want to make this statement," Boies said. "That I gave notice to the [defense] counsel that if he was going to assume his theory of this case to the witness, that we should leave to assume ours, and he said there would be no objection. I have stated nothing to this witness that the evidence of this case does not maintain."

Judge Burnham agreed.

"Call your next witness," he ordered the defense, and the trial moved forward.

In a surprising move, Tom Milner announced, "The defense rests." The prosecution was wholly unprepared for this and asked for a continuance until that afternoon. The newspaper reporters were also shocked as they left the courtroom. "It Was a Day of Surprises," one headline stated, describing the events that had occurred in the dank little courthouse.[38] Another reporter wrote, "If a bomb shell had been dropped into the courtroom, it could not have had caused greater surprise."[39]

After all the defense team's carefully planted leaks insisting that the defendant would explain everything, Novak would not be taking the stand. No courtroom audience would ever hear his side of the story. Ultimately, every detail of what really happened in Walford during the night of February 2 and early morning of February 3, 1897, remained known only to Frank Alfred Novak.

FOURTEEN

The Summing Up
and Verdict

On Saturday, November 20, both sides made their closing arguments. The little courtroom was filled once again as everyone listened to the prosecution's summary while straining to catch a glimpse of Novak's face. Reporters sat elbow to elbow at a long table, scribbling notes at top speed while courtroom artists sketched each of the principals. Even with the windows open, the rank air inside took its toll, causing one woman to lose consciousness. When water was sprinkled on her face and she still did not awaken, two bailiffs pushed through the crowd and carried her outside. Several others had to leave before they were overcome by the foul air, which now seemed to affect everyone, including the portly John Ney, who swayed a little as he stood and gave the defense's summation, completing it with great effort.[1]

M. J. Tobin had spent months preparing for his closing remarks on this case and he conducted himself in a "masterly manner."[2] In an interesting sidelight, Ney requested that the court reporter take notes on Tobin's remarks, something that was uncommon at the time. The defense attorney was clearly interested in having Tobin's summary put into the court records, in case there was a need to appeal the verdict in the future. It also could have been an attempt to rattle the young prosecutor, who was wrapping up his first major case.

If this was Ney's goal, it appeared to have no impact whatsoever on Tobin, for the county attorney stood and delivered a strong summation, going over the circumstantial evidence and connecting all of the pieces one last time for the jury. He began by outlining Novak's actions, paying particular attention to his behavior prior to the fire—obtaining the insurance policies, allegedly sleeping in the store to guard against burglars, and studying a map of the United States, supposedly looking at potential escape routes.

Tobin also reviewed the forensic evidence in the case, describing the fractured skull and the exposed brain tissue once again. He reminded the jury that Novak had signed the Union Pacific ticket "Frank Alfred" and asked the jury, "Why would he flee?" Further, Tobin debunked the defense team's claim that Novak had carried Murray up to the cot on the second floor. If this were true, Tobin asked, then how could the little bed fall down to the basement with the body still on top? He noted that there was no proof that the boiler or gas plant had leaked any fumes, and so there was no reason to believe the defense's theory that the gases from burning wood and coal could disorient a man. He called the testimony from the defense team's expert witnesses regarding this issue "a monumental farce."[3]

Tobin made a special point of singling out Red Perrin's testimony, noting that the defense didn't question one scintilla of the detective's story but instead mounted an *ad hominem* attack in an attempt to discredit Perrin himself. The detective was telling the truth, Tobin said, and the truth in the case had come out throughout the course of the trial.

Then the young prosecutor outlined the list of facts that he and Boies had presented to the jury. He went back to the timeline of that fateful February night, reviewing Novak's actions that evening—how he changed clothes and took a shotgun, money, and some food before leaving the burning building. He questioned why Novak, supposedly an innocent man, fled the state instead of helping Ed Murray escape from the burning store. Why would Novak adopt different aliases as he transferred from one train to another, and then finally to a steamer, and why would he travel from Walford to a place thousands of miles away, about as far removed from civilization as any other spot in the world?

When he reached the conclusion of his arguments, Tobin weighed each word carefully: "I say to you, gentlemen of the jury, that . . . the acts on that night were planned; that the deeds of that night were premeditated. That the man who did it knew exactly what he was doing."

Tobin then cut to one of the key points in his argument—Novak's motive for murder:

"It was done for money. It was done for money and I submit to you that there have been numerous crimes, horrible crimes, done for the very same thing that this was committed for. I say to you that ever since the Savior of the world died upon the cross; ever since the Son of God was betrayed and crucified for a few pieces of silver, crimes dark and damnable have been committed for the same purpose; for money, red-handed murderers have crouched in dark places at midnight ready to make the fatal blow. . . . In my judgment, for money, for twenty-seven-thousand dollars, Ed Murray's soul was hurled into eternity and his poor body burned beyond recognition."[4]

After a break for lunch, the defense team summarized its arguments. First, John Ney spoke about their friendly relationship with the Benton County prosecutor and hoped that he and Milner's efforts were not seen as a personal attack against either M. J. Tobin or E. L. Boies. "As I said at the beginning of this case in making the opening statement, it is not our purpose to defeat justice. We are law-abiding citizens, Mr. Milner and myself, and nobody would desire to uphold the officers of the law more heartily and readily than he or I." Having defended the defense attorneys' own honor, Ney turned to their goals in advocating on Novak's behalf: "We have come here to give this man a clean trial for his life before this jury. We have here twelve citizens and one upon the bench hearing the evidence and upon that evidence to determine the guilt or innocence of the

accused. Nothing extraordinary, nothing strange, and we would dis-
abuse your minds or anything of that kind."[5]

Ney then explained to the jury that Novak had no motive to kill
Ed Murray. "Murder? Bosh." In the insurance policies he had taken
out, "You find love and solicitude both for the property there and
for the wife of his bosom and for his children and his parents and
his sisters." Novak was in the "heyday of his existence" and had nothing to gain by destroying his own store. Furthermore, there was no
evidence introduced that Novak was bankrupt; he was not "pressed
for money." Lastly, Ney pointed out that Novak and Murray held no
grudges against each other. And while it was tragic that Murray died,
Novak was not guilty of causing that death.[6]

Before he finished his closing argument, Ney couldn't resist one
last swipe at the two prosecuting attorneys seated across from him.
Earlier in the trial, he had called the prosecution's arguments "buncombe," and now again took umbrage at what he thought was Tobin's
everything-but-the-kitchen-sink approach in the trial. Ney compared
Tobin's efforts to the wide-ranging scope of the Bible, and argued
that "we have [seen] injected into this case nearly everything from
Genesis to Revelations by the county attorney."[7]

❦ ❦ ❦

Later that night, an astonishing story broke that threatened to stop
the trial. An Associated Press article reported that a man named
Charles Wood had walked into a police station in Seattle and said
that he had met with Edward Murray in late February 1897, several
weeks after the fire. He was absolutely positive that the man he met in
a saloon was Murray. Furthermore, Wood asserted that he spoke to
Murray for several minutes. After the discussion, Wood—who knew
all about the Walford fire—said that he told someone he thought was
a policeman about the incident, but that nothing ever happened. So
Wood decided to repeat his story and this time went directly to the
police. Seattle Police Chief C. S. Reed, who had been working fever-

ishly to maintain order in that town since the Klondike gold rush began months earlier, wired Sam Metcalf, the Benton County sheriff, and assured the Iowa lawman that they would investigate Wood's statements.

"Every effort will be made to discover Murray," one paper declared. "Wood says he has known Murray for years and he was there at the time of the burning of Novak's store and knows all the particulars. Wood is apparently a man of standing, and his word is believed."[8] Another paper concluded that "the case has been wrapped in seemingly more impenetrable mystery for the time being than it was for days last February."[9]

Although the news caused a furor, the disruption of the Novak case turned out to be short-lived. A few reporters discovered that while Wood in fact did hail from Vinton and had left for the Klondike about three weeks earlier, his family admitted that the fifty-year-old Iowan was "addicted to the drink habit" and would sometimes go off on an alcoholic binge and disappear for weeks at a time.[10] His story of meeting Edward Murray was proven to be false. The *Vinton Eagle* commented, "Altogether, Wood managed to kick up quite an excitement. Charley is evidently having a fly time and will do well if he sees nothing worse than ghosts."[11]

Rumors swirled around Vinton that Wood had been sent to Seattle by the defense in a last-ditch ploy to produce either a mistrial or a postponement of the case. As it turned out, the Seattle police never found any evidence that Novak's defense team was involved with Wood or his story.

This diversion concluded, Judge Burnham called the court to order on Tuesday, November 23, and Tom Milner continued the defense team's summation. The mercurial Milner, a man who thrived in the white-hot spotlight of the courtroom, was in his element. He was an expert at taking the pulse of a jury and, like his counterparts across the aisle, had spent considerable time organizing his summary remarks.

Milner began by describing the case over the past two weeks "in panoramic view," pointing out that besides the twelve jurors, millions of other Americans from "the Passamaquoddy Bay to the Golden Gate" were interested in the details.[12] He slyly added that while he could not "play with words" the way Tobin did, he would nevertheless refute all of the state's points regarding Frank Novak and Edward Murray. The defense team leader noted that everything the prosecution said was almost impossible to prove, from Novak's motives down to whether he had defrauded any insurance companies.

For example, if in fact Novak wished to travel undetected, Milner said, why did he wander around the Iowa countryside in broad daylight? Why would he go to Iowa City to catch a train when he knew there was a good chance that someone would recognize him? One by one, Milner countered the prosecution's theories, trying to rebut every point, and concluded that all of the alleged facts strung together by Tobin and Boies still did not equal direct proof, but amounted merely to "hearsay."[13]

He commented that Novak carried insurance, but this was not unusual, emphasizing again that Novak had even sold insurance himself. On Novak's flight, Milner remarked, "his course is aimless, his identity unconcealed." The attorney stressed that Novak signed the name "Frank Alfred" on the Union Pacific train ticket not as a means to hide his identity but simply by mistake. He had meant to write his entire name but neglected to do so. Milner also attempted to cast doubt on the identity of the corpse itself, noting that a hundred men might have worn the same type of shirt that Edward Murray had on that day. He also claimed that many Catholics wore a St. Joseph cord, like that found around the body's waist. Milner also raised questions about the skull, stating that the prosecution had not really proven that Ed Murray's body was the one found in the wreckage.[14]

After a lunch break, E. L. Boies gave the state's final comments. Contentious to the last, Milner objected, saying that Boies could not perform this task legally as that was the job of the Benton County attorney. Judge Burnham overruled, and Boies began the prosecution's final summation. He quickly went over the key points from the prosecution and concluded his closing arguments by stating that No-vak's explanation regarding the events on the night of February 2 was "teeming with lies and falsehoods." Boies simply asked, "When did it become necessary for an innocent man on this earth to make up a story which is in conflict to undisputed evidence as to the truth?" adding that "innocent men tell the truth and innocent men may plan their defense upon the eternal rock of truth and no living man, and no living power, can ever reach them, if they do."[15]

It was now 10:30 AM on November 23. Judge Burnham ordered the jury to be sequestered one last time. Now, after nearly two full weeks of testimony and almost one hundred witnesses, the twelve men finally had the case.

A little more than thirteen hours later, at shortly before midnight, the jurors returned with their verdict. The courtroom, which now gave the appearance of "some old cave," was barely lit by the flickering oil lamps.[16] The light fell only on the front portion of the room, illuminating Tobin clearly but casting a shadow over the defense table. Novak leaned forward expectantly, his face barely visible. The jurors' bodies were outlined in the faint light but their faces were concealed in the darkness.

J. T. Heath, foreman of the jury, passed the verdict to the clerk of courts, as instructed by Judge Burnham. Due to the poor light, the clerk strained to read the writing on the form, but cleared his throat and announced what Heath had written:

"We, the jury, find the defendant guilty of murder in the second degree, and that his punishment be imprisonment in the penitentiary for ten years at hard labor." The jury had found Novak innocent of first-degree murder, which requires premeditation and carries the death penalty. Second-degree murder, which is not premeditated, is a lesser charge and carries with it a lesser sentence.

Everyone looked at Frank Novak, who slouched back into his chair as "a ghastly pallor overspread his face." He tried to steady himself by gripping the corners of the table and seemed to be focused at something on the floor.[17]

Judge Burnham noted that the jury had filled out the paperwork incorrectly. "Your verdict not being in the proper form, you will have to retire. The court cannot receive this verdict in the form in which it is presented," he said. The judge instructed the bailiff to leave with the jury and explain the differences among the three forms that the twelve men possessed. After a few more minutes, the jury returned with its verdict separate from its recommendation. Again, the jurors found Novak guilty of second-degree murder.[18]

"Shall I read this recommendation that is here?" the clerk asked Judge Burnham.

"Yes," Burnham said.

"We, the jury request that the punishment of this defendant be ten years in the penitentiary."[19]

A short time later, out on the street, a *Gazette* reporter cornered Novak, who had regained a little composure since hearing the verdict a few minutes ago. Novak listened to the *Gazette* man's questions and then paused for a moment. "I suppose there is no use in trying to question the verdict; it can't be helped now, but I say, as I have said all the time, I am innocent of the crime with which I am charged."[20]

Novak then repeated the identical phrase he had uttered ever since his arrest four months earlier. Since then, these words had become his personal litany. "There are some things which I cannot explain." He then added, "And which I never will be able to explain, but I must abide by the decision of the jury. I must suffer for something of which I am not guilty." As he was led back to his cell, he stated, "Time will show to the world that I am right."[21]

FIFTEEN

After the Verdict

The people of Vinton had hoped that a small bell in the court-house tower would ring when a verdict was reached, but the bell was silent. Instead, one of the bailiffs visited the hotel where many reporters and lawyers were staying and told several people about the jury's decision. Curiously, none of the jurors initially spoke about the verdict; later, a few of them later explained that it was a result of a compromise.[1] A rumor surfaced that one of the twelve jurors might have been bribed, but nothing was ever proven in this regard.[2]

The reporters called in their stories to their respective newspapers in Iowa and other parts of the country as the scene in Vinton began to settle down. After the verdict was read, Agnes McKinnon, court stenographer for the seventeenth judicial district, was no doubt much relieved. For two weeks, she had worked feverishly. When her notes were typed up in the following year, they were found to total slightly more than sixteen hundred typewritten pages (four hundred twelve thousand words) of court proceedings and testimony.[3]

E. L. Boies, the hired gun who had assisted M. J. Tobin in planning the prosecution's strategy and had done an admirable job in summarizing the case, boarded the afternoon train back home to Waterloo. Tom Milner, a man who reveled in the bright spotlight of courtroom drama, commandeered the office of the three-story Ralyea House, and leaned back in a rocking chair with his feet perched on a steam radiator. Although he had lost the case, Milner assumed the role of the victor, puffing on a big cigar. "For two weeks the man who like General Grant cannot enjoy himself without his cigar . . . was making up for lost time as he sat receiving the congratulations of friends and telling stories of his many interesting experiences." About an hour later, Tobin arrived and the two men who had just finished a courtroom battle worthy of the Kilkenny cats casually smoked a few cigars together. Neither lawyer talked about the case but instead swapped stories concerning their days at Cornell College in Mount Vernon.[4]

🍂 🍂 🍂

The verdict in the Novak case made headlines across the state, as it was one of the first times that anyone had been convicted of murder based solely on circumstantial evidence. As the story broke in different papers, some articles were filled with inaccuracies and misspellings. For months, the papers had tripped over the Bohemian names, stumbled on the spelling of various towns, and botched other facts associated with the case. Their reports on the verdict continued to include errors. Even the *New York Times* was not immune, as its brief story described the murder of Edward Murray by his "room-mate" Frank Novak, who had, the *Times* reported, set fire to "the house in which they lived."[5]

Back in Iowa, the general consensus was shock and anger at the jury's verdict, as many people were outraged that Novak did not receive the death penalty. Some newspaper stories seemed to echo Mark Twain's sentiments that "the jury system puts a ban upon intelligence and honesty, and a premium on ignorance, stupidity and perjury."[6] An editorial in the *Cedar Rapids Daily Republican* pulled no punches. The paper quoted humorist Artemus Ward, who once wrote, "If there was anything hidden from an inscrutable Providence, it was the mind of a petit juror," the term for someone who sits on a civil or criminal trial jury. The *Republican* also pointed out that "Frank Novak was either guilty of one of the most cold-blooded and deliberate murders ever perpetrated in Benton County or he was innocent. By no logical process whatsoever, could the jury reach a conclusion that he was guilty of murder in the second degree."[7]

The editorial writer added, "Is this not fresh proof and striking proof that our jury system is for the most part a farce?" The writer further noted, "It is said by those personally acquainted with the jury in the Novak case, that it was an average jury and yet no one will contend that they arrived at anything like a logical or a decent conclusion in the matter. The writer concluded that "ninety-nine percent of those who have followed this trial were disgusted with the outcome."[8]

Several other newspapers in the state also howled in dismay. Out in western Iowa, the *Sioux City Tribune* reported that the jury's vote "lacks the first hint of consistency," while the *Iowa State Register* concluded, "We are nothing if not a sentimental people." According to the *Des Moines Leader*, "From many points of view this verdict seems worthy of being set aside for it can be reconciled neither with the theory of guilt not with the one of innocence. If Novak is guilty of anything it is the kind of murder for which the law prescribes capital punishment; if not guilty of anything he should be set at liberty."[9]

Few Iowans seemed to doubt that Novak was guilty of first-degree murder. Many believed that the verdict was a gross miscarriage of justice and that he had an inappropriately light sentence. Writing about the case roughly seventy-five years after the verdict, M. J. Tobin's son, John, himself a well-known lawyer and judge in eastern Iowa, believed that his father had proven that Novak had murdered Ed Murray. "His [Novak's] guilt was more clearly established by the surrounding facts than if half a dozen witnesses had testified to seeing him strike Murray on the head and place his body in the basement before starting the fire. Under the indisputable facts there simply could be no question as to guilt."[10]

☙ ☙ ☙

There was one notable exception to the coverage of the jury's verdict, and that was the *Belle Plaine Union*, Tom Milner's hometown newspaper. Rather than emphasize Novak's conviction, the story carried the headline, "TOM MILNER'S VICTORY!" and called his defense of Novak "a Herculean task . . . almost a forlorn hope . . . especially since it was almost a waste of time to defend [Novak]. . . . We do admire the pluck and vim of our friend Milner." Still, the paper admitted that "the [verdict] was a great surprise to thousands of people."[11]

At this point, it would have been easy for Milner not to contest the jury's decision, to admit defeat and say that he did the best he could. But the defense attorney was a long way from conceding this case. Accepting any loss in court was contrary to his nature. There was simply no "give-up" in the man.

Within a few days of the trial's end, he promised to file a motion for a new trial along with an appeal to the Iowa Supreme Court, since the defense attorney believed from the beginning that the case presented by the state was riddled with errors. On November 30, Milner and Ney filed for appeal, claiming thirteen different reasons that Novak should be entitled to a new trial. Milner also had been quietly working to have all of Novak's remaining assets in Walford transferred to his wife, Mary, in case her husband had to serve any portion of the sentence that Judge Burnham would mete out next month.[12]

Novak himself passed a quiet Thanksgiving with his wife and two sons in the company of Sheriff Sam Metcalf's family. The sheriff, who had spent considerable time with Novak since the suspect's arrival in Vinton in September, had treated him well, bringing his prisoner books, cigars, and on most evenings over the past three months, taking him to family meals. In fact, the two were so close that some people in Vinton were critical of the chummy relationship between sheriff and prisoner.[13] One paper declared that "probably no prisoner —murderer or otherwise—has received such royal treatment,"[14] while another report noted that Metcalf "had a relationship more like father and son than officer and prisoner."[15]

After the trial, Metcalf reacted angrily when a *Gazette* reporter asked him about Novak's stay in the Vinton jail.

"I have been severely criticized by the press for allowing Frank so many privileges and for not shackling him when I was taking him from the jail to the courthouse, but he is not in here for punishment, simply being held here to await punishment."[16]

By this point, Sam Metcalf must have been mighty tired of the case in general. For three months he had fended off reporters, women visitors, other lawyers, and scads of obnoxious curiosity seekers trying to catch a glimpse of Frank Novak. Although he personally thought that Novak was pleasant enough, he couldn't wait for the case to wrap up and Novak to leave his jail, whether to go home or go to prison. The sheriff knew that Judge Burnham would pass sentence in early December and then the whole storm that surrounded the placid little town of Vinton would pass. Ever since February, the sheriff had to work hard for his salary and despite criticism in the papers, probably believed he was earning every cent of his wages.

☙ ☙ ☙

Money was a constant thread that ran through the Novak case, and while Sam Metcalf was doing his job guarding his now-famous prisoner, the sheriff was concerned about a financial issue. Earlier in the year, when the search for Novak began, Metcalf had ordered a reward of two hundred dollars for the fugitive's capture, but he had done so with no legal authority. When C. C. Perrin claimed the money, the Benton County board of supervisors refused to pay, until M. J. Tobin pressured it to make good on the reward. In fact, it was not until April 1898 that this matter was resolved and Perrin was given the money, minus fifty dollars for Tobin's work in securing the funds.[17] The other reward that had been offered, five hundred dollars as stipulated by Governor Drake of Iowa, had been paid to Red Perrin a few months after Novak was captured.

But the reward money paled next to the mountain of expenses generated in the pursuit. Perrin and a number of Thiel agents had spent months chasing Novak, a search that encompassed roughly twenty-five-thousand miles altogether. These detectives—Hurst, D. D. Anthony, Dr. Charles Peterson, D. L. Clouse, Perrin, and many other

Thiel operatives—carefully accounted for their expenditures, which included train and steamer fares, meals, entertainment expenses, telegrams, and other funds spent in the long pursuit. Perrin in particular was as thorough as a chartered accountant regarding his expenses. When everything was tabulated, the amount of his out-of-pocket costs alone added up to about twenty-four-hundred dollars. Combined with the agency's fee, the total amount came to just under four thousand dollars.[18]

Since the Travelers insurance policy on Novak was for ten thousand dollars, that company had spearheaded the search for him, hiring the Thiel agency and working with Tobin in the pursuit of the fugitive. Unfortunately for Travelers, the other four insurance companies that carried policies on Novak had, from the beginning, balked at providing any financial assistance. One firm, the Northwestern Mutual Life Insurance Company, declined to participate at all, since it could "mark off their policy now that Frank Novak was [found] alive."[19] The United States Casualty Company also was hesitant to assist in any expenses from the beginning. Andrew Van Wormer, president of the company, had outlined its position in a letter to Travelers: "if the amount to be offered the [Thiel] detective agency can be *fixed and certain* [his italics], we shall be willing to bear our proportionate amount thereof." Obviously, no one could have predicted that Novak would flee to the "arctic regions," as one company so quaintly put it, but the net result was that Travelers paid off the Thiel account with only a small amount of financial support from U.S. Casualty, which contributed two hundred fifty dollars. Travelers's president, Dr. J. B. Lewis, realizing that he had little likelihood of obtaining any additional funds from the other companies, accepted the check and closed his books on the matter.[20]

🌿 🌿 🌿

Meantime, as November rolled into December, people waited eagerly for the next step—Judge Burnham's sentencing of Novak. It had been a tumultuous two weeks as dozens of newspapers across the state had either sent their own reporters to the courthouse or picked up wire stories filed from papers and news services. In Vinton, it seemed like every street corner had a cluster of people debating Novak's guilt or innocence. Women continued to shower Novak with cakes and flowers but Judge Burnham refused to allow the women to hand any gifts to the defendant during the trial. The judge also banned the display of these flowers in court.[21]

On Saturday, December 4, the wait was finally over. Strangely enough, the once-packed courtroom only had about fifty spectators when the prisoner came in and took his customary position behind the defense table. Then Tom Milner stood up and read off the thirteen objections he had originally filed, along with an amended list that now totaled fifty-two different reasons for declaring a mistrial. After Milner finished, John Ney stood and castigated the newspapers of Cedar Rapids and Vinton for their allegedly slanted coverage of the case, which he believed had been extremely prejudicial against his client.[22] It was no coincidence that several of these papers had carried the full account of Red Perrin's trip to the Klondike and his journey back to Iowa with Novak. Ney also took this opportunity for one last swipe at Perrin, calling him a "scavenger" and claiming the detective was "born of a mother and father who hated each other."[23]

Even though the trial was over, both defense attorneys were still gunning for the detective, who had been seen slipping in and out of the Cedar Rapids area. Although Perrin's work on the Novak case was done, he had some unfinished business of a more personal nature. During the trial, he had met one of Ed Murray's cousins, an attractive twenty-year-old named Mary Agnes Murray. The detective courted Miss Murray for years, stopping to visit with her and her family whenever he passed through Cedar Rapids on business.

If one of Milner and Ney's goals during the arraignment was to upset Judge Burnham, they had succeeded. The judge listened to both of their arguments for retrial. Then it was his turn to speak. Choosing his words carefully—for Judge Burnham was a calm, deliberate man—he pilloried Ney, saying that the newspaper articles

the attorney cited had absolutely no bearing on the judge's interpretation of the law. Furthermore, Burnham said that as judge, he
had made sure to give careful consideration to the letter of the law,
both in regard to the witnesses' testimony as well as the admission of
evidence. After upbraiding the defense team, Judge Burnham overruled the motion for a new trial and was ready to pass sentence on
Frank Novak.[24]

He fixed the prisoner with a steady gaze and asked him to stand.
Novak's face was pale from three months in jail and showed signs of
fatigue, but he pulled himself up out of his chair and stared back at
the judge.

"Frank A. Novak, the jury in the case of *State vs. Frank A. Novak* returned a verdict of guilty of murder in the second degree. A motion
has been filed and argued for a new trial and overruled by the court
and nothing now remains for the court to do but to pass sentence.
Have you anything to say why sentence should not be passed?"

Novak cleared his throat and addressed the judge.

"If it please your honor, a man who would go through what I have
since my arrest and stand under it is made of different stuff than I
am. As to the charges here, I am as innocent of each and every one
as I was thirty years ago. That is all I believe. I would add that even
if I had been acquitted I would not have been satisfied. I will not be
satisfied until the guilty parties are brought to justice, whoever they
are, and my name cleared of the dark blot upon it. That may be a very
hard thing to do without me."[25]

Novak sat down.

Judge Burnham paused for a moment and spoke:

"I think that you have had a very fair trial as indicated by the remarks I made upon this motion [for a new trial]. I think you were ably
defended by able counsel. . . . You had the advantage of a fine personal appearance and in my judgment of strong intellectuality. . . . I
cannot see [any] mitigating circumstance surrounding the case in
your behalf. . . . I know that today I feel more compassion for your
sorrowing wife and little children than you have exhibited here dur-

ing the entire trial. . . . I have taken counsel alone with myself, counsel with my own conscience and from my own sense of right and the
duty I feel that has been placed upon me. . . . Feeling as I do upon
passing a sentence that will satisfy my conscience; so that I have done
my duty in this respect, is that you be confined at the Anamosa penitentiary at hard labor for the period of your natural life."[26]

The judge had overridden the jury's recommendation of ten years
hard labor, as he believed that it was not a sufficient punishment
for the severity of the crime. The life sentence for Novak was the
harshest penalty Burnham could mete out legally, because Novak
had not been found guilty of first-degree murder and thus could
not be sentenced to death. It was obvious that Burnham had given
considerable thought to his decision and felt it was the proper one in
this particular case.

Novak's reaction to Burnham's sentence was muted. He stood "un-
moved," as one paper reported, and heard Burnham's words with
"calmness and stolidity."[27]

But no sooner had the judge finished speaking than Tom Milner
popped up again. He had several more legal arrows in his quiver, and
he was determined to shoot every one of them. First, Milner asked
for an arrest of judgment, a motion that is made to stop a verdict
from being entered. He also requested that a transcript be made of
the trial and that all of the evidence in the case be kept for the appeal. Then Milner asked the judge to set Novak's bail. Tobin urged
that it be fixed at fifty thousand dollars, while Milner argued for the
amount to be twenty to twenty-five thousand dollars.[28]

Milner also filed for a writ of *habeas corpus* from the Iowa Supreme
Court. This legal term, which translates as "you have the body,"
means that any prisoner has the right to challenge the terms of his
imprisonment.

After a few days, Judge Burnham set bail at $37,500. Novak and Sher-
iff Metcalf left Vinton for Cedar Rapids, where they would change
trains for the Anamosa State Penitentiary, where Novak would serve

out his life sentence. He spent the night in Cedar Rapids, but while in the Clifton Hotel, he received a piece of good news. The chief justice of the Iowa Supreme Court, a judge with a name straight out of an O. Henry short story: LaVega G. Kinne, had issued a writ of *habeas corpus*, and ordered that Novak be returned temporarily to the Benton County jail in Vinton to await the outcome of Milner's appeal.[29]

As he was taken out of the hotel, the prisoner was smoking a cigar and in high spirits; one reporter wrote that Novak was "cheerful and chipper."[30] Despite the bad weather and the early departure time, friends and dozens of curious onlookers accompanied him as he walked down to the street to the depot. "Altogether," one reporter declared, "it was quite a Novak day."[31]

🌿 🌿 🌿

The news of the case reverberated around the state for months afterward. Thousands of words were written about Novak's flight and arrest, with thousands more on the trial itself. Dozens of small papers across Iowa as well as large-circulation ones like the *New York Times* and the *Chicago Tribune* covered the case, with some publications carrying daily transcripts of the trial. The Associated Press also filed stories of Novak's arrest and subsequent trial.

The AP's transmission of the story through telegrams underlined an important aspect of the case—the use of both old and new inventions. The telegraph, a technology more than fifty years old, had played a vital part in keeping Tobin and the Thiel agency apprised of several clues discovered during Novak's flight. But the telephone had now begun to replace the somewhat old-fashioned telegraph key. Because of its speed—it was used a few times to relay some timely information to the detectives in this case—the telephone had other benefits, particularly with newspapers and wire services. Twenty years after Alexander Graham Bell made the first long-distance telephone call from Salem, Massachusetts, to the *Boston Globe*, the telephone had become an essential part of a breaking news story. The phrase,

"Hello sweetheart, get me rewrite," entered the common vocabulary of many reporters as they called in stories.[32]

The *Cedar Rapids Evening Gazette* highlighted the impact of the telephone. A few months after the trial, in a story coinciding with the opening of the local telephone exchange in Cedar Rapids, the *Gazette* marveled at this device, claiming that the newspaper held the world's record "for the greatest amount of actual news matter ever transmitted over a telephone wire for thirteen days." The record was set during the Novak trial, the paper pointed out, adding that one reporter used almost twenty hours of telephone time as he dictated to a stenographer the "testimony, incidents, evidence and verdict in that remarkable case."[33]

Another technology used successfully in the case was photography. From the beginning of the investigation, photographs played an important part in the search and capture of Frank Novak. By this time, photographs were routinely used as a means of catching criminals. Allan Pinkerton was a pioneer in this facet of police work. For decades, he had been using photographs as a method to identify suspects, and other detectives and police departments had discovered that photography served as an accurate and inexpensive tool that could be used as evidence in court. In the Novak case, the Thiel agents were originally armed with an undated photograph of a younger, thinner Novak when they began their search in Iowa. Photos were duplicated and sent around the country to law enforcement officials in major cities and seaports. Photographic copies also were made of some of the evidence, in particular the steamship ticket for the *Al-Ki* upon which Novak had signed his distinctive "A" in the alias "J. A. Smith." This ticket played a key role in his indictment months later. In addition, Red Perrin had the foresight to have many photographs taken of himself and Novak in Alaska as both men waited for the *Portland* to take them to Seattle. The detective had wanted proof that Novak had been captured and took great care to have Novak photographed with and without the thick reddish beard that he had grown while traveling through the Yukon Territory. William Ogilvie, the Canadian surveyor who took the pictures, carefully marked the glass plates and the negatives with the correct date and Perrin's initials, so that there would be no doubt as to the authenticity of these photographs.[34]

Lastly, the advent of the transcontinental railroad enabled the detectives to follow Novak's trail in a much quicker fashion than at an earlier time. Red Perrin's speedy trip across Canada—from Vancouver to Ottawa and back for the extradition papers—would have been impossible without the trans-Canada railroad, which had been completed only twelve years earlier, in 1885. But just as important was the development of a number of transcontinental rail lines in the United States along with the expansion of regional and local railroads. This shortened the time that it took for the detectives to move around the country as they gathered information, as overland travel by stagecoach or wagon alone would have slowed down the pursuit for months. And once Novak had returned to the West Coast, the Northern Pacific railway and the BCR&N from St. Paul made sure that he was safely ensconced in the Vinton jail, just ninety-six hours after the *Portland* had docked in Seattle.

❧ ❧ ❧

While Novak returned to Vinton early in the morning of December 10, happy that he had dodged a trip to the penitentiary, Milner also was pleased to receive Supreme Court Justice Kinne's granting of the writ of *habeas corpus*, a delaying tactic that would enable Milner to argue for an appeal. He also thought that the bail of $37,500 was excessive and traveled by rail to Des Moines to argue that the amount should be reduced.[35]

Novak received an early Christmas present when his attorney succeeded in having the Iowa Supreme Court lower the bail to eighteen thousand dollars, an amount that Milner noted would be relatively easy to raise, based on Novak's own collateral and funds from his family members. Even so, there was so much interest in this matter that the Benton County clerk, who was attempting to close his books for the year, had had enough. He posted a brief note in his office that read: "Novak has not filed his bond. Yes, the weather is fine."[36]

But despite the efforts of his family and relatives, Frank Novak could raise only about sixteen thousand dollars, two thousand dollars short of what he needed. By December 28, Milner had exhausted all of his legal recourses for any further delays in Novak's incarceration, including the writ of *habeas corpus*, which became null when Novak could not make bail. Now there was nothing left for the court to do but arrange Novak's transfer to Anamosa.

"DONS THE STRIPES" exclaimed a headline in the *Gazette* on December 31, 1897. On that evening, as the rest of the country prepared to celebrate the New Year, Novak and Sheriff Metcalf boarded a night train from Cedar Rapids to Anamosa State Penitentiary, where they arrived at 10:37 PM. Waiting expectantly with its cold white limestone maw open was the forbidding castle-like prison with its lofty carved crenelations, towers, and medieval-looking turrets. The structure was known in eastern Iowa by the mellifluous phrase, "The White Palace of the West," but its inmates simply called it "the Colony."[37]

As soon as Novak arrived, prison officials placed him in a holding cell. On the next day, January 1, 1898, they gave him breakfast and a shower, shaved his head and mustache, and fitted him with a coarse, striped woolen uniform and matching cap. His shoe size—nine—was entered into the prison logbook, along with notations on age, height, weight, and a few small identifying scars on his head. Officials took several photographs of him, and Novak was measured with the Bertillon system, the standard method of categorizing criminals, which included two photographs—later known as "mug shots"—plus five different anatomical measurements, ranging from the dimensions of Novak's head to the length of his left foot.[38] Finally, they assigned him a four-digit number. From that point forward, Novak would be Number 3896. Then they took him down a corridor to be "tucked in," as the prisoners said, to cell 157. This cellblock was part of the prison known as "Murderer's Row."[39]

A guard opened the heavy metal door and gestured for Novak to enter the cell. After the door clanged shut, he listened to the guard's footsteps fade away as they echoed off the cold stone floor. Then there was silence in the cellblock.

PART FOUR

THE WHITE PALACE
AND THE FORT

SIXTEEN

•———————————————————•

Life in the Colony

When Novak walked through the massive entrance gates shortly before midnight on December 31, 1897, he entered a state penitentiary that had been under construction for almost twenty-five years—and it was still years away from completion.

Construction of the fifteen-acre compound began in 1873, when twenty-four inmates arrived from Fort Madison and started work on what was formally called the Additional Penitentiary. It was given this rather odd name because it was to take additional prisoners from the overcrowded penitentiary at Fort Madison. At first, Anamosa's cellblock consisted of a crude wooden stockade and thus was prone to frequent escape attempts. But these living quarters were temporary as plans already had been completed for a more permanent structure. The new penitentiary would be constructed of dolomite limestone from a nearby quarry, located a few miles away in a little town named, appropriately enough, Stone City.[1]

Most of the prisoners worked as stonecutters. For more than thirty years—well into the 1900s—hundreds of inmates quarried the limestone and transported it by rail to the penitentiary, where others offloaded the heavy cargo and chipped the rock into carefully measured blocks. It was tough, backbreaking work done with primitive tools under the worst kind of working conditions. One by one, the prisoners cut the stones and built the foundation and walls of Anamosa's fortress-like penitentiary. The immense structure was typical of penitentiaries of that time and in fact was modeled after the prison at Wethersfield, Connecticut.[2] Several states, including Ohio, Pennsylvania, New Jersey, and Massachusetts, had constructed similar imposing buildings. Like these other prisons, the style was Romanesque Revival, with crenulations, parapets, towers, turrets, and high thick walls. With its medieval appearance, the intimidating high limestone walls at Anamosa instantly conveyed a powerful image of unquestioned authority.

The original cellblock consisted of seventy-two cells, with each one constructed of six-inch-thick flagstone. With little ventilation or heat, the cells were blazingly hot in the summer and miserably cold during the long Iowa winters. These cells measured roughly eight feet in length and about four-and-a-half feet in width.[3] Until the late nineteenth century, the number of prisoners varied between about four hundred to more than six hundred (including a few female inmates and some prisoners judged to be insane). During Novak's first year at Anamosa, the number peaked at six hundred and twenty-five prisoners, and sixty-three guards were on hand to keep the inmates in line.[4]

Because of the construction specifications at Anamosa, escape attempts were rare and seldom successful. There was little chance of tunneling out, as each wall was forty feet high, four feet thick, and extended at least fourteen feet beneath the ground's surface.[5] Shotgun-toting sentries were posted inside turrets while other guards stood at key spots throughout the prison.

Life at the penitentiary was grim from the moment the sun peeked over the parapets until lights out in the evening. For many prisoners, most of their time was spent at grueling physical labor as a stonecutter either at the quarries or in the stone shed, where the large blocks of stone were shaped.

One new "lifer" described a day in the stone shed. First, an inmate showed him "how to cut a draft to the straight-edge. . . . The mallet was heavy. The chisel was nearly as cold as my feet. . . . Every time I cut over the draft, I would try the straight-edge on it. . . . The red chalk on the straight-edge pointed out the high places. . . . I looked at that stone and sighed again. All my life I had roamed at will. Now I was to confine my wanderings to a circuit the dimensions of a stone." The prisoner concluded, "I wished the stone were in a mill-pond with me under it."[6]

The stone shed symbolized life in the penitentiary. Everything at Anamosa was designed to cut down a prisoner, from the hard manual labor and poor living conditions to the food, which except for a few holiday meals was monotonous and tasteless. Each day began with the same breakfast—bean or potato stew with bread, coffee, and sorghum. Lunch and dinner were just as bland.

Because Anamosa utilized the "silent system, the men were not permitted to speak to each other. They used hand signals when they needed to communicate with the guards. In the dining room, they usually did this through a series of gestures if they wanted more food or drink. In addition to the silent system, the men also used the demeaning lockstep whenever they moved from their cells to other places inside the prison compound. In short, life in the penitentiary demanded "absolute obedience, bending the convicts' behavior to fit its own rigid rules."[7]

During this time period of the early to mid-nineteenth-century, other penitentiaries were built, including one in New York City and another in Auburn, New York. In these prisons, as in the separate system, the inmates slept in single cells. They worked together during the day but were not allowed to speak to each other. Everything was done in absolute silence.[8] The prisoners moved from one place to another in lockstep, a stiff kind of shuffle-step, in which each man kept his eyes downcast and shuffled his feet forward while keeping one hand on the shoulder of the man in front of him. This became known as the Auburn or "silent system." The hope was that the silent system, which became quite popular by the last third of the nineteenth century, combined with "unrelenting routine of hard work, moderate meals, silent evenings, and restful nights . . . would produce [men] who were, indeed, cured of all vices and excesses."[9]

❧ ❧ ❧

Another form of punishment was solitary confinement, with the prisoner locked into a dark cell with nothing to eat but bread and water. Although corporal punishment had been largely replaced by solitary at the close of the nineteenth century, this type of confinement was a powerful means of "maintaining order, enforcing discipline and preventing escape."[10] At Anamosa, a system of five iron rings was used in the solitary cells. Depending on the offense, a prisoner would be chained to one of the five rings, which were hammered into the wall at different heights. If the prisoner had committed a lesser offense, the lowest ring was used and he could lie down if he wished. The most serious charge resulted in the prisoner being locked to the highest ring, which meant that he would be standing for long periods of time.[11]

Many viewed solitary confinement as worse than any other type of punishment. One Anamosa warden, Philander Madden, wrote that he was ashamed of this method: "Solitary confinement is . . . simply a slow, hideous process of execution. The physical, mental and moral faculties slowly sink, till all of manhood is submerged."[12]

❧ ❧ ❧

The iron rings in each of Anamosa's solitary cells were clear evidence of the continuing harsh treatment of prisoners. General conditions in the penitentiaries and jails in the United States were at best primitive and in some cases resulted in facilities not fit for human habitation. For much of the nineteenth century, "prisons were filled to overflowing with everyone who gave offense to society from committing murder to spitting on the street. Men, women and children were thrown together in the most atrocious conditions."[13]

The term "penitentiary" originally came from William Penn and the Quakers, who believed that those people incarcerated should become penitent and "be removed from the temptations of free society, subjected to religious instruction, and forced to perform hard labor in solitude, meditating on their sins."[14] Living conditions in these early prisons, such as the Walnut Street jail constructed in Philadelphia in 1773, were horrific. It was not uncommon for inmates to die of starvation or freeze to death. Meals were delivered to their cells and the prisoners were never let out. In an experimental portion of the Walnut Street jail, prisoners lived alone in single person cells, performing piecemeal vocational work such as sewing and weaving. More than fifty years later, the Eastern State Penitentiary, which opened just outside Philadelphia in 1829, copied this program, which became known as the "Pennsylvania system" or more commonly the "separate system," since the men were kept in separate individual cells.[15]

The construction of the new penitentiary at Anamosa came during the growing prison reform movement. According to Zebulon Reed Brockway, a noted prison reformer who gave a keynote speech at the National Prison Conference in 1870, "The central aim of a true prison system is the protection of society against crime, not the punishment of the criminals." His goal, through prison reform, was to make convicts into "useful citizens." This conference developed a document called the Declaration of Principles, a set of guidelines for reforming prisoners. One important reform that emerged after this landmark conference was the indeterminate sentence system. This plan meant that a range of time could be used as the basis of each crime. Then it was up to the judge to pronounce sentence within those guidelines. With this system, parole boards and elected officials would determine a prisoner's release date. If he was deemed sufficiently reformed, he would be released earlier. If not, he would complete his sentence. The aim of this plan was to "give inmates a sense that their behavior controlled their fate."[16]

Brockway also favored a classification system of three different grades. When he became superintendent of the new reformatory in Elmira, New York, in 1876, Brockway instituted this program. New prisoners entered the reformatory in the second grade. If they obeyed the rules and did what they were told, they could advance to the first grade, where they would enjoy more benefits. If they did not abide by the rules and if they did not work hard, they dropped to the third grade. Corporal punishment was abolished at Elmira, along with striped uniforms and the hated lockstep, methods that had long been used to "humiliate or degrade inmates."[17]

The progressive techniques used at Elmira and a few other prisons generally bore favorable results. Although it would be years before many other state penitentiaries would adopt these programs, change was coming, slowly but surely, and Anamosa would be swept along with the rising tide of prison reform.

❦ ❦ ❦

The first day of 1898 was frigid in eastern Iowa, with dull-grey clouds moving in and winds whipping across the broad farmlands. As is the custom with newspapers at this particular time of year, front pages recapped the top stories of the previous twelve months. According to statistics cited in one article, about nine percent fewer murders occurred in 1897 in the United States than in the previous year (9,520 versus 10,652). However, there were three thousand and five fires reported in the country, resulting in losses by fire that topped one hundred twenty-nine-million dollars, about eleven million more than in 1896.[18]

If he had seen any of these stories, none of them would have mattered much to Frank Novak, sitting in his cell during his first full day at Anamosa State Penitentiary. It's hard to know what was going through his mind, but perhaps he was thinking of the rush of activities that had taken place the day before. The train trip from Cedar Rapids was a short one, leaving little time to prepare him for the sight of the penitentiary stone walls surrounded by the town of Anamosa. Writing about a similar view more than one hundred years later, an inmate commented, "When I arrived here . . . the first thing I noticed . . . was how exactly in the middle of town this penitentiary is located. . . . I'm sure soon enough it will feel rather isolate[d], but for now it seems to stand on the corner of a neighborhood."[19] The grim, castle-like stone structure dominated the scene. It seemed to threaten any onlooker, evoking a "forbidding mien to both prisoners and the outside community."[20]

Still, based on his conversations with Tom Milner, Novak was hopeful that he would not remain in this horrible place for more than a few days. The forceful lawyer from Belle Plaine was confident that Novak would soon make bail and be released. Moreover, there was some additional news that must have made Novak smile. For months, he had been obsessed with seeking revenge against the man who had put him in the Benton County jail. But M. J. Tobin wasn't the object of Novak's rage; he understood that Tobin was simply carrying out his duties as Benton County attorney. Tobin and Novak actually had much in common, since they were both sons of immigrants and ambitious young Iowa businessmen who were trying to make their respective marks in the world. Novak held a grudge against the man who brought him back to Iowa—Red Perrin. Novak wanted to hurt the Thiel detective's reputation and, as a parting gift to Perrin, had given an exclusive story to the *Gazette* through an anonymous source—most likely Milner.

Published on New Year's Day 1898, the article claimed that Perrin had bungled the chase from the beginning and could have picked Novak up only eighty miles from Juneau, instead of trekking all the way to Dawson City through more than six hundred miles of wilderness. Moreover, the story went on, Perrin's whole account of chasing Novak to Dawson was "a fairy tale"; Perrin had merely wanted to see the Yukon country, and stayed close to the Swift scow with Novak aboard until they both reached the Klondike.[21]

Novak also insisted that the detective had handled him roughly, although D. L. Clouse had been "very kind." The story also made a thinly veiled threat: "It is an assured fact that if Frank A. Novak is ever granted a new trial all these facts will be brought out." Finally, the article intimated that Novak was not in trouble financially and that his bail would soon be raised, allowing him to leave Anamosa State Penitentiary in a few days. If that happened, the source concluded with some acrimony, "We all hope that . . . the people who have been so anxious to see Frank Novak go to the penitentiary will now feel satisfied."[22]

In the same article, the *Gazette* countered most of these points, stating that Novak was not telling the truth. He had only been in Juneau for a few days, and at that time, the detectives on his trail were still at least three weeks back. And even if the money for his bail was raised, Novak would be arrested again, charged with arson, and immediately sent back to the Benton County jail.

🌿 🌿 🌿

Given the legal and journalistic efforts on his behalf, Novak may well have been optimistic as he sat in his cell on January 1. Perhaps he tried not to think about all his niggling doubts that seemed to ooze out of the cracks of the thick limestone walls. Milner had explained to him that bail would be met somehow, but even if it was not, the attorney promised that he would appeal the case to the Iowa Supreme Court. Then Milner hoped that it would declare a mistrial and a new trial would begin, perhaps in a different county, one where people were not prejudiced against his client. This time, Milner believed, Novak would be found completely innocent, and would go free. In the meantime, Prisoner #3896 would just have to find a way to kill time.

But when almost two weeks went by with no news of his bail being raised, Novak grew increasingly nervous about his prospects. Rumors of his anxiety began to seep out into the press: "Novak has a horror of remaining behind the bars, and there are many who are expecting daily to hear of his confessing the entire story of the crime," one report said.[23] Maybe he wondered what his life would be like if all of Milner's legal gyrations came to naught. For now, he probably believed that he could mark off the days until Milner succeeded. Even the idea of going back to the cell in Vinton was most likely far more appealing than the penitentiary.

While he waited, Novak had begun work as a stonecutter, chipping away at limestone slabs, forming them into blocks for use in the penitentiary's ongoing construction. After a short period of time, perhaps due to his rather weak physical condition, he became a helper and rotated between various buildings, bringing tools to the others and performing light duties. This was clearly an easier job more befitting his white-collar roots.

Meanwhile, Milner was keeping his promise to pursue the case. At the end of January, a reporter for a Marshalltown newspaper asked the attorney if he had accepted defeat. "Not much," was Milner's terse reply. "I am now getting out the transcript of an appeal and will carry the case up." He was close to raising the bail, Milner went on, and "we are going to fight to the last ditch. . . . If I get licked in the state Supreme Court the case will be taken to the United States Supreme Court, if Novak lives long enough."[24]

Milner's comments appeared at the end of January. At Anamosa, the days passed by slowly, as if each day was etched into the cold stone walls of Novak's cell. Perhaps he felt frozen in time, like a fossil in amber. As weeks rolled by, the stark realization sank in that he could spend the rest of his life at Anamosa, or so the newspapers reported. One commented that Novak was not in good health while another source said he was "failing fast."[25] But the truth was that he would have to remain at Anamosa at least until October, when the Iowa Supreme Court would decide whether to grant a motion for a new trial. Despite this remaining possibility, he had, as another newspaper decided, "lost all hope."[26] These descriptions of Novak's mental state may have been tinged by yellow journalism, as the papers that had covered the case were still trying to keep readers' interest piqued.

❦ ❦ ❦

On April 1, 1898, William A. Hunter, a strong advocate of the prison reform movement, became warden at Anamosa. The youngest of six children, Hunter had been a drummer boy at the battle of Shiloh. Ironically, he had worked as a pharmacist in Tom Milner's town of Belle Plaine and was a postmaster there for two terms.[27]

Hunter immediately instituted several changes at the penitentiary. The warden later commented, "When I assumed charge, I found the prison without any rules or system of management. . . . On the first day of April [1898], I distributed a system of stringent rules that was almost revolutionary."[28]

To him, the place was not a penitentiary, it was a festering sewer. The new warden saw that his job was to flush out the pipes, so he and his guards swept through the cells, confiscating money, books, jewelry, and other personal items while turning up dozens of homemade weapons. In short, the warden took almost everything that belonged to the prisoners.

Having removed all of the prisoners' possessions, Hunter's next step was to impose a new disciplinary program. He believed that a system of grading would motivate the inmates to improve their own station. Having studied a similar plan used in Australia, England, and Ireland known as the Crofton method, Hunter also was aware of the success of this approach at the Elmira Reformatory. Hunter copied Brockway's system and established three grades, with each new prisoner assigned to the second grade. A system of marks would determine if and when he should be moved up or down a grade. Those in the first grade, who were allowed to wear plain woolen gray suits, had special privileges. They could eat their meals at certain designated tables with other first-grade men; they could have a supply of tobacco and were allowed to write a letter a week. They also could receive mail and newspapers. Men in the second grade wore plaid uniforms and could write letters only every two weeks. The third-grade men wore the classic prison stripes and had very few privileges. In fact, they had to take their meals in their cells.[29]

The prisoners hated these changes. They despised the new classification system that the warden had installed. Moreover, they were incensed that all of their goods and money were confiscated, a fact that Hunter acknowledged. "The men chafed under [the new rules]. They complained that they were too severe. . . . It was hard to stand it but they are in line now."[30]

No prisoner seemed to be under as much pressure as Frank Novak, who appeared to be falling apart. According to prison records, this began in May 1898, when he was sent to solitary confinement for lying about the chief engineer and being argumentative with the deputy warden.[31]

Then, in July, an incident caused Novak to lose his grip and completely break down. By then, seven months into his sentence, Novak was part of the prison routine, working at a "small-boy" job as a mechanic's helper, carrying tools to the workers in the machine shop. While working in the shop, Novak had had several clashes with another inmate, a man he referred to disparagingly as an "Irish hobo." Finally, their disagreements came to a head on one blisteringly hot July day, and they started fighting. Novak picked up a club and assaulted the other prisoner, who immediately turned and grabbed a sharp tool from his workbench. A guard stepped in and separated the two men before the fight escalated into bloodshed.[32]

Because he had started the fight and then lied about it later, Novak was sent to solitary confinement for the second time in two months. When he emerged from "the hole," he found that the new warden had changed Novak's job duties. He had transferred Novak from the easy job as a helper to the stone sheds, where, for eight hours each day, he was assigned the backbreaking task of breaking up spalls, or chips, into smaller stones to be used for road construction.[33]

As always, Tom Milner was quick to leap to his client's defense. He called the reports of Novak's fight completely false, an example of yellow journalism, and said there was no truth to any part of the story. Further, Milner insisted that Novak was a "well-behaved ward" and claimed that he was well respected by the guards and the warden at Anamosa.[34] The newspapers defended their version of the story and pointed out that Novak had been in solitary confinement before.[35]

In the meantime, Milner continued to prepare the paperwork for the Iowa Supreme Court, but he argued that he was hampered by the prosecution, which had not yet completed its written abstracts. Part of the delay was due to answering a large number of legal abstracts that Milner had brought up for appeal, and it was an arduous task for Tobin to complete. Until the abstracts were finished, Milner could not present the case in Des Moines. Milner was able to obtain a continuance and promised that he would be ready with all documentation from the prosecution by January of 1899.[36]

This delay meant that the "notorious murderer," as one paper called Novak, would have to wait months before his appeal would be heard.[37] The news may have been a crushing blow for Novak, but he had learned an important prison rule—it was best to keep quiet and do what he was told. More and more, he understood the lifer's mentality and worked through each day, crossing them off one by one.

On February 2, 1899, exactly two years after the fateful night in Walford, Milner submitted the case to the Iowa Supreme Court. Although M. J. Tobin was on hand and ready to begin arguments against a new trial, the court accepted the paperwork without any additional oral statements. It did so partly due to the voluminous amount of printed material that both sides submitted to the court, which added up to more than six hundred pages of testimony and documentation. Milner spoke to the court about Novak's mental state in February 1897, which the defense attorney had always claimed was a temporary insanity brought about by the "gaseous effects of the burning wood."[38]

Now he argued that Novak had been insane all along. Pleading insanity to a murder charge was certainly nothing new and Milner was well aware of the legal precedents. In one of the more famous cases, in 1859, Congressman Daniel Sickles had shot his wife's lover, Philip Barton Key, in broad daylight and within view of the White House. Sickles's lawyer entered a plea of temporary insanity and the congressman was acquitted.[39]

Milner also claimed that Novak's confession to Red Perrin, made on the steamer from Dawson City to St. Michael, should never have been accepted in court. The attorney enumerated more than four dozen points in pushing for a new trial. On the other side, Tobin replied that he was satisfied that Judge Burnham had done everything according to law and had made sure that the trial was legally proper.

After some debate, the Iowa Supreme Court agreed with Tobin. In May 1899, the court handed down its decision. The majority opinion affirmed that Judge Burnham had conducted the trial fairly and properly. Although two dissenting judges believed that the jury had been prejudiced by Burnham's actions in court, Novak was denied a new trial and the sentence was upheld.[40]

Milner had exhausted all legal options. It appeared that Frank Novak was to remain at Anamosa for the rest of his life.[41]

SEVENTEEN

The Redemption Dance

After Novak was imprisoned, his family, which had lost thousands of dollars through his poor investments, shady business dealings, and a mountain of legal fees incurred in the case, barely managed to eke out an existence. In 1901, a story broke that Mary Novak was preparing to file a petition for divorce. Struggling to support her two young boys, she had converted her small home into a boarding house, and had allegedly fallen in love with one of the boarders. Another article quickly dismissed this story as merely an "ugly rumor," and no divorce suit was filed, but Mary's brother, Joseph Shunka, who had worked with Frank Novak at Walford, was arrested for firing five shots at his sister's alleged lover, hitting him once. As a result, Shunka was found guilty of attempted murder and sentenced to two years in prison.[1]

Meantime, at Anamosa, Novak became more used to life in the Colony. In addition to his work duties, he had organized a prison orchestra and served as the group's conductor and first violinist. His good behavior, after the fight in 1898, had earned him a transfer from the backbreaking work on the spall pile to light administrative duties. Novak was now employed in the records department, logging in the prisoners when they arrived at Anamosa and assisting in the Bertillon method of measuring and categorizing each new inmate. Since photography was part of this system, he learned the process from another convict named John Bellew, a man from Webster County, Iowa, who operated the bulky wooden portrait camera, developed the negatives, and then made prints for the files. Bellew took three photographs of each prisoner—one in civilian clothes plus one front and one side view in a plaid prison uniform.[2] Besides being responsible for these pictures, Bellew snapped other photographs of the prison buildings as well as the town of Anamosa itself, along with many casual photos of inmates and guards. He was well liked by the prisoners and possessed considerable skills in the art of photography.[3]

Paroled in 1902, Bellew used these skills to open a photography studio in Woodbury County, Iowa.[4] Frank Novak then became the photographer at Anamosa. Although he still employed the antiquated Bertillon system of classification, he spent considerable time carefully photographing each new inmate.[5]

By then, the prisoners had begun to reap the benefits of Warden Hunter's progressive system of rewards for good behavior. The *Prison Press*, a newspaper that the prisoners had started shortly after Hunter became warden, was thriving and was sold on a subscription basis to prisoners at seventy-five-cents per year or forty cents for six months. One of several newspapers in the country that was written and printed solely by inmates, the *Prison Press* was an attempt to keep the men and women inside informed of world events. The newspaper also contained religious readings, blurbs about various prisoners, and bits of folksy advice that resembled a "Dear Abby" column.

One frequent contributor to the *Prison Press* was the recently appointed photographer. While he was photographing new prisoners, Novak was constantly thinking of other pictures he could take inside the prison walls. His omnipresence became something of a joke among the inmates and guards, who watched him constantly roaming the prison grounds with his camera, taking portraits and documenting prison life. In 1903, when a group of tourists passed through the prison—by then, two railroad spur lines brought visitors into the grounds—the ubiquitous Novak was among the inmates who took photographs of the trains and passengers. It seemed that "Frank and his box" were everywhere.[6] Eventually, the warden trusted Novak enough to let him amble outside the penitentiary walls, where he shot more photographs of the prison. One of his pictures of the administrative building was praised in the prison newspaper as "sharp and well-developed and suitable for framing. It appears," the *Prison Press* reporter added, "that Frank has found his work, for the pictures are far superior to much of the work done [by photographers] outside."[7]

Over the years, Warden Hunter had grown fond of Novak and wished to show him off as a model prisoner, someone who had done well under Anamosa's grading system. Hunter made sure that his budding photographer had whatever supplies he needed. At this time, the receiving area of the administration building was too cramped for a real photography studio, and Novak asked for a complete darkroom with adequate lighting facilities. The warden assured his prized inmate that he would have both and assigned carpenters to make a skylight in the room above the receiving area, so that Novak would have enough light. Then some prisoners ran a water line into a special sink for the chemical baths needed to develop the negatives. When it was completed, Novak was able to print whatever size photo that he needed.[8]

Novak also became involved with a spiritual organization within Anamosa, a relatively new group called the Volunteer Prison League, or VPL. As part of the prison reform movement, the VPL attempted to address the religious needs of men and women in many of the jails in the United States. The VPL's first chapter was founded in 1896 by a diminutive expatriate Englishwoman named Maud Ballington Booth. The daughter-in-law of William Booth, founder of the Salvation Army, Maud Ballington Booth had a special place in her heart for all prisoners, whom she believed were greatly neglected in the United States penal system. After a trip to Sing Sing, the infamous New York state prison known for its abysmal conditions, she realized the need for a national organization to help prisoners, not only while they were incarcerated but especially after they were released. She understood that in most cases a paroled prisoner had no idea how to survive in the outside world. Booth quickly became known throughout penitentiaries as a pocket-sized saint who was deeply interested in the souls of the inmates, for as she once wrote, the prisoners needed "something that would carry their thoughts away beyond the gray walls, and some message from Christ's dear heart of love that would part the dark clouds."[9] To many of the prisons she visited, she was known fondly as the "Little Mother." Once she started the VPL, chapters sprang up in many penitentiaries throughout the Northeast and Midwest. Thousands of prisoners joined the VPL, each one striving to live up to her standards while remembering the watchwords of the organization—"Look Up and Hope!"[10]

Because Booth spent much of her time visiting many penitentiaries, each VPL chapter vied for her attention, hoping that she would come. For many, having her make an appearance was like seeing their own mothers again. Prisoners sent letters to her and urged the warden and prison officials to arrange a visit, especially around Thanksgiving or Christmas. Like many other prisons, Anamosa State Penitentiary had a VPL chapter and it was not surprising that one of the leaders in the effort to bring Maud Ballington Booth to the penitentiary was Frank Novak. Although the VPL chapter was only a few years old, its presence was already quite strong at Anamosa and the *Prison Press* news sections mentioned frequent efforts to arrange a meeting with the Little Mother.[11]

Novak's VPL activities, which focused mainly on prayer meetings, Bible study, and rehabilitation efforts of prisoners, underscored his busy life at Anamosa. Even so, he still had other things on his mind. Like every other inmate, his foremost thought concerned leaving the penitentiary. Although he had ample chances to slip away from Anamosa, especially with his outside photography work, the considerable risk and repercussions of even attempting an escape apparently discouraged him from doing so. There had been some attempts before and during the time he was at Anamosa but few of them were successful. Besides, Novak believed that there still were legal channels left for his attorneys to explore.

Perhaps encouraged by John Bellew's release and knowing that

Bellew had also been sentenced to life in prison, Novak decided to see whether he might become eligible for parole. He asked Tom Milner to explore this possibility. The defense lawyer, who had the stubbornness of a snapping turtle, had never stopped working for his client. At this point, Novak's impoverished family probably could no longer afford an attorney, but Milner still kept pushing the legal process forward and in March 1903 traveled to Des Moines and filed paperwork seeking either a pardon or parole from Governor Albert B. Cummins.[12]

Novak's future at Anamosa was further muddied by a letter allegedly from Judge Burnham, who had presided over the original trial. In the letter, which had surfaced in 1902, the writer—supposedly Burnham—wrote that if he had accepted the jury's recommendation that Novak serve ten years in jail, the prisoner would now be eligible for parole. With a sentence of this length, prisoners could apply for parole after six years and three months, and Novak had already served that long. But the authenticity of the letter was in doubt due to Burnham's strong statements before he pronounced sentence, and since the judge was on an extended European trip, Governor Cummins agreed to withhold any decision until Burnham returned.[13]

When the news of Novak's parole efforts broke, the reaction from many angry Iowans was swift. A number of residents in Benton and Linn Counties were infuriated by Novak's brazenness, as they still remembered the events of that cold night in Walford years earlier. To them, Novak's crimes were an abomination and should have resulted in the death penalty. Some newspapers declared that the sentence of life imprisonment was one of the worst miscarriages of justice in the history of the state and, in that light, freeing the man who committed the crime would be an even greater mistake than not finding him guilty of first-degree murder. Among the apoplectic Iowans who sent letters to Governor Cummins were Congressman M. J. Wade; Edward Swan, deputy marshal of Cedar Rapids; and J. M. Terry, a former state senator from Linn County. In addition, several people hired a Cedar Rapids attorney named H. L. Wick to make sure that Novak remained behind bars.[14]

M. J. Tobin, who by now had established a thriving legal practice in Vinton, did not join the initial letter-writing campaign, but earlier had responded to a letter from H. W. Garrett, the governor's pardon secretary in Des Moines. As usual, Tobin didn't mince his words: "The murder for which Mr. Novak was convicted was unusually cold-blooded; hence I am opposed to extending to him executive clemency."[15]

But Novak still had many supporters as well, and some of them were quite powerful. One was F. W. Faulkes, editor of the *Cedar Rapids Evening Gazette*. Faulkes had a personal relationship with Governor Cummins, and the newspaperman had always believed that Novak was innocent. In a letter to the governor dated January 14, 1903, he called Novak's imprisonment "a rank injustice" and alluded to "some strange facts" that would come to light later. He urged Cummins to parole the convict and wrote that "I will stake my life that a parole for Novak would result in good in more ways than one."[16]

But of all the letters sent to various Iowa newspapers, perhaps none were as poignant as one published on August 13, 1904: "I want to enter my protest on any clemency on part of F. A. Novak, who is now seeking a pardon at your hands for the cold, deliberate murder . . . at Walford in February 1897, a date never to be effaced from my memory. . . . There is not one good word to be said in favor of this fiend . . . and if you should investigate the facts you will most certainly find that he had committed many crimes before the one in question."[17]

The writer recited the other crimes and mistakes Novak had been accused of, including the theft of money from an express company in Cedar Rapids; outstanding bills owed to others as well as mounting debts due to playing the Chicago grain market; fires that had been set in Walford prior to the burning of the general store; the mysterious death of Novak's brother-in-law and part-owner of that store;

and many other strange occurrences that Frank Novak had been implicated in during his years in eastern Iowa.

Finally, the writer concluded: "I speak not only for myself but for the county and the people in this matter when I say that the sentiment is unanimously against any pardon for this man who shed an innocent man's blood for mere gain."[18]

The author of this letter was William Murray, father of Edward Murray. Now ninety years old, the white-haired, frail patriarch of the Murray clan had led a long and arduous life and had suffered a great deal of hardship. Besides losing two sons—Daniel and Edward—within six months, a third son, Charles, was judged legally insane and had been committed to an asylum in Independence, Iowa, in 1899. The young man was deeply troubled by the murder of his brother Edward and suffered nightmares for years, dreaming that an unseen enemy was stalking him and that he would suffer a similar grisly death. Sometimes he had horrible visions about being electrocuted by lightning strikes. Finally, these nightmares "dethroned his mind," as one newspaper put it.[19]

With all the tragedies that William Murray had endured, he was especially aggrieved over the loss of his son Edward, a death that he was never able to overcome. Within two years of writing this letter, the heartsick old farmer would die a broken man.

🌿 🌿 🌿

Meanwhile, the misfortunes of the Novak family continued. In 1904, Milo Novak, Frank's oldest son and now fourteen years of age, ran away from home. He had been missing for two weeks before a notice appeared in the *Gazette* on February 13. Later that year, Mary Novak filed for divorce. It had now been seven years since her husband was sentenced to life imprisonment, and she might have been contemplating legal action for some time. The timing of the suit was interesting, considering that it occurred at about the same time that Novak was appealing his sentence. She sought custody of both their children—older son, Milo, who was still missing, and Leo, age twelve. She also sued to obtain Frank's real estate holdings as she had little money of her own and was barely able to provide for her family.[20]

Although the divorce was granted and Mary Novak began to distance herself from her former husband and his family, others in the Novak clan as well as some friends still believed in his innocence. Nowhere was this sentiment stronger than among people in the area around Iowa City and Cedar Rapids. Papers in both cities—the *Iowa City Republican* and the *Cedar Rapids Evening Gazette*—had editors who had long been convinced that Novak was innocent, and made a persistent effort to exonerate the famous Anamosa prisoner.

In May 1904, Tom Milner visited Anamosa State Penitentiary. Besides taking an extended tour of the facility and marveling at the large eight-by-twelve-foot Gordon printing press that cranked out the prison newspaper, he consulted with his longtime client about the chances for a pardon or parole. Although most people believed that the matter was now a dead issue, counting out Tom Milner on anything was a serious mistake. The Belle Plaine attorney had never given up in carrying the case forward and promised Novak that he would continue to work for his release.[21]

The year closed with Maud Ballington Booth's second appearance at the penitentiary, the result of the prisoners' constant lobbying of the warden. The *Prison Press* was most vocal in this effort and in both regular columns and editorials constantly pleaded for her return to Anamosa. Finally, the prisoners were rewarded. After stopping in the prison in Joliet, Illinois, a few days earlier on Thanksgiving Day 1904, Maud Ballington Booth visited "her boys" at Anamosa.

The Little Mother's schedule was a full one. After a brief chat with the warden, the visiting party and the prisoners moved into the chapel, which had been rebuilt after a fire eight years earlier. The orchestra, led by first violinist Novak, played a piece from Franz von Suppe's opera *Poet and Peasant*, and then Father Coffin, a frequent visitor to Anamosa, read the Twenty-third Psalm. Following a few opening remarks by Judge Kenyon, the Little Mother stood and delivered a stirring speech, dwelling on hopefulness and the power of prayer.

The speech was met with thunderous applause. Leading the group of prisoners in the chapel was Frank Novak, who, as past chairman of the VPL chapter, had lobbied to have Booth return to Anamosa and now basked in the glow of her speech. After the service, everyone retired to the dining room, where a Thanksgiving meal was served. Before she left, Maud Ballington Booth gave a long interview to a *Prison Press* reporter, inmate #5152. A stenographer from the warden's office fought to keep up as the words poured out of the small English-woman whom, the reporter acknowledged later, "easily outdistanced us."[22] Then Booth stood up, said a few warm good-byes, and boarded a carriage back to the Anamosa train station.

The account of her visit in the *Prison Press* illustrates the many hats that Frank Novak now wore. First and foremost, he was the official prison photographer, a position that he relished. While the *Prison Press* did not include a photograph of Booth in the following issue, the paper did print a portrait that Novak took of Father Coffin. But Novak also served as a VPL leader, helping to persuade prisoners to join the Little Mother's organization. In addition, he had used his musical talents to organize an orchestra as well as a band, while teaching inmates how to play various instruments. But perhaps most importantly, Novak's various activities achieved two results. He now was able to fill each day with many chores, including letter writing, organizing the prison library, working with the orchestra and band, and assisting the VPL chapter. He had become a model prisoner for Anamosa, quite possibly its most famous and most rehabilitated con-vict. As one account noted later, "in the prison school and library, Mr. Novak was a moving spirit. If [Anamosa] was without a soul, Frank Novak put one there by means of music, study and good reading."[23]

☙ ☙ ☙

In 1905, Governor Cummins decided to visit the penitentiary. War-den Hunter was thrilled because he could show the governor how successful the prisoner classification system had become. The war-den was positive that the pecking order he had established was working and had resulted in a more cooperative prison population. There were now two hundred forty-six members in the first class, one hundred twenty-three in the second class, and only five in the third or lowest class. Of course, Hunter singled out Novak, Anamosa's prized prisoner, and introduced him to the governor. Although he was now more comfortable than when he had arrived there eight years earlier, Novak was certainly nobody's fool. He saw the visit as an opportunity to make a good impression and insisted that the governor sit for a formal portrait, appealing to Cummins's barn-sized ego. Novak took a series of photographs and promised to send copies as soon as he developed and printed them. One of the photographs was later reprinted in the *Prison Press*, where it was noted, "Of course, Frank claims his Art is what makes the governor so good-looking."[24]

Unfortunately, the overall quality of the portraits was quite poor. Warden Hunter wrote an apologetic letter to B. W. Garrett, the pardon secretary in Des Moines, stating that "Novak has [developed] several [photographs] but they seem to be such failures that I have not sent them in." He added, "However, by Novak's request, I send you three of the recent prints." Novak also took advantage of the opportunity and cleverly slipped in a photograph of himself and a family snapshot with his two sons.[25] But despite Novak's attempts to make up to the governor and despite Milner's efforts, no parole or pardon was forthcoming.

Warden Hunter died in 1906 and Marquis Barr was elected to fill his spot, beginning in November. Shortly thereafter, the Iowa General Assembly voted to convert the Anamosa State Penitentiary into the Iowa State Reformatory. The effective date for this conversion would be no later than July 4, 1907. This change in the prison's status meant that all prisoners sentenced to life imprisonment, plus others serving long terms for such crimes as burglary and armed robbery, would be transferred to Fort Madison, which would then be designated as the only state penitentiary in Iowa.

On May 20, a special railroad car was brought up to Anamosa and fifty prisoners in chains boarded the train, which left the Anamosa station that morning. The trip was cut short, however, as several lawyers temporarily halted the train's progress. The lawyers had filed writs of *habeas corpus* on behalf of two prisoners, Novak and a man named Louis Busse, arguing that the transfer to Fort Madison was illegal since the sentence for both men stipulated that they should serve their time at Anamosa State Penitentiary. Two sheriffs boarded the train at Marion with court documents ordering the train to stop, but after some discussion and because the hearing over the writs of *habeas corpus* would not be held for at least another week, it was decided that the transfer of prisoners should continue.

Under the watchful eyes of Warden Barr, Deputy Warden Smith, and armed guards, the men were unchained at the Cedar Rapids station and permitted to smoke, while sandwiches, cookies, and gingerbread were given to them. A crowd pushed up against the rail car, surging forward to get a glimpse of the prisoners, especially Novak, who had already expressed his unhappiness about the transfer to aging Fort Madison, which one reporter described as "an unfit place to keep prisoners for any length of time."[26] A reporter for the *Cedar Rapids Daily Republican* commented sarcastically, "Apparently, the worship of notorious criminals is not always confined to women. If Csolgoz [Leon Czolgosz, who assassinated President McKinley] had not been electrocuted, it is probable that by this time there would have been petitions galore for his pardon and we should have been told with much unction of his 'great love for his children.'"[27]

One eyewitness reported that Frank Novak's father, John, had boarded the train. The old Bohemian immigrant, now sixty-eight, who had spent practically all of his life's savings in an effort to free his son, spoke with Frank for a few minutes. Seeing his son in chains was too much for him, and he broke down and wept uncontrollably. Because of his age and his infirmities, John Novak was sure that it was the last time he would ever see his son alive.[28]

Frank Novak's reaction to seeing his father was muted, as the prisoner was probably preoccupied with what lay down the tracks ahead of him. Anamosa had the reputation of being a "play house," in convicts' terminology, but Fort Madison, thirty-three years older than Anamosa, was a much rougher, more primitive place. "The Fort," as it was called, was ruled by Warden James C. Sanders, a man who believed in prison reform but was hamstrung by the wretched conditions at the aging penitentiary.

After an hour, the prisoners were manacled together again, the guards were stationed in the special car, and the wheezing engine huffed and slowly picked up speed, clattering down the track to Fort Madison at the southeastern tip of the state. A few hours later, the train arrived and Novak and the other forty-nine convicts were marched into the facility, stripped, given new clothes, measured with the Bertillon system, and photographed. Their names were entered into the prison logbook.

Anamosa's ledger on Frank Novak was closed. He would serve the remaining portion of his life sentence at The Fort.

EIGHTEEN

•———————————————•

Novak's Second
Disappearing Act

As hard as it was to "do the book"—prison slang for a life sentence—at Anamosa, marking time was much worse at Fort Madison State Penitentiary. With cramped, filthy cells and a well-deserved reputation for draconian punishment, the old prison was a much rougher facility than its newer sister penitentiary one hundred twenty-five miles to the north.

Workers broke ground for the Fort Madison Territorial Penitentiary in 1839, seven years before Iowa became a state. Known as the oldest prison west of the Mississippi, The Fort was perched on a small ridge about four hundred yards from the Big Muddy. Before a crude wooden stockade was completed, the first prisoners were kept in the cellar of the warden's house. "Each night, with ball and chain dangling from their legs, they were [lowered] into the cellar through a trap door," but the makeshift jail had immediate security issues, for "in spite of precautions, seven of the first twelve prisoners escaped before the cells were ready."[1]

The warden's cellar was a harbinger of the squalid conditions of the stone cellblock, which was completed in 1841 and could hold one hundred thirty-eight convicts.[2] A prisoner later described the cells as "vermin-infested" and crawling with bedbugs.[3] "The house is damp and dark," he wrote. "We live and die in those steel and stone apartments. We curse and pray in them, plot future crimes and cry bitterly in them."[4]

Each dimly lit cell measured about six feet in length and eight feet in height, more like a small cave than a cell, with little natural light filtering through the barred window. Dozens of noxious lard- and coal-oil lamps made a feeble attempt to illuminate the building's interior. Also, since there was no indoor plumbing, a wooden bucket stood in each cell until morning, when the inmates carried them down to the lower yard and dumped the waste into a trough.[5]

On the outside, although The Fort was not as distinctive as Anamosa, it displayed a similar appearance of complete authority. Thirty-foot high stone walls ran about four hundred feet on each side, forming a square around the compound. At the entrance, an enormous stone watchtower guarded a pair of heavy iron gates while several smaller, medieval-looking turrets were built along the perimeter walls.

From the beginning, living conditions at the penitentiary were abominable. As early as 1845, just six years after its founding, once "the public realized that prisoners were crowded into small quarters and that violent punishment was used to control the unruly, a committee was appointed to investigate [the problems]."[6] Even so, it wasn't until twenty-four years later, in 1869, that Dr. George Shedd, a member of the Iowa State Prison Board, headed east to study conditions at other prisons and penitentiaries. But despite his findings and despite the first seeds of prison reform sprouting in other parts of the country, little was done to improve life at The Fort. In fact, shortly after Shedd's report, a warden named Martin Heisey was investigated for malfeasance. In 1870, a special joint committee of the Iowa Senate and House of Representatives examined thirteen charges against Heisey, ranging from neglect, fraud, and nepotism to dereliction of duty. Although the charges were dismissed by the investigating committee, which cheerfully reported that Heisey's "faithful, efficient and untiring devotion to his official duties has but few parallels," the complaints underlined some of the ongoing issues at the old prison.[7]

By 1874, two hundred sixty-four prisoners were jammed into Fort

Madison. Twenty-two years later, the cellblock had grown to three hundred seventy-two cells with plans to add one hundred twenty more, making a fourth level.[8] All of these prisoners still were housed in the original cellblock building. By 1907, there were five hundred twenty-six inmates with only forty guards, much higher than the ten-to-one ratio mandated by state law.

As at Anamosa, much of each prisoner's day was filled with work. From the beginning, the directors at Fort Madison were instructed to make sure that each inmate "now convicted [and] in the confines of this place [should be] sentenced to hard labor."[9] However, most of the prisoners' labor consisted primarily of working at small manufacturing shops in the compound, the first one being a shoe factory. Later, the Fort Madison Chair Company established a shop at the penitentiary, as did the Iowa Farm Tool and Implement Company. As with all prisons, wages were extremely low, with each prisoner collecting about forty-five cents a day for his efforts.[10]

From the beginning, discipline was an ongoing issue at The Fort, with corporal punishment used on a regular basis. Besides wearing a ball and chain—employed well after the stone cellblock was completed—some prisoners were later forced to wear a tortuous invention that appeared to be straight from the Middle Ages. It was called the "necklace." This painful device consisted of an "iron band around the neck, with two iron horns . . . with points extending upwards," thus limiting the wearer's head movements. These iron collars were later described as "barbarous" and "would not be tolerated in any civilized land at the present time." Besides these forms of corporal punishment, a basswood tree that stood just beyond the prison wall was used as a whipping post for many years.[11]

But perhaps in a nod to the reform movement, whippings at The Fort had most likely ceased by the 1870s and solitary confinement had emerged as the prime method of punishment. Once in solitary, a man would be chained to the cell door with his hands "placed between the rods of the inner door and fastened together from the outside which prevents the prisoner from walking about or from lying down."[12] Of course, the harshest form of corporal punishment—the death penalty—had been on the books in Iowa for many years. Fort Madison was the only site in the state where executions had taken place, beginning in 1894, when prison officials hanged sixteen-year-old James Dooley, who had been convicted of first-degree murder.[13]

❦ ❦ ❦

While the general use of corporal punishment appeared to lessen over time, Fort Madison's abysmal conditions had remained virtually unchanged for more than six decades. In 1906, the year before Frank Novak's transfer, a government report on the prison summed up the current situation at The Fort: "The prison cell house of Fort Madison was erected many years ago before many of the modern improvements were known and has outlived its usefulness. . . . [It] is entirely unfit to be used as such and in the judgment of your committee is a disgrace to the great state of Iowa, being unfit for human habitation and should be replaced by a new one at the earliest possible time."[14]

Despite Novak's disappointment at being sent to the aging penitentiary, he immediately began working to duplicate his success at Anamosa. He tried everything he could to ingratiate himself with James C. Sanders, the new warden, by playing the violin in the prison orchestra—Sanders himself was a talented cornet player—and working with the prison photographer. In all of his actions, Novak strived to portray himself as a model prisoner. At the same time he continued to send out letters requesting a pardon while Tom Milner also petitioned the governor for his client's early release.

After a year at The Fort, Novak's prayers were answered. In August 1908, William Boyd Allison, an Iowan who had served in the United States Senate for 35 years, passed away unexpectedly, just a few months after the state's Republican Party endorsed his reelection. Governor Cummins, who had run against Allison in the primary, was now picked by the state legislature to succeed him. Time was short, and Cummins had to clear up some legal matters before he could leave Des Moines and settle into his new Washington office.

Among the remaining papers on the governor's desk was Novak's petition for pardon. Clearly, Cummins was familiar with Novak's case, as he had been pestered by Tom Milner for years. In fact, Milner's activities amounted to so much badgering that one paper referred to it as an "incessant assault."[15] Inundated with other requests from convicts across the state as well, Governor Cummins called for a meeting of the board of pardon and parole. At the very least, he most likely saw it as a chance to rid himself of this legal gadfly once and for all.

The governor had had a past history of making controversial decisions. After meeting with the board, and possibly discussing the case with Judge Burnham, Cummins decided to commute Novak's sentence, reducing the time to twenty-five years instead of life imprisonment. Novak had served ten years already and had earned considerable time off thanks to his good behavior. As a result, the former Walford storeowner and banker would be released in 1911.[16]

Pardoning Novak was one of Cummins's last official acts before he left for Washington, and it resulted in a firestorm of rage across eastern Iowa. The *Vinton Eagle* noted later that the governor's ears must still be "tingling" from the shouts of many angry Benton County residents, especially since no new evidence had been introduced in the past eleven years.[17]

In Iowa City, another paper questioned why the governor had changed his mind, pointing out that five years earlier he had refused to sign any pardon for Novak, stating at the time that "no punishment could be severe enough for the enormous crime Novak committed, and that commutation would not be pleasing to the people of Benton County." It was hard to fathom, the paper added, "that a murderer like Novak can ever earn the right to mingle freely with his fellow man."[18]

Nevertheless, the commutation was now on the books. Within three years, Novak was slated to walk out of Fort Madison Penitentiary as a free man.

Tom Milner had done his job. With a drive that bordered on obsessive-compulsive behavior, he had spent more than a decade arguing for Novak's release. While he had taken on many other clients and had even worked on cases with his former adversary, M. J. Tobin, the Novak case was never far from his mind. To Milner, losing a lawsuit, especially one of this magnitude, was a personal indignity, and the Novak case had gnawed at him throughout the appeals process. He had promised the Novak family that Frank would be freed, and he had finally delivered. After all these years, the self-described "Napoleon of the Slope" had come through.

All that remained for Novak was to serve out the rest of his time. To someone who had become quite adept at crossing off days, it was simply a matter of discipline. By immersing himself in his usual prison activities—playing in the orchestra, taking photographs, and serving in the VPL chapter—Novak kept busy, working hard to make the time pass as quickly as possible.

Knowing that his sentence was winding down, many newspapers revived the story, wondering what he would do after his release, but Novak, who seldom passed by any visiting reporters without speaking to them, refused to do any interviews. His new plan was to keep his mouth shut and work as hard as he could to keep the days and weeks sliding off the calendar.

Although the overall physical conditions of the old penitentiary had not changed much, Warden Sanders had instituted several reform measures. He abolished the lockstep in about 1910 and removed the hated striped uniforms and replaced them with two-piece gray suits. Sanders also altered the silent system, so that prisoners now could speak to each other in many areas of the prison. In addition, the warden implemented the grading system that had proved to be successful at Anamosa. Sanders organized the prison orchestra, expanded the school, and, by some accounts, attempted to improve the lives of the prisoners. A full-page article in the *Gazette* concluded: "Well may Iowa congratulate herself on her board of control and the man they selected to introduce the humanitarian policy they decided upon."[19]

In September 1910, David Brant, a controversial editor of the *Iowa*

City Republican, made a concerted effort to have Novak released one year earlier than his designated parole date. First, the editor wrote to Governor Beryl F. Carroll, asking that Novak be freed as soon as possible. Convinced of Novak's innocence, Brant wrote, "In fact I have always believed there was something in this case not brought out. I do not think he ever committed murder." Brant concluded his letter by reassuring Governor Carroll that "nobody would have cause to complain [if Novak was released early]."[20]

The Iowa City editor also included a portion of a letter from Novak himself, pleading for an early parole. The prisoner's focus was on his two sons, Milo—who had returned home after living on the road for five years—and Leo. "I have in mind," Novak wrote, "taking steps towards giving the boys an education, if released soon, so that I can work—I am afraid they are *drifting*"–Novak underlined this word—"and that, you know, would be a final blow to the many [disappointments] incident to my present misfortune. . . . I think you will understand—and I hope you will have it within your power, and your inclination, to seek my relief."[21]

Someone, perhaps Governor Carroll himself, scrawled across the bottom of Novak's letter "Sept. 1911." That was the original parole date set by Governor Cummins three years earlier. In a note to David Brant, Carroll wrote, "I do not know whether I ought to in any way modify the conclusions reached by Governor Cummins or not, but I will take the matter up when I have more time and look into it."[22] Brant would not let this issue rest. He peppered Governor Carroll with more letters, urging Novak's early release.

Finally, the governor had had enough. On November 18, he sent a lengthy response to the Iowa City editor, refusing to move up Novak's release date: "If I have figured correctly," Carroll wrote, "Novak's term will expire next August. . . . It seems to me, upon investigating the records in this office, [Governor Cummins] has been very liberal with him. . . . There are many objections on file to any clemency whatever being extended to Novak, and from the records I find, both the Judge and County Attorney were against the exercising of any clemency."[23]

Carroll's response did not satisfy Brant, who also had other issues with the governor. By the following year, the editor, who was once described as "original, aggressive and forceful" and may have thought of himself as a crusading journalist in the mold of Lincoln Steffens and Ida Tarbell, was himself an advocate of prison reform and wrote a scathing open letter in the *Iowa City Republican*, attacking Governor Carroll for the deplorable living conditions at Fort Madison State Penitentiary and Anamosa.[24] Brant stated that Iowa's prisons "are certainly rotten" and he promised his readers that he would get to the bottom of the issue, penning several philippics against the governor.[25] Carroll responded angrily, saying the blame lay not with him but with the Iowa legislature. Furthermore, the governor thundered that the real reason that Brant was upset was not due to poor prison conditions but because Carroll would not reduce Novak's sentence any further.[26]

By July, a few other papers had picked up Brant's crusade and ran articles complaining about the treatment of prisoners at Fort Madison and Anamosa. One of the largest newspapers in the state, the *Des Moines Daily News*, decided to put one of its best journalists on the story, an investigative reporter named Sue McNamara who was well known for her scoop concerning the actress Sarah Bernhardt. According to McNamara, Bernhardt had not been born and raised in France as the actress had claimed. Her real name was Sarah King and she used to work as a milliner in the small town of Rochester, Iowa, before becoming famous.[27]

McNamara spent many days at Fort Madison and wrote a five-part series about the old penitentiary; overall, the stories shed little light on the grim conditions there. One headline underscored the incongruous and euphemistically cheerful tone of the articles: "Prisoners Happy Behind Stone Walls."[28] McNamara worked to put a positive spin on this series and, rather than dwell on the wretched cramped cells, she wrote about how the prisoners attempted to make their living areas brighter by painting the walls. She mentioned the orchestra and various book clubs, while also praising the warden for some of his numerous reform efforts, such as banning the use of billy clubs and setting up the system of different grades for the prisoners based on their behavior. The reporter did touch briefly on the need for a new cellblock, commenting that the individual jail cells were small, about the size of a tomb, and hardly large enough to house one man. She added that the light in the cells was particularly bad, but these problems would be solved when a new cell house was built. Until then, the men would have to make do with their current living arrangements.[29]

The penultimate article in the series was an exclusive interview with Frank Novak. With less than two months left in his sentence, Novak was arguably the most famous prisoner in the state. He had always had a fondness for women reporters [possibly because he felt that he could manipulate them] and immediately granted an interview with the veteran newspaperwoman. In this article, McNamara summarized the chase across North America and his arrest in the Klondike, noting that he was still as "cool and indifferent as when he threw down his violin in the Alaskan roadhouse." When she asked what he had in mind upon his release, Novak paused for a moment and then answered, "The first thing I will do when I get out of here is to put up a little tent on the banks of some river and camp out for several weeks. . . . I want to get my lungs full of fresh air and walk over miles of open country."[30]

To anyone who recalled the details of the case, this remark brought up the memory of his actions immediately after the Walford fire. On that day, he walked roughly twenty-two miles across "open country" in the general direction of Iowa City.

Novak turned his back on McNamara and began working on a photograph that he was framing. Then he said, "After I've had enough of camping I shall continue my work of picture-making." He spoke fondly of his two boys but said nothing about his wife, who had divorced him many years earlier.

When the reporter asked him if he was keeping track of how much time he had left in prison, he replied, "Oh, no, I'm not counting the days till I get out. What's the use?"[31]

But whether he admitted it or not, Novak was probably keeping track. He was less than two months away from his release date and the days passed by quickly. They seemed to accelerate until finally, at exactly midnight on September 3, 1911, Fort Madison's big iron gates swung open. Dressed in a cheap suit and clutching a suitcase and a five-dollar bill, Novak walked out into the darkness. His own redemption, as some had called it, was now complete. He had done his time. Now he was back in the real world, trying to imagine the changes that had taken place in the past fourteen years.

Once he passed through the gates, the usual controversy surrounding his early release erupted again. Each time Novak had pushed for his freedom, beginning with his request for parole in 1903 and culminating in Governor Cummins's grant of clemency in 1908, many furious Iowans had responded with letters arguing that the life sentence should be upheld. But this time, now that he was actually out, the anger was even more intense. Once again, several newspapers decried the miscarriage of justice that allowed Novak to go free. As usual, a few other newspapers published articles that claimed Novak's innocence. The *Waterloo Reporter* went as far as to comment, "Had he remained at home; had he given the alarm while the building was on fire, [then] he would never have been convicted."[32]

For many, the lengthy pro-Novak article in that Iowa City paper was the last straw. One anonymous reader, who called himself "Yours for the Truth," wrote a long, angry letter denouncing all who attempted to whitewash the crime. The letter recapped the entire story from the time the Walford store burned down to the present. Point by point, the letter writer rebutted each of the statements in the *Republican* article and made a strong effort to set the story straight:

"A recent article in the *Iowa City Republican* pretends to tell Novak's side of the story, and it appears that the writer wants to impart the fact upon the people of Iowa that Novak served these years as an innocent man, and that the man for whose murder he was convicted was some worthless person for whom no one had any respect. . . . It was a careful, cunning, scheming plot worked up by Novak and the testimony found in the dull court records of Benton County can still tell that heart-rending story. . . . The crimes of the [James Gang and] Younger Brothers in Minnesota were not as dastardly as the one committed by Novak. . . . [He] is as guilty of that crime today as he was on the day the judgment entry was made on the records. . . . A criminal should not be lauded as a hero and certainly no attitude should be displayed on the part of the public that he suffered 15 years as an innocent man."[33]

If Novak had any reaction to this controversy, he kept it to himself, for now he was too busy deciding on his next course of action. Despite his professed love for his two boys, it appeared that he had little interest in living near them, as rumors surfaced that he had closed a deal to purchase a photography studio in St. Louis. In fact, when he was still in jail, Novak and an armed guard had taken the train from Fort Madison down to St. Louis to talk to a photographer there. Another article noted that he had been spotted in Des Moines, while a third story mentioned that he was considering setting up a studio in Cedar Rapids.[34]

Novak needed funds to start his new photography business. But John Novak, who was still alive, had little money left to support his son in any more business endeavors. From this point on, Frank Novak would have to manage his own finances.

Even so, after trips to different cities and despite his efforts to purchase a photography studio, Novak found himself back at the town of Fort Madison in November 1911, just two months after his parole, living on the other side of the thick penitentiary walls. He had carefully preserved the negatives from some of his prison photographs, including some from the bungled hanging of John Junkin the year before, and placed a few small advertisements in the *Cedar Rapids Evening Gazette*, trying to make money by selling a set of twelve photographs of the penitentiary for fifty cents. Novak also advertised a collection of four prints of the Junkin hanging, which he offered for one dollar.[35]

Although he was a free man, Novak could not avoid trouble. Apparently, he and Warden Sanders had had some disagreements over the last three years and now that Novak was outside the walls, he intended to settle a few old scores with the guardian of The Fort. He began circulating stories that Sanders was incompetent, and that morale and discipline at the old penitentiary were at an all-time low. This was, he charged, a direct result of Warden Sanders's inability to run the prison smoothly.[36] Novak wasn't alone in these claims, as others had complained about the warden's incompetence. One prisoner named Haley had even filed charges against the warden, stating that Sanders was excessively cruel to the prisoners and had mismanaged the penitentiary.[37]

Bad feelings between Novak and Sanders erupted in December 1911. According to one report, the trouble began when Novak came to the warden's house on December 20. The warden was not home, but Sanders's wife and little boy were present. Novak demanded to see a convict named Wallace, but Mrs. Sanders told him this was not possible and Novak left. He returned a week later, on December 27. This time, the warden was at home and none too pleased to see Novak, who had upset Sanders's wife on his previous visit.

There are many different accounts of what happened next. One story was that Novak asked Sanders about some money that he believed the warden owed him. Another article reported that the recently discharged prisoner demanded to speak with some other inmates. In any case, Novak became abusive and cursed the warden and everyone else at the penitentiary. Warden Sanders decided that he had enough and physically picked Novak up and deposited him outside the front door. Then an inmate named James Dimmitt, who was working in the warden's kitchen and overheard Novak's remarks, followed the two men out and took this opportunity to reach over the warden's shoulder and land a hard right hook to Novak's jaw, knocking him down and breaking two teeth. Apparently, Novak had made more than a few enemies at the prison. Dimmitt expressed considerable satisfaction that he had "laid Novak out," as one paper put it, and was not concerned as to whether or not he would be punished for the punch. In fact, Dimmitt's only regret about the incident was that he hadn't completed the job and killed Novak, "even if [I] had to swing for it."[38]

The Iowa Board of Control, which oversaw all prison operations, received a letter from the warden detailing this episode. After discussing the matter, the board decided to accept the warden's account. Nevertheless, Warden Sanders was criticized in several papers. One was in his hometown of Emmetsburg, Iowa, where the *Democrat* printed a nasty version of the incident, noting that Sanders had gone berserk, slapping Novak twice without provocation and then picking him up and throwing him out of the house. After Dimmitt's haymaker punch, a surgeon had to repair Novak's torn lip. "If we dare believe half the reports about Sanders," the paper summarized, "it is high time that Fort Madison prison gets another warden and Iowa another governor."[39]

In any case, Novak probably left Fort Madison soon after this incident. He disappeared from sight, which was odd, since he was usually a man who seemed to enjoy the hot spotlight of publicity. Then about two years later, in November 1913, an announcement was published in the *Cedar Rapids Daily Republican* that a Miss M. Ella Johnson of Cedar Rapids had married Frank A. Novak, "a successful Chicago real estate merchant and banker." They were wed in the Presbyterian Manse in Marion, Iowa, by the Reverend Charles F. Ensign. After the ceremony and a special three-course supper, the couple boarded a train to Chicago, where they would take up residence in a new house. Miss Johnson, who was born in Atkins, Iowa, was described as being a childhood sweetheart of Novak's.[40]

❦ ❦ ❦

Although details of his remaining years are somewhat sketchy, Frank and Ella Johnson Novak lived in Chicago for many years. During that time, Novak worked as a real estate broker. One account noted that the last part of his life was "quiet and uneventful."[41]

Frank Novak died on July 12, 1930. He was sixty-six years old. Novak's great-granddaughter, Lani Novak Howe, recalled that her family members were ashamed of him and that he was regarded as the black sheep of the family. She added that when he passed away, no one wanted to claim the body.[42] But after a few days, Novak's remains were taken to a cemetery in Cedar Rapids, where he was buried alongside his father, mother, and a few other family members. Oddly enough, the year of his birth on his tombstone—1865—is incorrect, as Novak was born in 1864.[43]

NINETEEN

•————————————————————————•

The Measure of Their Lifetimes

Of the three literary club members from Cornell College who played a major role in the trial, E. L. Boies, who so ably assisted M. J. Tobin, was the first to die, passing away in 1903 at the age of forty-two after a bout of typhoid fever. His death was greatly mourned throughout Iowa but especially in his home town, where the *Waterloo Daily Courier* devoted most of its front page to his passing, calling him a giant in the legal profession, a brilliant man who "thought in syllogisms" and a great orator.[1]

Years later, in 1912, Tom Milner, the hardheaded lawyer who never gave up his defense of Novak, died of anemia. He lived long enough to see Novak released from Fort Madison. With his perpetual stubbornness, for fourteen years, from 1897 to 1911, Milner was a constant advocate for Novak.[2] Called "eccentric," "flamboyant," "witty," and just plain "peculiar," Milner once summed up his life in a brief, colorful note in the *Waterloo Daily Courier*:

> I [first] saw the light in Highland Town, O[hio] on December 1,
> 1856. . . . I commenced practicing law in Iowa Falls in 1880. . . .
> I studied law in Dubuque, Iowa. I like it and would rather be
> poor at that business than a millionaire at anything else. . . .
> I am freckled, ambitious, red-headed and happy. I am a Russell
> Sage on vacations, never having taken one in my life, and haven't
> time if I did want to take one. . . . I never lay down, get licked
> oftener than I ought to, but universally die in the ditch when

there is no hope beyond and no beyond to go to. My teeth are still good.[3]

Despite the scores of cases in which Milner served as defense attorney, many of the lawyer's obituaries led with the Novak case, pointing out that he was "famous as Novak's counsel."[4] Milner probably would have been less than pleased to have been most remembered for a case that he had lost.

The ace tracker, Red Perrin, rode his success in the Novak case to the top of the detective profession. Several papers in the United States and abroad had carried the story of his trip to the Klondike and the pursuit and capture of his prey. The Travelers portrayed him as a hero, and featured his diary in its newsletter for many months. Gus Thiel, head of the detective agency, was especially pleased that Perrin had "got his man."[5]

The quiet, auburn-haired detective had developed a fondness for Iowa, but it was not due solely to the Novak case. He had fallen in love with one of Ed Murray's cousins, Mary Agnes Murray. She was twenty years old at the time of the Novak trial, a smart young woman who had attended private school in Dubuque and was a student at St. Mary's College in South Bend, Indiana. Perrin courted her for many years, until he was named general agent of Thiel's office in Montreal. After that, his visits to Iowa became fewer and fewer until he finally decided that the current situation with Mary was intolerable. And so, after about a six-year courtship, on November 15, 1904, Red Perrin and Mary Agnes Murray were married.[6] The ceremony was short and low-key, as her mother had died recently, and was held in the home of her father at 757 Fifth Avenue in Cedar Rapids. After the wedding, the couple boarded the evening train to Denver for their honeymoon, and planned to be back in Cedar Rapids for Thanksgiving, before Perrin had to return to Montreal.[7]

But the ace detective was not destined to stay in Canada for much longer. Gus Thiel moved him to New York, where he became managing director of the agency's New York branch, located at 170 Broadway in lower Manhattan.[8] By then, he and Mary had moved into an apartment in Brooklyn, as even then the cost of living in Manhattan was prohibitive.

In 1909, the couple had a child, a daughter whom they named Helen, and shortly thereafter, the family left Brooklyn and moved into a larger apartment at 611 West 111th Street in Manhattan. During that time, Mary Agnes Perrin still made frequent trips back to Cedar Rapids to see her family while her husband still roamed around the country, working cases for Gus Thiel.

On January 13, 1911, Red Perrin was traveling west on the *Boston and Buffalo Special*, stopping in Batavia, New York, a small town between Rochester and Buffalo. He had finished his dinner, relaxed for a few hours, and retired to a berth in the last Pullman car. It was just before dawn, and the train's big steam-powered engine was idling in the station, waiting for the conductor to give the all-clear signal. Many miles away, J. B. Lydell, a forty-year veteran engineer, was holding down the throttle on the New York Central's *Western Express*. For Lydell, even with his years of experience, this particular run had been a nightmare. The engine's windows were covered in thick ice, and visibility was further reduced when a heavy fog settled on the tracks. It was so thick that the engineer could barely see past the engine's headlight. Despite the poor weather conditions, Lydell was on a tight schedule and he kept the train going at a fast pace. The *Western Express* was one of the most prestigious trains on the New York Central line, and the crew worked to make sure that it always ran on time. Lydell pushed hard, heading west at a fast clip.[9]

Some four thousand feet from the Batavia station, Lydell missed a caution signal and then a stop sign. By the time he saw the red lights of the stopped train, it was too late. He jammed on the brakes, threw the big engine into reverse, yelled at the fireman to jump and leaped from the cab. With a sickening crunch, the *Western Express* slammed into the idling train, tossing the cars like so many dominos and sparking a fire.

Rescuers helped more than twenty wounded passengers out of the wreckage and then turned their attention to the four dead. One was described as about five feet eight inches tall and one hundred seventy pounds, with reddish hair and a sandy-colored mustache. Under his body was a silver Masonic charm with an inscription that read: "Cassius C. Perrin, #9,581, Mecca Temple, New York."[10]

Red Perrin's adventurous life, which had stretched from the rough-cut southern part of the Arizona Territory, down to Monterrey, Mexico, and up to the Klondike, a life that had him crisscrossing the continent many times on detective work, was over. He was fifty-four years old. Ironically, Perrin passed away during the same year that Frank Novak was paroled.

After her husband's death, Mary Agnes Perrin returned to Cedar Rapids and spent the rest of her life in her father's house on Fifth Avenue. She outlived her husband by nine years, leaving their only child, eleven-year-old Helen, an orphan in 1920.[11]

🌿 🌿 🌿

Of all the *dramatis personae* involved in the Novak case, only one man lived out the full measure of a lifetime—M. J. Tobin. His successful prosecution boosted his legal career and he became well known in eastern Iowa. For many years, Tobin had frequently been portrayed in the newspapers as a gifted, ambitious young man of great intelligence and courage. He was reelected to a second term as Benton County attorney and after that returned to private practice in Vinton.[12] He cemented his reputation as a trial attorney by successfully handling several celebrated cases, although none was as famous as the Novak lawsuit.[13]

Tobin and his wife Lucy had three children, all boys. Each of his sons followed in his father's footsteps and became a lawyer. All three graduated from the University of Iowa, with two of them going on to receive their law degrees from the same institution.[14] M. J. Tobin himself had a solo legal practice until 1914, when his oldest son,

Hamilton, joined the firm. He was followed by Tobin's second child, Louis, and finally John Tobin in 1921. The firm was appropriately named Tobin, Tobin, Tobin & Tobin. In later years, John Tobin, who became a prominent judge in an Iowa district court, laughingly referred to himself as "the '& Tobin'" in the firm.[15] M. J. Tobin served as the trial and appellate attorney; Louis handled the municipal work; while Hamilton and John did a mix of legal work, building up a roster of clients for the firm. Of the three brothers, John may have been the best lawyer, and after his father was the most respected of the Tobin attorneys.[16]

M. J. Tobin was interested in many other areas besides law. In his early forties, Tobin was named as U.S. collector of internal revenue for the northern half of Iowa, holding that position from 1905 to 1913. An avid Republican, he was a temporary chairman of the Iowa state Republican convention and later served as chairman. Later on, he also was selected as a delegate to several national Republican conventions. Tobin also was active in local civic affairs. He helped organize the Vinton Country Club and was a member of the Greater Vinton Club. Tobin's office was located above the State Bank of Vinton—a good spot, since he was a director of that bank and served on the institution's board for many years.[17] All in all, M. J. Tobin lived a long, satisfying, and productive life. He died after a series of heart problems on May 20, 1945, at the age of eighty.

The town of Vinton prospered as well. The stuffy old courthouse, which was reviled by so many, was finally torn down and a new one was built in 1906 on the same site. Designed by Charles Emlen Bell, the structure, which still dominates the Vinton downtown area, was constructed in a beautiful Beaux-Arts style and finished in sandstone. A few years ago, the courthouse was placed on the National Register of Historic Places.[18]

But of all of Tobin's accomplishments, it was the story of his courtroom tenacity in the Novak case that was passed down through the family for generations. Elizabeth Fischer Hadley, a great-granddaughter of M. J. Tobin, remembered discussions about the case and said, "I was less impressed with the legal part of it than I was with the gold rush in Alaska. As a child and a young adult, that was the part that was really interesting to me. But although they didn't talk much about former cases, we all knew about the trial. I don't know if it was a result of this, but we used to recite some poems by Robert Service like *The Cremation of Sam Magee*."[19] Her father, Karl W. Fischer Jr., who also was a prominent attorney in the Tobin firm, added, "I think that M. J. was like a bulldog, and that he would hang on for dear life when he was in the middle of something." He further noted, "I went through the details of the Novak case many times with M. J.'s son, John. M. J. Tobin wasn't going to let this man Novak get away with it. They knew that he had fled and felt he must have been guilty for that reason, along with many others, of course. The forensics showed it."[20]

❦ ❦ ❦

Mary Novak never remarried. For many years, she ran a boarding house on First Avenue in Cedar Rapids with her two sons, Milo and Leo, and just managed to stay afloat financially. It was a tough way to make a living, but she persevered. Milo, her oldest son, who had run away from home for five years, came back and worked for many years at the Quaker Oats plant. Leo dropped out during his sophomore year of high school and worked as a fireman, shoveling coal on the Milwaukee Road for three years. He then returned to Cedar Rapids, finished high school, and enrolled at Coe College, where he became a star football player. After doing some postgraduate work at Notre Dame and Iowa State, he became a famous coach at Washington High School, where his football teams won many championships.

But Leo Novak was destined for greater things than high school athletics. He left Cedar Rapids and in 1926 was hired by the United States Military Academy at West Point, staying there for 23 years as a football, basketball, and track coach. While at the Academy, Leo

Novak produced a winning percentage of .690, the highest ever in the history of West Point basketball. As coach of the cadet track team, he also developed two world-record holders. Knute Rockne, a longtime friend, once called Leo Novak "the greatest interscholastic coach of his time."[21]

❦ ❦ ❦

There is one last piece to the puzzle of Frank Novak. To find it, one must go to Norway, a small town about five miles from Walford. Once entering Norway, a visitor crosses over several pairs of Union Pacific railroad tracks, turns left, and drives down the main road, a street similar to hundreds of other Iowa towns. "Norway," a web site notes, "is a town with a gas station, a bar, three baseball diamonds, three churches and a video rental store."[22] The gas station, just past the tracks, functions as an oasis in the small town and does a big summer business selling soda, beer, and snacks.

From Railroad Street, a nondescript dirt road named County Trunk Highway W24 branches off and winds out of town. A mile or so from the heart of Norway, perched high on a small grassy ridge, is St. Michael's Cemetery. A rusted, filigreed gate half-heartedly guards the entrance to the old graveyard, which has some headstones dating back to the Civil War. Looking out from atop the hillside, one can see for miles, far across the Iowa plains. Farmhouses lie casually across the view, strewn here and there, and in the summer, the corn tassels forming a soft yellow blanket spread out below the graves.

A line of ragged old cedar trees stands guard, offering a little bit of shade under the blazing midday sun. Next to the trees, a gravel road neatly cuts the graveyard in half, with "Catholics buried on the left side and everybody else on the right," according to one local resident.[23]

Not too far from the road, on the left side—the Catholic side—is a weathered gray marble obelisk about three feet high. Decades of harsh heat and extreme cold have not been kind to the aged grave marker. The single shaft of inch-thick iron that once fastened it to its base has snapped and the obelisk has toppled over, lying face up in the tall green grass. The family name "Murray" is engraved on a square stone base nearby.

On the marker is an inscription below the dates that at first glance looks like Gaelic. On closer inspection, the faded words are carved in English script: "May thine soul rest in peace." The last few letters on the old stone are worn away.

Buried near the fallen stone are the remains of poor Edward Murray, an innocent man who by fate, providence, or just plain bad luck was absolutely in the wrong place at the wrong time.

ACKNOWLEDGMENTS

In writing a book on a murder case, whether the crime took place last year or a century ago, the author must be prepared to do a considerable amount of detective work. In fact, during the course of my research, one person I interviewed referred to me as a "historical sleuth," and I suppose that there is some truth to that. For much of the time, I felt I was gumshoeing Novak in much the same fashion as Red Perrin did, but obviously I didn't have to pack goods over the Chilkoot Trail, build my own boat, and navigate six hundred miles down the Yukon River to Dawson City. However, in many ways, I *was* following Frank Novak, from the time he was born until his marriage to Ella Johnson in 1913. But unlike Perrin, tracking Novak wasn't my goal. I wanted to learn everything I could about the man—what made him tick, his business successes and failures; and most important, what his motives were.

During the past six years, my research journey has taken me to dozens of places in Iowa, the West Coast, Alaska, the Yukon, and several European countries. I talked to many Iowans and visited libraries, historical societies, and chambers of commerce. In doing so, I realized that I would never have been able to complete this book without the assistance of many people and organizations.

First, I thank the State Historical Society of Iowa (SHSI) for its assistance in both Des Moines and Iowa City. Two SHSI library resource technicians, Heather Hildreth and Charles Scott in Iowa City, were immensely helpful in locating microfilm of old newspapers and periodicals. In particular, Scott was instrumental in finding the musty sixteen-hundred-page, two-volume set of court testimony that had been lying in archival repose for the past one hundred and ten years. Moreover, he graciously let me take digital photographs of each page. I'm also most grateful to Sherri Stelling, Rosie Springer, and Bruce Kreuger at the SHSI Des Moines office for their assistance in providing additional historical documents for my perusal.

Many of the libraries that I visited were extremely helpful in ferreting out detailed information about the case as well as background information on eastern Iowa. I especially thank Virginia Holsten of the Vinton Public Library, who took time from her busy schedule to answer my questions as well as patiently search through back issues of the *Vinton Eagle*; Kristi

Sorenson of the Belle Plaine Public Library; and Pat Erger of the Norway Public Library.

I also received assistance from Jennifer Albin and Wendi Goen, archivists at the Arizona State Library in Phoenix, Arizona. They discovered rare photographs of Red Perrin as well as archival information on his days spent as a deputy sheriff in Tucson in the early 1890s.

John McGlothen, research analyst of the *Cedar Rapids Gazette*, assisted me regarding background information on the early days of that newspaper. He also forwarded to me several clippings on the career of W. I. Endicott, a city editor of the *Gazette* during the Novak case.

I owe a large debt of thanks to Jennifer Rouse, consulting librarian and college archivist of Cornell College, and Peggy Hill, records coordinator of Coe College. Jennifer passed along information to me about three of the four lawyers involved in the case—M. J. Tobin, E. L. Boies, and Tom Milner— all of whom graduated from Cornell. Peggy sent me copies of her files on Leo Novak, Frank Novak's son, who graduated from Coe College and whose amazing life is probably worthy of a separate book.

The archivists at Library and Archives Canada were extremely helpful in providing information on the North West Mounted Police post in Dawson City as well as copies of Perrin's arrest warrants and a typed report from Inspector Charles Constantine detailing Novak's arrest in July, 1897. Thanks also to Melanie Quintal and, in particular, Claire Banton for assistance in tracking down William Ogilvie's fascinating photograph of Perrin and Novak together in St. Michael, Alaska.

I am especially grateful to Mary Beth Davidson, director of records management at Travelers insurance company. From the beginning, she was extremely helpful and gave selflessly of her time in digging out information on the case. She also made copies of background records from the company's files, including the original coroner's report, the Thiel Detective Agency's notes on the case, and a sheaf of letters to and from Dr. J. B. Lewis, president of Travelers in 1897.

In addition, Dick Snavely, director of the Anamosa State Penitentiary Museum, was an excellent source for information on the prison. Both he and Steve Wendl were vital in supplying documentation regarding Novak's stay at Anamosa. Ironically, Dick's great-uncle, a man named M. D. Snavely, installed the gas boiler in Novak's store and was quoted extensively in the court documents.

For information on John Farley and some of the early days of the Thiel Agency, I am grateful to Scott S. Taylor, from the Special Collections Division at Georgetown University Library in Washington, D.C., who assisted in locating the unpublished scrapbook that was compiled by one of Farley's ancestors. Thanks also to Kathryn Hodson, Special Collections Department manager at the University of Iowa Library, for giving me access to John W. Tobin's papers. In addition, I appreciate the work of Jason Stratman from the Missouri Historical Society.

My research efforts would have been incomplete without the invaluable assistance of many Vinton residents. These were Patricia Tobin Fischer, the granddaughter of M. J. Tobin and daughter of John Tobin; her husband, the late Karl W. Fischer Jr., an attorney at Tobin's law firm for many years and who, like Patricia, shared memories about M. J. and John Tobin; and Elizabeth Fischer Hadley, M. J. Tobin's great-granddaughter. Besides loaning me some family photographs and other documents of the case, they also lent me a scrapbook that M. J. Tobin's wife, Lucy Dosh Tobin, compiled almost fifty years after the verdict. The scrapbook contained photographs, letters, notes, and clippings from some long-lost newspapers, as well as M. J. Tobin's handwritten comments on the 1899 appeal. Special thanks also to Betsy's husband Rick, who provided a great deal of enthusiasm during the course of my research in Iowa. He also took the time to photograph the unique "Hero of Vinton" hand-carved walking stick with Tobin's likeness.

On the Novak side, Lani Novak Howe, a great-granddaughter of Frank Novak, provided some useful information on her infamous ancestor and his first wife, Mary Novak; her grandfather, Leo Novak; and her father, Jack Novak.

I had several email exchanges with Ramesh Nyberg, a retired detective with the Miami-Dade police department. Ram's insights regarding the sociopathic mind of a criminal were most illuminating.

John Hiers, Paul Allen, and Charles M. Biscay Jr. were of great assistance in helping me with other aspects of the book. John's advice regarding story flow and his peerless photo restoration work, particularly in the pictures after the Novak and Jilek fire, is much appreciated.

I would be remiss if I neglected to offer my sincere appreciation to the "Iowa Gang"—Frank, Wally, and Jean Maher; Ann and Wayne Mallie; and the late Bob Erusha. Wally and Jean graciously opened up their home to me while I was in Iowa and followed with great interest my research in Benton County, Linn County, and other parts of the state. I also am especially grateful to the late Lee Tow for his efforts in shedding additional light on Frank Novak in Walford and taking me to the site of the fire.

I owe a special thanks to Jim McCoy, director of the University of Iowa

Press, for believing in the book and offering advice and encouragement along the way. I also acknowledge the assistance of Charlotte Wright, managing editor of the University of Iowa Press, and Catherine Cocks, acquisitions editor. Their diligence in proofreading the manuscript is much appreciated. In particular, Catherine did a herculean job in shaping the flow of the book. Moreover, her thoughtful comments and questions were always on the mark, from beginning to end. I also enjoyed working with editor Arnold Friedman and am very grateful for his time and effort in producing the final version of the book.

Lastly, I thank my wonderful wife Donna for her steady support. As with my other writing projects, she has been a source of unending encouragement. Her patience and understanding regarding the amount of time spent researching and writing this book, along with her suggestions, are much appreciated and, as always, I am indebted to her.

NOTES

1. Death in Flames

The chapter title comes from a headline in the *Marshalltown Evening Times-Republican (METR)*, February 3, 1897, p. 1.

1. *Testimony before the Coroner's Jury*, State of Iowa, Benton County, p. 1. Travelers Archives, reproduced with permission.

2. *Testimony*, p. 4.

3. *Testimony*, p. 1.

4. *State of Iowa* v. *Frank A. Novak*, pp. 1079, 1119, and 1120. Also, see *Testimony*, p. 2.

5. *Des Moines Daily News (DMDN)*, May 27, 1899, p. 2.

6. *Investigation of Alleged Death of Frank Novak*, part 1, p. 1. Two of the five insurance companies (Travelers and the Economic Life Association of Clinton, Iowa) investigated the case, but only Travelers was determined to continue the search for Novak. Travelers Archives, used with permission.

7. *METR*, February 3, 1897, p. 1.

8. *Testimony*, pp. 2 and 8. Identification checks were common in the latter part of the nineteenth century. They were typically rented on a yearly basis from special registry companies. If something happened to the wearer, the number could be traced to the issuing company and the person could be identified. The check cost one dollar per year. Novak purchased the check from the Standard Registry Company of Chicago on July 31, 1896, about seven months prior to the store fire.

9. *Daily Iowa Capital*, February 5, 1897, p. 1.

10. Conversation with Karl W. Fischer Jr., August 11, 2007.

11. *Cedar Rapids Evening Gazette (CREG)*, March 5, 1888, p. 4.

12. William J. Tilstone, Kathleen A. Savage, and Leigh A. Clark, *Forensic Science: An Encyclopedia of History, Methods, and Techniques*. Santa Barbara, CA: ABC-CLIO, 2006, p. 161.

13. Suzanne Bell, *Crime and Circumstance: Investigating the History of Forensic Science*. Westport, CT: Praeger Publishers, 2008, p. 4.

14. *Crime and Circumstance*, pp. 62–63.

15. Kathleen Ramsland, *Beating the Devil's Game: A History of Forensic Science and Criminal Investigation*. Waterville, ME: Thorndike Press, 2007, pp. 90–91.

16. *Beating the Devil's Game*, p. 129.

17. Douglas Starr, *The Killer of Little Shepherds: A True Crime Story and the Birth of Forensic Science*. New York: Alfred A. Knopf, 2010, p. 19.

18. www.enotes.com/forensic-science.

19. John W. Tobin, "Murder: A Persistent Pursuit," *Palimpsest* 51.10 (October, 1970), p. 417. Also see *State v. Novak*, p. 1376.

20. *Testimony*, p. 5.

21. *Testimony*, p. 4.

22. *Testimony*, p. 4. Also see *Investigation of Alleged Death of Frank Novak*, part I, p. 6, for a description of the fabric.

23. According to the Thiel investigation, W. I. Endicott of the *Gazette* had asked several of Novak's friends about him when he met Hasek, who explained to the editor about Novak's bridgework. It was Endicott who pushed to have Hasek testify at the coroner's jury. See *Investigation of Alleged Death of Frank Novak*, part I, p. 10.

24. Louis M. (or Alois) Hasek eventually went to dental school at the University of Iowa, the first of several generations of Haseks to do so. For more than one hundred years, a Hasek practiced dentistry in the Cedar Rapids area. See the obituary for Dr. Ondrej Hasek, *Cedar Rapids Gazette* online, October 2, 2009.

25. *Testimony*, p. 6.

26. *Testimony*, p. 8.

2. The Bohemian Immigrant's Clever Son

1. www.preservationiowa.org//downloads/BohemianHD_2.pdf.

2. Luther B. Hill, ed., *History of Benton County, Iowa*. Chicago: Lewis Publishing, 1910, vol. 2, p. 803.

3. www.travel.cz.guide/73/ndex_en.html.

4. Karel Kysilka, "Emigration to the USA from the Policka Region in 1850–1890." Presented at the Genealogy Seminar of the Czech Heritage Society of Texas, Hillsboro, TX, July 31, 1999, p. 1.

5. "Emigration to the USA," p. 16.

6. Dr. Jan Habenicht, *History of Czechs in America*. St. Paul: Czechoslovak Genealogical Society International, 1996, p. 211.

7. www.dvoraknyc.org/Dvorak_Trip_to_Spillville.html. The famous symphony was composed in 1893.

8. Federal Writers' Project of the Works Progress Administration for the State of Iowa, *Iowa: A Guide to the Hawkeye State*. New York: Viking Press, 1945, p. 189.

9. *History of Czechs*, p. 216.

10. Email correspondence from Michael Gould, May 10, 2007.

11. Hill, *Benton County*, p. 803.

12. 1880 United States Census.

13. Benton County Historical Society, *The History of Benton County, Iowa*. Dallas, TX: Taylor Publishing Company, 1989, p. 33.

14. *Chicago Times-Herald*, August 28, 1897, p. 1.

15. *DMDN*, September 11, 1897, p. 1.

16. *Investigation of Alleged Death of Frank Novak*, part 1, p. 1.

17. *Cedar Rapids Daily Republican (CRDR)*, February 4, 1897, p. 5.

18. *DMDN*, September 11, 1897, p. 1.

19. *CREG*, July 24, 1893, p. 5; *CREG*, December 21, 1893, p. 5.

20. *CREG*, February 19, 1894, p. 8.

21. *METR*, November 9, 1897, p. 1.

22. John W. Tobin, "Murder: Circumstantial Evidence," *Palimpsest* 51.10 (October, 1970), p. 422.

23. William B. Haskell, *Two Years in the Klondike and Alaskan Gold-Fields*. Fairbanks: University of Alaska Press, 1998, p. 384.

24. *Investigation of Alleged Death of Frank Novak*, part 1, p. 2.

25. *CRDR*, February 4, 1897, p. 5.

26. *State* v. *Novak*, p. 1081.

27. *State* v. *Novak*, pp. 1077ff.

28. *State* v. *Novak*, p. 1135.

29. *State* v. *Novak*, pp. 1135 and 1149. It took roughly thirty days for a team of workers to build the store.

30. Correspondence from John L. Way to Dr. J. B. Lewis of Travelers, February 4, 1897. Way wrote that Novak was an agent of that firm but had not done very much business in Walford. Novak took out his largest insurance policy—ten thousand dollars—with Travelers. Note: all correspondence between Lewis, Gus Thiel, M. J. Tobin, and others in 1897 is from Travelers Archives. Reprinted with permission.

31. *DMDN*, May 6, 1896, p. 3.

32. *Sioux Valley News*, September 2, 1897, p. 1.

33. *State* v. *Novak*, p. 1056.

34. *State* v. *Novak*, p. 1058. In addition, some states like Washington and Oregon still require a form of this poison register.

35. *State* v. *Novak*, p. 372 and p. 39. The amount was roughly two hundred twenty dollars in paper money and eighty dollars in silver coins.

36. Correspondence with Christopher P. Leary, DDS, October 9, 2007. According to Dr. Leary, any dentist would have quickly seen that the dental bridge discovered under the cot was not made for the dead man's mouth.

37. *State* v. *Novak*, pp. 529 and 638.

38. *State* v. *Novak,* p. 638.

39. *State* v. *Novak,* p. 622.

40. *Investigation of Alleged Death of Frank Novak,* part 1, p. 3.

41. John W. Tobin, *Murder: Circumstantial Evidence,* p. 419.

42. *State* v. *Novak,* pp. 298 and 861.

43. *State* v. *Novak,* pp. 298 and 521.

3. Down on the Ground

1. *Chicago Times-Herald,* September 28, 1897, p. 1.

2. *Investigation of Alleged Death of Frank Novak,* part 2, p. 1.

3. *CREG,* February 5, 1897, p. 3.

4. *Sioux Valley News,* September 2, 1897, p. 1.

5. *Investigation of Alleged Death of Frank Novak,* part 1, pp. 8, 14.

6. *Vinton Eagle (VE),* February 12, 1897, p. 1. The story originally ran in the *Gazette* on February 9.

7. *CREG,* February 5, 1897, p. 3.

8. James Clark Fifield, ed., *The American Bar: Contemporary Lawyers of the United States and Canada.* Minneapolis, MN: Byron Printing Company, 1918, p. 213.

9. Connie LaGrange, "Tilford Academy, 1871–1916," unpublished manuscript, 1971.

10. *Syracuse Herald,* May 5, 1912, Section B, p. 7.

11. *The Sibylline.* Mt. Vernon, IA: Cornell Publishing Company and Edson Fish, 1888. There are no page numbers for this edition of the Cornell College yearbook.

12. John W. Tobin, *Murder: Circumstantial Evidence,* p. 422.

13. Harley Ransom, *Pioneer Recollections: Stories and Pictures Depicting the Early History and Development of Benton County.* Cedar Rapids, IA: Historical Publishing Company, 1941, p. 139.

14. The total amount of insurance that Novak carried with the five companies was $27,000. In 2012 dollars, this would be the equivalent of about $752,000. U.S. Department of Labor, Bureau of Labor Statistics, *Handbook of Labor Statistics*. Also, see the web site of the Federal Reserve Bank's Minneapolis branch: http://www.minneapolisfed.org/community_education/teacher/calc/hist1800.

15. *State* v. *Novak*, p. 940.

16. *CRDR*, February 12, 1897, p. 5.

17. *CREG*, February 3, 1897, p. 6.

18. *CREG*, October 12, 1918, p. 6.

19. library.thinkquest.org/C0111500/spanamer/yellow.html.

20. library.thinkquest.org/C0111500/spanamer/yellow.html.

21. newscoma.com/2010/02/21.

22. Robin Dunbar, "The Detective Business." Chicago: Charles H. Kerr, 1909, p. 4.

23. Dunbar, "The Detective Business," p. 3.

24. *CRDR*, February 4, 1897, p. 5.

25. *CREG*, February 6, 1897, p. 8.

26. *Waterloo Daily Courier (WDC)*, February 17, 1897, p. 12.

27. *WDC*, February 17, 1897, p. 12.

28. *Investigation of Alleged Death of Frank Novak*, part 3, p. 1. Years after the case had faded from the papers, a story on Kroulik referred to him as the man who was once mistaken for Frank Novak.

29. Jo Novak was once charged with embezzling forty thousand dollars but before the case went to trial, his father allegedly reimbursed the money to Jo's accuser. See *Investigation of Alleged Death of Frank Novak*, part 1, p. 8.

30. Correspondence from Tobin to W. I. Endicott, date unknown. Referenced in *Investigation*, part 1, p. 12.

31. Correspondence from John L. Way to Dr. J. B. Lewis of Travelers, February 4, 1897. In one of the many ironies in the case, the physician who examined Novak on behalf of Travelers was a doctor from Norway, Iowa, named J. A. Smith. This was the name that Novak later used as one of his aliases. See a letter dated October 22, 1897, from Dr. Lewis to M. J. Tobin in Travelers Archives.

32. Correspondence from Dr. J. B. Lewis to Bayard P. Holmes, February 8, 1897.

33. Correspondence between Frank Thornburg and Dr. J. B. Lewis, February 8, 1897.

34. Correspondence from Frank Thornburg to Travelers, February 8, 1897.

35. Correspondence from Dr. Lewis to the Northwestern Mutual Life Association, March 1, 1897.

36. Correspondence from Andrew Van Wormer to Dr. Lewis, March 3, 1897.

4. Thiel's Men Move In

1. Mary M. Farley and Marcella E. Dillon, *Biography of John F. Farley*, unpublished, pp. 1 and 21. Also, see the Records of the Pinkerton National Detective Agency, Library of Congress, Manuscript Division, ID #MS536301, Administrative File, 1857–1899, Box 32. The information on Thiel in Chicago is from a caption on a photograph taken in 1868.

2. These offices were listed on Thiel stationery in correspondence dated at the time of the Novak case.

3. J. Anthony Lukas, *Big Trouble: A Murder in a Small Western Town Sets Off a Struggle for the Soul of America.* New York: Touchstone, 1997, p. 84.

4. Martin Wheeler, *Judas Exposed: or, The Spotter Nuisance, An Anti-Secret Book Devoted to the Interests of Railroad Men.* Chicago: Utility Book and Novelty, 1889, pp. 27 and 13.

5. Wheeler, pp. 127 and 179.

6. Lukas, *Big Trouble*, p. 84.

7. *Biography of John F. Farley*, pp. xvii and 22. Farley was born in 1849. Even though Thiel was able to expand the number of his offices to fourteen, Pinkerton still held the upper hand in terms of overall business income, with twenty offices across the country.

8. *Biography of John F. Farley*, p. 59.

9. *Biography of John F. Farley*, p. 59.

10. *Investigation of Alleged Death of Frank Novak*, part 2, p. 4.

11. *Investigation of Alleged Death of Frank Novak*, part 2, p. 7.

12. *CREG*, February 20, 1897, p. 5.

13. *Investigation of Alleged Death of Frank Novak*, part 1, p. 6.

14. *Investigation of Alleged Death of Frank Novak*, part 1, p. 8. There is no evidence that the Thiel agents followed up on this information.

15. *Chicago Times-Herald*, August 28, 1897, p. 1.

16. *Investigation of Alleged Death of Frank Novak*, part 1, p. 8. "Jack-leg" or "jackleg" is a slang term for an unscrupulous or dishonest individual. It can also mean an amateur, which could have referred to Jo Novak's lack of legal training.

17. *Investigation of Alleged Death of Frank Novak,* part 1, p. 9. A blind is a gambit, something that is put forward that is intentionally misleading.

18. *Investigation of Alleged Death of Frank Novak,* p. 12.

19. *Investigation of Alleged Death of Frank Novak,* pp. 13–14.

20. *Investigation of Alleged Death of Frank Novak,* p. 16.

21. *Investigation of Alleged Death of Frank Novak,* p. 17.

22. *Investigation of Alleged Death of Frank Novak,* p. 17.

23. *Investigation of Alleged Death of Frank Novak,* p. 17. On the same day, February 24, Edward Murray's father, William Murray, filed an information form with L. S. Miller, a justice of the peace, accusing Frank Novak of murder. See State Historical Society of Iowa (Des Moines), Governors' Criminal Correspondence, 1838–1910, file folders on Frank Novak.

24. *Investigation of Alleged Death of Frank Novak,* part 2, p. 2.

25. *Investigation of Alleged Death of Frank Novak,* part 2, p. 3.

26. The word "hack" is a shortened form of the word hackney, defined as a horse that is hired or rented, usually with a buggy.

27. *State* v. *Novak,* p. 694.

28. *Investigation of Alleged Death of Frank Novak,* part 2, p. 3.

29. *Investigation of Alleged Death of Frank Novak,* part 2, p. 4.

30. Correspondence from Bayard P. Holmes to Dr. J. B. Lewis, March 5, 1897.

31. http://politicalgraveyard.com/geo/ZZ/GR.html#CONSUL.

32. Correspondence from Holmes to Lewis, March 9, 1897.

5. Following the Trail

1. *Investigation of Alleged Death of Frank Novak,* part 3, p. 1.

2. *CREG,* February 20, 1897, p. 5.

3. *Investigation of Alleged Death of Frank Novak,* part 3, p. 2.

4. *Investigation of Alleged Death of Frank Novak,* part 3, p. 5.

5. *Investigation of Alleged Death of Frank Novak,* part 3, pp. 6–7.

6. *Investigation of Alleged Death of Frank Novak,* part 3, p. 7.

7. *Investigation of Alleged Death of Frank Novak,* part 3, p. 8.

8. *Investigation of Alleged Death of Frank Novak,* part 3, p. 8.

9. *Investigation of Alleged Death of Frank Novak,* part 3, p. 9.

10. *Investigation of Alleged Death of Frank Novak,* part 3, p. 8.

11. *Cedar Rapids Weekly Gazette (CRWG),* September 8, 1897, p. 1.

12. Pedro, a popular card game roughly similar to Hearts, was prevalent

in the nineteenth century and is still played in many countries today. See http://www.pagat.com/allfours/pedro.html.

13. *Dubuque Herald*, September 4, 1897, p. 4.

14. Correspondence from G. H. Thiel to M. J. Tobin, April 4, 1897.

15. Correspondence from G. H. Thiel to M. J. Tobin, April 4, 1897.

16. *CREG*, September 2, 1897, p. 1.

17. *New York Times*, January 14, 1911, p. 2. Also see *CREG*, September 2, 1897, p. 1, for Tucson reference.

18. *CREG*, September 2, 1897, p. 1.

19. A search of records reveals no one named C. C. Perrin in the military at that time. In fact, there is very little evidence of Perrin's early days in Arizona. According to the Arizona History and Archives Division, Archives and Public Records, in Phoenix, there is no documentation that he served as a U.S. marshal at Tucson. The only information in the state archives shows that Perrin was a constable in precinct one in Tucson from about 1890 to 1892. He also served as deputy sheriff. Two photographs of Perrin exist in the Arizona State Library, Archives and Public Records. On the back of the photographs are the words, "Cash Perrin, 1890–1892." Correspondence with Nancy Sawyer, archivist, Arizona State Library, May 29, 2007.

20. *Arizona Republic*, January 19, 1891, p. 4.

21. See *Pima County Civil Case Numbers #1835; #1883*, Arizona State Library, Archives and Public Records.

22. *CREG*, September 2, 1897, p. 1. The *Gazette* noted that Perrin drifted around the West for several years, but the paper is incorrect. Perrin left Arizona sometime in 1892 or 1893, as he was at the Chicago World's Fair by 1893.

23. *CREG*, September 2, 1897, p. 1. For information on the fair, see *The Chicago World's Fair of 1893: A Photographic Record, with Text by Stanley Appelbaum*. New York, Dover Publications, 1980.

24. *State* v. *Novak*, p. 813.

25. *Chicago Daily Tribune*, March 19, 1895, p. 1.

26. *Elgin (IA) Echo*, April 23, 1896, p. 4. One account noted that the cost of the chase far exceeded the amount of money that Larrabee embezzled.

27. *WDC*, August 30, 1897, p. 1.

6. Klondike Madness

1. Murray Morgan, *One Man's Gold Rush: A Klondike Album*. Seattle: University of Washington Press, 1967, p. 28.

2. Haskell, *Two Years in the Klondike and Alaskan Gold-Fields*, p. 63.

3. *The Travelers Record* (newsletter), November 1897, p. 6. Clouse was from Mount Pleasant, Iowa. See *CREG*, September 8, 1897, p. 5.

4. *Travelers Record*, November 1897, p. 6.

5. Inspector Charles C. Constantine, Report, July 26, 1897. Library and Archives Canada, Ottawa, Ontario, 1897. Inventory No. 13-12. Extradition Files R188-42-8-E.

6. Perrin was a meticulous man who kept precise records of his entire trip to Canada and Alaska. Besides his diary, the detective made sure to jot down every expense he incurred, from entertaining officials in Ottawa and Victoria to purchasing materials in Juneau for sealing a boat. His detailed report survives due to the records preserved by Travelers.

7. Despite amassing a large supply of goods, Knudson and Perrin were still traveling relatively light. Just two months later, the Mounties clamped down on the Alaska-Canada border and refused to let anyone in unless he (or she) had about two thousand pounds of essentials—tools, warm clothing, and most importantly, about five hundred pounds of food. Everyone was afraid of starvation during the upcoming winter and it was a legitimate fear. As it was, Dawson City barely made it through, hanging on until the first steamboat, *May West*, reached the city on June 8, 1898. See Pierre Berton, *The Klondike Fever: The Life and Death of the Last Great Gold Rush*. New York: Alfred A. Knopf, 1972, p. 284.

7. Inside, Hell Begins

1. *The Travelers Record*, November 1897, p. 6. Perrin displayed a long-standing prejudice against Indians throughout his diary. The manhunter had spent several years in Arizona and his abiding hatred of Indians could be traced back to his days when he was allegedly fighting Apaches. Interestingly, no concrete evidence survives regarding Perrin's involvement in any skirmishes, although he claimed to have several scars from Indian arrowheads.

2. Haskell, *Two Years in the Klondike*, p. 67.

3. www.skagway.com.

4. Martha Ferguson McKeown, *The Trail Led North: Mont Hawthorn's Story*. New York: Macmillan, 1948, p. 101.

5. Morgan, *One Man's Gold Rush*, pp. 35 and 47.

6. Pierre Berton, *The Klondike Fever: The Life and Death of the Last Great Gold Rush*. New York: A. A. Knopf, 1972, p. 245.

7. *The Travelers Record*, November 1897, p. 6. According to the company,

the *Record* was a monthly newsletter that circulated to libraries, hotels, barber shops, and other places. Email correspondence from Mary Beth Davidson of Travelers, April 6, 2011.

8. Adney, *The Klondike Stampede,* p. 44.

9. *The Travelers Record,* November 1897, p. 6.

10. Edwin C. Bearss, *Proposed Klondike Gold Rush National Historical Park Historic Resource Study.* Washington, D.C.: National Park Service, 1970, p. 54.

11. Archie Satterfield, *Chilkoot Pass: The Most Famous Trail in the North.* Anchorage: Alaska Northwest Publishing, 1988, p. 22.

12. *The Travelers Record,* November 1897, p. 6.

13. From about July 1897 to roughly the end of 1898, roughly thirty to forty thousand men, women, and even some children made their way to Dawson City, with thousands of these going over the Chilkoot Pass. Berton, *The Klondike Fever,* p. 417.

14. *The Travelers Record,* November 1897, p. 6.

15. R. S. Williams, "Botanical Notes on the Way to Dawson City, Alaska," *The Plant World: A Monthly Journal of Popular Botany* 2 (August, 1899), p. 178.

16. *The Travelers Record,* November 1897, p. 6.

17. Morgan, *One Man's Gold Rush,* p. 111.

18. Oakum is a type of hemp or jute fiber that is used along with tar or pitch to seal seams in boats. Wooden mallets were used to pound the oakum into the seams, making the boat waterproof. Oakum is still used in the repair or restoration of wooden hulls.

19. *The Travelers Record,* November 1897, p. 6.

20. *The Travelers Record,* November 1897, p. 6. News of the strike traveled up and down the Panhandle and there were a few reports earlier in the year about a strike, but it wasn't until July, 1897, when the *Excelsior* and *Portland* docked in San Francisco and Seattle, respectively, that Klondike Fever burst out across America.

21. *The Travelers Record,* November 1897, p. 6.

8. Down the Yukon

1. *The Travelers Record,* November 1897, p. 6. Although Perrin's diary says they were in Alaska, Caribou Crossing, now called Carcross, is in present-day Yukon Territory. At the time, this part of Canada was embroiled in a border dispute with the U.S. To the consternation of the thousands of Americans who headed to the Klondike, the gold strike was located in Canada. Of course, this meant that each prospector had to pass through

customs. A Mountie outpost was set up on the Canadian side of the pass a few months after Perrin's trip.

2. Haskell, *Two Years in the Klondike*, p. 390.

3. Melody Webb, *The Last Frontier: A History of the Yukon Basin of Canada and Alaska*. Albuquerque: New Mexico Press, 1985, p. 103. The quotation listed in her book is actually from Johan Adrian Jacobson, *Alaskan Voyage, 1881–1883: An Expedition to the Northwest Coast of America and the Bering Straits*, translated by Erna Gunther. Chicago: University of Chicago Press, 1977, p. 91.

4. Mark Zuehlke, *The Yukon Fact Book*. Vancouver, BC: Whitecap Books, 1998, p. 139.

5. *The Travelers Record*, December 1897, p. 6.

6. Haskell, p. 119.

7. *The Travelers Record*, December 1897, p. 6.

8. Miner Wait Bruce, *Alaska: Its History and Resources, Gold Fields, Routes and Scenery*. New York: G. P. Putnam's Sons, 1899, p. 156. London carried the 1895 edition of this book on his trip to Dawson City.

9. Haskell, pp. 119–20 and 122.

10. John W. Leonard, *The Gold Fields of the Klondike: Fortune Seekers' Guide to the Yukon Region of Alaska and British America*. Whitehorse, Yukon Territory: Clairedge, 1994, p. 122.

11. Jack London, "Through the Rapids on the Way to Klondike," in *Jack London's Tales of Adventure*. Garden City, NY: Hanover House, 1956, p. 40.

12. *The Travelers Record*, December 1897, p. 6.

13. *The Travelers Record*, December 1897, p. 6.

14. Berton, *The Klondike Fever*, p. 280.

15. Adney, *The Klondike Stampede*, p. 141.

16. Berton, *The Klondike Fever*, p. 281.

17. *The Travelers Record*, December 1897, p. 6.

18. http://www.virtualmuseum.ca/pm.id.

19. The town of Ogilvie, Yukon Territory, and the Ogilvie Mountains are named for this humble Canadian civil servant.

20. Both Ogilvie and Perrin admired each other's professionalism and struck up a friendship immediately.

21. See Berton, *The Klondike Fever*, p. 172, and Adney, *The Klondike Stampede*, pp. 162–63.

22. *The Travelers Record*, January, 1898, p. 6.

23. *The Travelers Record*, January, 1898, p. 6.

24. William Ogilvie, *Early Days on the Yukon: And the Story of its Gold Finds*.

Whitehorse, Yukon Territory: Wolf Creek Books, 2002, p. 279. In addition to their friendship, there is evidence that Ogilvie and Perrin were Masons. See the following web site: http://freemasonry.bcy.ca/biography/ogilvie_w/ogilvie_w.html.

25. Even today, because of its remote location, the cost of goods in the Yukon and Alaska is typically much higher than in the Lower 48. There are still no rail lines from the continental U.S. and few highways that serve this part of the world.

26. *The Travelers Record*, January, 1898, p. 6.

27. Perrin later told a reporter that he saw some miners pan sawdust from a barroom floor. They cleared about eleven dollars in gold dust. See *Cedar Rapids Evening Gazette,* September 2, 1897, p. 5.

28. Ogilvie, p. 279.

29. *The Travelers Record*, January, 1898, p. 6. The number of miles that Perrin said he traveled seems to be a trifle optimistic.

30. Constantine was already aware of the Novak case. A letter dated May 2, 1897, was sent from Commissioner Lawrence W. Herchmer of the NWMP's Regina headquarters urging Inspector Constantine to render "any assistance you can" to D. L. Clouse, who at that time was the only Thiel agent in Alaska. Letter from Library and Archives Canada, Reference Number R196-48-2-E, File number 169-1897.

31. *The Travelers Record*, January 1898, p. 6.

32. *The Travelers Record*, January 1898, p. 6.

33. *State* v. *Novak*, p. 828.

34. *State* v. *Novak*, p. 828. There are three different accounts of Novak's capture. Besides the version here, the most colorful one has Novak playing violin in a dance hall when Perrin stopped him in mid-song and arrested him. The third story—and one that Perrin told his friend Ogilvie—was that the detective was suspicious of a certain tent where three men lived. One man did not go out until it was twilight, and pulled his cap down over his face so that he could disguise himself, which, the story goes, was a tipoff. The actual description of the arrest here is taken from Perrin's testimony under oath at Novak's trial. The detective's diary contains virtually the same details as he stated in court.

35. *State* v. *Novak*, p. 829.

36. *CREG*, September 2, 1897, p. 5.

37. *State* v. *Novak*, p. 833.

38. Constantine, see note 30.

39. *State* v. *Novak*, p. 839. Interestingly, the Dawson City Museum has several thousand documents from this time period. A census of Dawson City from 1901, which was a compilation of police records, government indexes, and other sources from before that time as well, lists a "Frank Novak, American born in Iowa." Under occupation, it listed him as a "Criminal/Gambler."

40. Constantine. See note 34.

41. *State* v. *Novak*, p. 840. Mathew Robinson Gowler was born in 1871 and had served in the Klondike for several years. He "took free discharge" on July 15, 1897, due in part to a leg injury he suffered in the Yukon. See www .rcmpgraves.com/database/search.html.

42. *The Travelers Record*, January 1898, p. 6.

43. *CREG*, September 2, 1897, p. 5.

44. *The Travelers Record*, February, 1898, p. 7.

45. *The Travelers Record*, February, 1898, p. 7.

46. *The Travelers Record*, February, 1898, p. 7 and *CREG*, September 2, 1897, p. 5. Novak was always unlucky in card games. He was a consistent loser wherever he played and was an especially bad poker player, according to Lu Gong, the Chinese gambler who had traveled with Novak from Seattle to Juneau.

47. Ogilvie, p. 281.

48. Ogilvie, p. 281.

49. *The Travelers Record,* February, 1898, p. 7.

50. Ogilvie, p. 282.

51. Ogilve, pp. 282-83.

9. The Long Journey Home

1. *The Travelers Record*, February, 1898, p. 7.

2. Berton, *The Klondike Fever*, p. 122.

3. *The Travelers Record*, February, 1898, p. 7.

4. See http://www.vintagephoto.tv/patents.html. For "Kodak Fiends," *CRDR*, September 2, 1897, p. 5.

5. The popular Pocket Kodak was released in 1895 and was one of the first small and inexpensive cameras sold in America. http://www.vintagephoto .tv/patents.html.

6. *CREG*, September 2, 1897, p. 1.

7. Benjamin F. Shambaugh, *Biographies and Portraits of Progressive Men of Iowa.* Des Moines: Conaway & Shaw, 1899, vol. 2, pp. 395–96.

8. *CRDR*, September 2, 1897, p. 5.

10. Setting the Stage

1. *DMDN,* July 14, 1897, p. 3.

2. *Hull Index,* July 16, 1897, p. 6.

3. *VE,* March 9, 1897, p. 4.

4. *CREG,* August 28, 1897, p. 5. The *Gazette*'s first story on Novak's arrest was in the previous day's edition.

5. *CREG,* August 28, 1897, p. 5.

6. *CREG,* August 27, 1897, p. 1.

7. *CRDR,* August 28, 1897, p. 5.

8. *Oswego Daily Palladium,* August 28, 1897, p. 1.

9. *CRWG,* September 1, 1897, p. 3.

10. *CRDR,* August 28, 1897, p. 5.

11. *WDC,* August 30, 1897, p. 3. Dr. H. H. Holmes and Harry Hayward were two notorious murderers during the last decade of the nineteenth century. For a detailed description of serial killer Holmes, see Erik Larson's riveting book, *The Devil in the White City: Murder, Magic and Madness at the Fair That Changed America.* New York: Vintage Books, 2004. For Hayward, see Walter N. Trenerry's account of the case in *Murder in Minnesota: A Collection of True Cases,* St. Paul: Minnesota Historical Society, 1985.

12. *CRDT,* August 28, 1897, p. 1.

13. *Daily Iowa Capital (DIC),* August 28, 1897, p. 2.

14. *WDC,* August 30, 1897, p. 1.

15. *CRWG,* September 1, 1897, p. 3.

16. *CREG,* September 2, 1897, p. 1.

17. *Dubuque Herald,* September 4, 1897, p. 4.

18. *VE,* September 3, 1897, p. 5.

19. *CREG,* September 2, 1897, p. 1.

20. *State* v. *Novak,* p. 877.

21. Lukas, *Big Trouble,* p. 86.

22. *Butler County News,* December 2, 1897, p. 1.

23. John W. Tobin, *With No Intention . . . and Other Stories.* Cedar Rapids, IA: Laurance Press Company, 1979, p. 135. Thoreau's observation was from his *Journal,* November 11, 1850.

24. *State* v. *Novak,* p. 941.

25. www.associatepublisher.com/e/h/ho/horace_boies.html.

26. John C. Hartman, *History of Black Hawk County, Iowa and its People.* Chicago: S. J. Clarke Publishing, 1915, vol. 2, p. 138.

27. *WDC,* April 17, 1903, p. 1.

28. *Waterloo Evening Courier (WEC),* September 15, 1897, p. 10.

29. *CRDR*, September 9, 1897, p. 1. *Qui vive* is a Latin term that means "on the alert" or "on guard."

30. *CRDR*, September 9, 1897, p. 1.

31. *New York Times (NYT)*, June 19, 1904, p. 28.

32. Jean Newland Swailes, comp. *Belle Plaine Centennial History Book*. Belle Plaine, IA: Belle Plaine Century Corporation, 1962, p. 38.

33. Ransom, *Pioneer Recollections*, p. 178.

34. *CREG*, August 21, 1912, p. 4.

35. *Butler County News*, quoted in the *Vinton Eagle*, December 24, 1897, p. 8.

36. *CREG*, August 21, 1912, p. 4.

37. *Proceedings of the Twenty-Eighth Annual Session of the Iowa State Bar Association, Held at Sioux City, Iowa, June 22 and 23, 1922*. Des Moines: Iowa State Bar Association, 1922. Also, see *Butler County News*, December 9, 1897, p. 4.

38. *CREG*, September 10, 1897, p. 6. Billy Wilhelm's account of his meeting with Novak was not the only time that the spiked-whiskey story would surface. During the trial, Dr. Woitishek, a Cedar Rapids druggist, would testify that Novak had asked him about morphine dosages and how many grains would kill a man. See *State* v. *Novak*, p. 1056. Although there is no firm evidence as to what was in this envelope or even if it ever existed, I believe (as did Tobin and Milner) that the substance referred to was morphine and have cited court testimony to support this theory.

39. *CRDR*, February 12, 1897, p. 5.

40. *VE*, September 14, 1897, p. 4.

41. *VE*, September 17, 1897, p. 4.

42. *DIC*, September 10, 1897, p. 3.

43. *CREG*, September 18, 1897, p. 8.

44. *CREG*, September 22, 1897, p. 8.

45. *CRDR*, September 24, 1897, p. 1.

46. *CREG*, September 23, 1897, p. 3.

47. *CREG*, September 24, 1897, p. 2.

48. *VE*, September 28, 1897, p. 1.

49. *VE*, September 28, 1897, p. 1.

50. *CRDR*, September 25, 1897, p. 1.

11. Orange Pumpkins and Yellow Journalism

1. *CREG*, October 20, 1897, p. 4.

2. John Henry Wigmore, comp., *The Principles of Judicial Proof, As Given by Logic, Psychology and General Experience and Illustrated in Judicial Trials*. Boston: Little Brown and Company, 1913, p. 827. Also, see Robert Loerzel,

Alchemy of Bones: Chicago's Luetgert Murder Case of 1897, Urbana: University of Illinois Press, 2003, a comprehensive account of the Luetgert case. Evidence also exists that like Novak, Luetgert was a ladies' man and may have had an affair with his wife's cousin, Mary Siemering.

3. Wigmore, *The Principles of Judicial Proof,* p. 828.

4. Loerzel, *Alchemy of Bones,* p. 67.

5. Wigmore, p. 828.

6. Loerzel, p. 253.

7. Loerzel, p. 279.

8. *VE,* November 2, 1897, p. 5.

9. Correspondence from M. J. Tobin to Dr. J. B. Lewis, of Travelers, October 20, 1897.

10. *VE,* October 1, 1897, p. 4. The interview originally appeared in the *Marshalltown Statesman-Press.*

11. *State* v. *Novak,* p. 858.

12. *VE,* October 12, 1897, p. 4. A portion of this article was originally published in the *Marshalltown Evening Times-Republican.*

13. *VE,* October 1, 1897, p. 4.

12. Inside the Courthouse

1. The courthouse was built in 1856 at a cost of roughly one hundred fifty thousand dollars. Although the structure was three stories high and had some interesting features—a one-hundred-twelve-foot tower and a fifteen-hundred-pound bell, conditions inside were primitive at best. See www.bentoncountyiowa.com/quality_of_life/attractions.html.

2. *METR,* November 10, 1897, p. 1.

3. *VE,* November 30, 1897, p. 2.

4. *CREG,* November 10, 1897, p. 6.

5. *CRDR,* November 10, 1897, p. 1.

6. *Portrait and Biographical Album of Benton County, Iowa, Containing Full Page Portraits and Biographical Sketches of Prominent and Representative Citizens of the County, Together With Portraits and Biographies of All the Governors of Iowa and of the Presidents of the United States.* Chicago: Chapman Brothers, 1887, p. 186.

7. *Proceedings of the Iowa State Bar Association's Third Annual Meeting, Held at Cedar Rapids, Iowa, July 7 and 8th, 1897.* Des Moines: Kenyon Printing & Manufacturing, 1898, p. 12.

8. Women could be jurors in 1920, after the passage of the nineteenth

amendment. In some states, however, women would not be seated in juries until dozens of years afterward.

9. *CREG*, November 10, 1897, p. 6.
10. *CRDR*, November 11, 1897, p. 1.
11. *VE*, November 19, 1897, p. 1.
12. *CREG*, November 11, 1897, p. 1.
13. *CREG*, November 12, 1897, p. 1.
14. *CREG*, November 10, 1897, p. 2.
15. *State* v. *Novak,* pp. 275–76.
16. *Testimony,* p. 5.
17. *Testimony,* p. 1.
18. *Testimony,* pp. 7–8.
19. *Testimony,* pp. 294–95.
20. *VE*, November 12, 1897, p. 12.
21. *State* v. *Novak,* p. 295.
22. *State* v. *Novak,* pp. 296–97.
23. *State* v. *Novak,* pp. 298, 301.
24. *State* v. *Novak,* p. 302.
25. *State* v. *Novak,* p. 303.
26. *State* v. *Novak,* p. 306.
27. *State* v. *Novak,* p. 318.

13. Point and Counterpoint

1. *State* v. *Novak,* p. 462. Also see *State* v. *Novak,* p. 612ff. regarding the handwriting samples.

2. *State* v. *Novak,* p. 488. Ney also touched on this point in his opening argument.

3. *CREG*, November 12, 1897, p. 3.
4. *WDC*, November 12, 1897, p. 12.
5. Ransom, *Pioneer Recollections,* p. 141.
6. *State* v. *Novak,* pp. 638 and 635.
7. *State* v. *Novak,* p. 640.
8. *State* v. *Novak,* p. 641.
9. *METR*, November 13, 1897, p. 8.
10. *CREG*, November 16, 1897, p. 1.
11. *State* v. *Novak,* pp. 970 and 976–77.
12. *State* v. *Novak,* pp. 725 and 807.
13. *State* v. *Novak,* p. 811.

14. "Noose," *METR*, November 12, 1897, p. 1; "Chain," *CREG*, November 12, 1897, p. 1.

15. *METR*, November, 11, 1897, p. 1.

16. *CREG*, November 12, 1897, p. 1.

17. *CRDR*, November 13, 1897, p. 1.

18. *State* v. *Novak*, p. 858. Perrin later detailed this discussion in *The Travelers Record*, January 1898, p. 7.

19. *State* v. *Novak*, p. 853.

20. *State* v. *Novak*, p. 867.

21. For Perrin's legal authority in Canada, see Charles C. Constantine, *Report to E. L. Newcombe, Deputy Minister of Justice, Ottawa*, July 26, 1897. Library and Archives Canada, Extradition Files R188-42-8-E, 1897 Inventory No. 13-12, Ref. No. RG13-A-5, vol. 989.

22. *State* v. *Novak*, p. 884. For Milner's response, see *WDC*, November 15, 1897, p. 1. Milner's remark is not in the court transcript.

23. *METR*, November 15, 1897, p. 1.

24. *CREG*, November 15, 1897, p. 1.

25. *WDC*, November 15, 1897, p. 1.

26. *WDC*, November 15, 1897, p. 1.

27. *State* v. *Novak*, pp. 834–35.

28. *State* v. *Novak*, p. 893.

29. *State* v. *Novak*, p. 903.

30. *CREG*, November 16, 1897, p. 1.

31. *CREG*, November 16, 1897, p. 3.

32. *CREG*, November 18, 1897, p. 1. This quotation mirrors what Novak told Edward Murray's father when the old man visited him in jail. Novak also used a phrase similar to "things that could not be understood" when he spoke with a reporter on the train back to Iowa. The meaning of these words would soon become apparent once Milner began calling defense witnesses.

33. *VE*, November 19, 1897, p. 8.

34. *State* v. *Novak*, p. 1464.

35. *State* v. *Novak*, p. 1493.

36. *State* v. *Novak*, pp. 1508–9.

37. *Dura mater* is the outermost of the three membranes of the brain and spinal cord. This would support the prosecution's view that Murray may have died from a blow to the head.

38. *CRDR*, November 20, 1897, p. 1.

39. *WDC*, November 24, 1897, p. 2.

14. The Summing Up and Verdict

1. *CRDR*, November 21, 1897, p. 1.
2. *CRDR*, November 21, 1897, p. 1.
3. *CREG*, November 20, 1897, p. 3.
4. *CREG*, November 20, 1897, p. 3.
5. *Cedar Rapids Sunday Republican*, November 21, 1897, p. 3.
6. *CREG*, November 22, 1897, p. 1.
7. *CREG*, November 20, 1897, p. 7. It should be noted that some of the summation arguments were not included in the court stenographer's transcript of the case. Some quotations from prosecuting and defense attorneys that appear here are taken from newspaper reports of the trial.
8. CREG, November 22, 1897, p. 1.
9. *Davenport Daily Leader*, November 22, 1897, p. 1.
10. *CRDR*, November 23, 1897, p. 1.
11. *VE*, November 23, 1897, p. 8.
12. *VE*, November 23, 1897, p. 8.
13. *VE*, November 23, 1897, p. 8. Milner's choice of this word was more than a little clever. The attorney was smart enough to know that by legal definition, hearsay could directly apply to Perrin's testimony, as the detective's account was based on the fact that Perrin had not only informed Tobin and Sheriff Metcalf of Novak's "confession" before the grand jury met, but also talked to reporters from the *Gazette*, which ran his diary in October detailing information on Novak's arrest. This was also part of Milner's continued attack on Perrin, whom he sarcastically referred to as Cassius Caesar Perrin, changing the detective's middle name deliberately in an attempt to link his betrayal of Novak's trust to Julius Caesar's betrayal by his friend Cassius. Ironically, throughout his summary arguments, Milner did not disagree with Perrin's account of the alleged spiked whiskey bottle. The attorney wanted to keep that seed firmly planted in the minds of the jurors.
14. *VE*, November 23, 1897, p. 8.
15. *State* v. *Novak*, pp. 1605–6.
16. *CRDR*, November 25, 1897, p. 5.
17. *CREG*, November 24, 1897, p. 1.
18. *State* v. *Novak*, pp. 1608–9.
19. *State* v. *Novak*, p. 1610.
20. *CREG*, November 24, 1897, p. 1.
21. *CREG*, November 24, 1897, p. 1.

15. After the Verdict

1. *Burlington Hawk-Eye*, November 24, 1897, p. 2.

2. In a letter dated January 14, 1971, to Dr. William Petersen of the State Historical Society of Iowa, John W. Tobin wrote that his father was convinced one of the jurors had been bribed. "[M. J. Tobin] always thought so, because the eleven other jurors told him they thought so. Through the entire deliberation of the jury this one juror merely sat mute, shaking his head and voting not guilty but not once stating one reason for his position. He held out alone for a very long time before finally yielding." According to the *Cedar Rapids Evening Gazette (CREG)* of November 24, 1897, p. 1, this dissenting juror was Nels Degn, who "would stand out until the case would result in a mistrial." John W. Tobin Papers, Box 7, Special Collections Department, University of Iowa Libraries, Iowa City, Iowa.

3. The two thick volumes of court testimony reside in the State Historical Society of Iowa in Iowa City. In 1898, Tom Milner requested that McKinnon's notes be typed and bound for the appeal process. The cost of doing so was about four hundred dollars and was paid for by the state. See *CREG*, March 30, 1898, p. 2.

4. *CREG*, November 24, 1897, p. 1.

5. *New York Times (NYT)*, November 24, 1897, p. 5.

6. Mark Twain, *Roughing It.* Berkeley and Los Angeles: University of California Press, 1972, p. 309.

7. All of these summary quotes were taken from the *Vinton Eagle (VE)*, November 30, 1897, p. 2.

8. *CRDR*, November 25, 1897, p. 4.

9. These newspaper quotations appeared in the *Vinton Eagle*, November 30, 1897, p. 2.

10. John W. Tobin Papers, University of Iowa Libraries.

11. *Belle Plaine Union*, November 25, 1897, p. 3.

12. *CRDR*, November 30, 1897, p. 1.

13. *CREG*, December 13, 1897, p. 8.

14. *VE*, December 7, 1897, p. 1.

15. *DMDN*, November 10, 1897, p. 8.

16. *CREG*, November 26, 1897, p. 5. The rival *Daily Republican* would also complain about the sheriff's "extreme leniency" in his treatment of Novak. See *CRDR*, December 31, 1897, p. 1.

17. Correspondence from M. J. Tobin to G. H. Thiel, April 16, 1898.

18. Correspondence from Dr. J. B. Lewis to U.S. Casualty Co., November 11, 1897.

19. Correspondence from M. N. McLaren to Dr. J. B. Lewis of Travelers, October 28, 1897.

20. Correspondence from Andrew Van Wormer to Dr. J. B. Lewis of Travelers, March 3, 1897. Also, see correspondence from Van Wormer to Lewis, December 11, 1897. In retrospect, Van Wormer was either perspicacious or just plain lucky regarding the tremendous amount of expense incurred in the case. Of course, no one knew in March that Novak was on his way to the Klondike, but the case was not without precedence in tracking fugitives. In fact, Red Perrin had no doubt incurred considerable expense when he chased and assisted in the arrest of Kit Larrabee in Monterrey, Mexico, the year before. It's also possible that Van Wormer may have known about Larrabee and the high costs incurred in that case.

21. The behavior of many of the women who attended the trial helped cement Novak's image as a ladies' man. He had received many gifts from women during his stay in the Vinton jail. In a humorous story, the *Cedar Rapids Weekly Gazette* ran an article in which a number of women had expressed their indignation that they were portrayed as overly sympathetic to the prisoner. While it was true that most of the females in the room appeared not to show any affection for the accused man, the paper added, nevertheless, "the fact remains that Judge Burnham was compelled to talk plainly to several women who asked permission to bring flowers to the courtroom to place upon the table of the prisoner and his counsel." *CRWG*, December 1, 1897, p. 9.

22. *Dubuque Herald*, December 5, 1897, p. 1.

23. *CREG*, December 6, 1897, p. 6.

24. *VE*, December 7, 1897, p. 8.

25. *WDC*, December 6, 1897, p. 1. According to a note from Ramesh Nyberg, a retired Miami-Dade, Florida, police detective, "Defendants make those statements because their defense attorneys tell them they should." Novak's remarks were similar to ones made during the O. J. Simpson trial, when Simpson vowed to find the killer of his wife and Ron Goldman. Email from Ramesh Nyberg, January 13, 2010.

26. *CREG*, December 6, 1897, p. 6.

27. *CREG*, December 6, 1897, p. 6.

28. *CREG*, December 8, 1897, p. 3.

29. *CREG*, December 9, 1897, p. 3.

30. *CREG*, December 10, 1897, p. 6.

31. *VE*, December 14, 1897, p. 4.

32. See A. A. Dornfeld, Tom Vickerman, and Archibald Leckie's *"Hello Sweetheart, Get Me Rewrite!" The Story of the City News Bureau of Chicago.* Chi-

cago: Academy Chicago Publishers, 1988. The bureau's origins can be traced back to 1890.

33. *CREG*, February 12, 1898, p. 5.

34. William Ogilvie, *Early Days on the Yukon*. Whitehorse, Yukon Territory: Wolf Creek Books, 2002, p. 282.

35. *CRDR*, December 16, 1897, p. 1.

36. *VE*, December 31, 1897, p. 4.

37. Email from Dick Snavely, January 29, 2010. The nickname of "the Colony" appears frequently in the *Anamosa Prison Press*. Dick is a retired prison psychologist at Anamosa State Penitentiary and the volunteer director of the Anamosa State Penitentiary Museum.

38. Invented in 1879 by a Frenchman named Alphonse Bertillon, this method of classification consisted of five measurements: head length, head breadth, length of the middle finger, length of the left foot, and length of the "cubit"—the forearm from the elbow to the tip of the middle finger. The standard photograph or mug shot was also part of this system. After a few more years, the Bertillon system would be replaced by the use of fingerprints as a primary form of identification. See www.nlm.nih.gov/visibleproofs /galleries/technologies/bertillon.html.

39. *CREG*, December 31, 1897, p. 6. The entry notes detailing Novak's physical appearance are from the Anamosa Penitentiary Records.

16. Life in the Colony

1. The name was changed in 1884 from the Additional Penitentiary to Anamosa State Penitentiary.

2. Joyce McKay, "Reforming Prisoners and Prisons: Iowa's State Prisons— The First Hundred Years." *Annals of Iowa* 60.2 (2001), p. 147.

3. www.asphistory.com/HTM/imrtime.html.

4. *Second Biennial Report of the Board of Control of the State of Iowa for the Biennial Period Ending June 30, 1901*. Des Moines: B. Murphy, 1901, p. 925. The ratio of prisoners to guards was supposed to be 8 to 1 at Anamosa and 10 to 1 at Fort Madison. See *Legislative Documents Submitted to the Twenty-Ninth General Assembly of the State of Iowa, Which Convened at Des Moines January 13, 1902*. Des Moines: B. Murphy, 1902, pp. 66–67.

5. R. M. Corbit, ed., *History of Jones County Iowa, Past and Present*. Chicago: S. J. Clarke Publishing Company, 1910, vol. 1, p. 344. The section on Anamosa was written by Judge H. M. Remley and originally appeared in the *Bulletin of Iowa Institutions* 3 (January 1901). It was updated by Clark Beems, clerk of the Anamosa Reformatory.

6. *Anamosa Prison Press,* January 14, 1905, p. 5.

7. David J. Rothman, *The Discovery of the Asylum: Social Order and Disorder in the New Republic.* Boston: Little, Brown, 1971, p. 103.

8. Rothman, pp. 82–83.

9. www.correctionhistory.org/html/chronicle/state/html//nyprison.

10. McKay, *Reforming Prisoners and Prisons,* p. 144. Information on bread and water in solitary was from Dick Snavely in an email dated July 3, 2012.

11. www.asphistory.com/HTM/imrtime.html. According to an email from Janice Pearson, a volunteer at the Anamosa State Penitentiary Museum, some prisoners were punished in solitary. One particularly vicious guard was a man named Passwater. This sadist once left a man hanging from the rings for forty-eight straight hours. Pearson noted that "Passwater's punishments were frequent and the solitaries were constantly full." Email correspondence from Janice Pearson, November 29, 2012.

12. Dellis Swartzendruber, *A History of the Anamosa State Penitentiary.* Anamosa, IA: IPI Graphic Arts Shop, 2006, p. 35. The quotation is from one of Warden Madden's biennial reports. The source of the quote was not cited by Swartzendruber.

13. www.ushistory.org/us/26d/asp.

14. www.answers.com/topic/prisons-and-prison-reform.

15. John W. Roberts, *Reform and Retribution: An Illustrated History of American Prisons.* Baltimore: United Book Press, 1997, pp. 32–37.

16. Laura Bufano Edge, *Locked Up: A History of the U. S. Prison System.* Minneapolis: Twenty-First Century Books, 2009, pp. 27 and 28.

17. Roberts, *Reform and Retribution,* p. 63.

18. *Cedar Rapids Evening Gazette (CREG),* January 1, 1898, p. 1.

19. Correspondence from Jordan Holm (inmate #6016946) to his brother Jason, April 20, 2005. www.freejordan.org.

20. McKay, *Reforming Prisoners and Prisons,* p. 147.

21. *CREG,* January 1, 1898, p. 2.

22. *CREG,* January 1, 1898, p. 2.

23. *Fort Wayne (IN) News,* January 11, 1898, p. 1.

24. *Humboldt County Independent,* January 27, 1898, p. 1.

25. *Perry Daily Chief,* February 18, 1898, p. 1. Also, see *Des Moines Daily News (DMDN),* February 17, 1898, p. 2.

26. *Algona Courier,* March 4, 1898, p. 6.

27. Swartzendruber, pp. 35 and 38.

28. Swartzendruber, p. 39.

29. Swartzendruber, pp. 38–39. Dick Snavely noted that the third-grade prisoners also received much less tobacco than first-class ones. He added

that by being confined to their cells, they received less to eat than first-class prisoners (Email correspondence from Dick Snavely, July 3, 2012). According to recollections from a guard named B. G. Rees in 1907, a first-grade prisoner received ten cents' worth of tobacco a week; second-grade men received five cents of tobacco per week, while third-grade prisoners went to "the hole" if they were caught with any tobacco. Rees also noted that when a prisoner came in at second grade, he received nine credit marks a month. To move up to first grade, one had to acquire fifty credit marks out of a possible fifty-four. If a prisoner received three demerit points in any thirty-day period, he would go back a grade. Thanks to Steve Wendl's web site, www .asphistory.com/1907.html, for this information.

30. Swartzendruber, p. 39. Hunter's quote apparently came from a prison Board of Control meeting.

31. Correspondence from Dick Snavely, March 9, 2007. The information is from the penitentiary's records. It is not known whether Hunter's system of rings in solitary was used on Novak.

32. *CREG*, July 23, 1898, p. 6. The term "small boy" goes back many years, possibly centuries. "Small boy" refers to one of the lowest rungs of an apprenticeship. Typically, a small boy was usually a nine-to-eleven-year old who was apprenticed to a master craftsman.

33. *CREG*, July 23, 1898, p. 6.

34. *Cedar Rapids Daily Republican (CRDR)*, August 31, 1898, p. 6. The blurb in the *Republican* was taken from the *Belle Plaine Union*, Tom Milner's hometown paper.

35. *CREG*, July 23, 1898, p. 6.

36. *Waterloo Daily Courier (WDC)*, October 24, 1898, p. 1.

37. *Algona Courier*, October 28, 1898, p. 6.

38. *Algona Upper Des Moines*, February 8, 1899, p. 4.

39. Philip Barton Key was the son of Francis Scott Key, composer of "The Star-Spangled Banner." For the story of Dan Sickles, see www.civilwarhome .com/sicklesbio.html.

40. *Des Moines Daily News (DMDN)*, May 26, 1899, p. 1.

41. John Tobin, M. J. Tobin's son, and himself a well-known judge, explained: "The Fifth Amendment to the Constitution of the United States, protecting an accused from admissions against his interest, was given careful consideration by the trial judge. The Supreme Court affirmed the instructions of the Trial Court. It further held that the circumstances of Novak's admissions were voluntarily made by him and were such that (Red)

Perrin's testimony of those admissions was properly received in evidence. The now famous Miranda Rule regarding 'the right to remain silent' was not to be expressly enunciated for another 67 years. But in 1899 the rights of an accused were given the careful protection which the Miranda doctrine now requires." *Palimpsest* 51.10 (October 1970), p. 427.

17. The Redemption Dance

1. *CREG,* October 19, 1901, p. 8.

2. The plaid pattern indicated a second-class prisoner. This was the classification that all Anamosa inmates received when they arrived.

3. John Bellew was sentenced to life imprisonment in 1894 for the first-degree murder of Joe Tiffany, in Fort Dodge, Iowa. In a case that was eerily similar to Novak's, the evidence was almost entirely circumstantial. Bellew fled and was tracked by detectives in Chicago. However, his defense was that he and Tiffany were both drunk and that Tiffany drank from a whiskey bottle. When apprehended, Bellew gave an alias, saying he was Jack Woods. At his hearing, Bellew told the judge that the whiskey they drank must have been spiked and that was what killed Joe Tiffany.

4. *Dubuque Telegraph-Herald*, April 24, 1902, p. 5. When Bellew was released, a rumor surfaced that he was engaged to a daughter of one of the Anamosa guards, but there appears to be no evidence to support this story.

5. According to Dick Snavely, "I suspect the prison trained lifers for (trades) like photography, since they would be around for a long time. Prison Industries still like to hire long termers for their shop jobs for that very reason." Email correspondence, May 12, 2010.

6. *Anamosa Prison Press (APP),* February 7, 1903, p. 6.

7. *APP,* February 28, 1903, p. 6.

8. *APP,* March 14, 1903, p. 6.

9. Susan Fulton Welty, *Look Up and Hope! A Biography of Maud Ballington Booth*. New York: Thomas Nelson, 1961, p. 132.

10. In her autobiography, *After Prison–What?* Booth wrote about the transformative experience she had at Sing Sing Prison in 1896. This led to her founding of the VPL. Today, the Volunteers of America, another organization that Booth founded, "maintains similar programs based on [her] ideas and programs." http://learningtogive.org/papers/paper213.html.

11. Booth had made a previous trip to Anamosa State Penitentiary in 1903. Novak was chairman of the VPL chapter at that time.

12. *Waterloo Daily Reporter*, March 27, 1903, p. 1. Novak's father would wind up spending almost everything he had in an effort to free his son and was still paying Frank's legal fees.

13. *WDR*, August 11, 1904, p. 2. Burnham's letter has apparently not survived. There is no copy of it in Novak's pardon file at the State Historical Society of Iowa in Des Moines. However, Burnham did write a letter to Governor Cummins in January, 1903, stating that "I cannot see any reason for extending executive clemency to this man. . . . I believe him to be guilty of cold blooded, premeditated murder." See *Cedar Rapids Daily Republican,* September 27, 1911, p. 9.

14. *Des Moines Daily Capital,* August 12, 1904, p. 5.

15. Correspondence from M. J. Tobin to B. W. Garrett, January 26, 1903. Cited in *Cedar Rapids Daily Republican*, September 27, 1911, p. 9.

16. Correspondence from F. W. Faulkes to Governor A. B. Cummins, January 14, 1903. State Historical Society of Iowa (Des Moines), Governor's Criminal Correspondence, 1838–1910, file folders on Frank Novak.

17. *CRDR,* August 13, 1904, p. 2.

18. *CRDR,* August 13, 1904, p. 2.

19. *CREG,* July 29, 1899, p. 1. The headline for this article was succinct: "His Mind Unhinged."

20. *Iowa State Reporter,* March 15, 1904, p. 2.

21. *APP*, May 21, 1904, p. 6.

22. *APP*, November 26, 1904, p. 1.

23. *METR*, September 5, 1911, p. 8.

24. *APP*, December 23, 1905, p. 6.

25. State Historical Society of Iowa, Des Moines, Governor's Criminal Correspondence.

26. *WDC,* May 21, 1907, p. 7.

27. *CRDR,* May 18, 1907, p. 5. Czolgosz was electrocuted on October 29, 1901.

28. *Waterloo Semi-Weekly Reporter,* May 21, 1907, p. 3.

18. Novak's Second Disappearing Act

1. *Iowa: A Guide to the Hawkeye State,* p. 538. Interestingly, although Fort Madison has always referred to itself as the oldest prison west of the Mississippi, that claim appears to be incorrect. The Missouri State Penitentiary, located in Jefferson City, opened its gates about three years earlier, in March, 1836. The prison closed in 2004 so Fort Madison is *currently* the oldest prison west of the Mississippi.

2. *The History of Lee County, Iowa, Containing A History of the County, its Cities, Towns, Etc.* Chicago: Western Historical Company, 1879, p. 194.

3. Corbit, *History of Jones County Iowa*, p. 341. For the description of prisoners in the warden's cellar, see Bob Neese, *Prison Exposures, First Photographs Inside Prison by a Convict*. Philadelphia: Chilton Company, 1959, p. 5. Information on the first cellblock completion is from an online article in the *Burlington Hawkeye*, July 20, 2007, "Legislative Committee Tours Iowa State Penitentiary," by Nicholas Bergin.

4. Bob Neese, *Prison Day by Day*. Fort Madison, IA: Penal Press, 1957, pp. 43 and 85.

5. Neese, *Prison Day by Day*, p. 15. Just before a prison inspection in 1911 or 1912, these old wooden buckets were replaced by steel ones. See George Cosson, M. A. Roberts, and Farley Sheldon, *The Report of the Committee Appointed to Investigate the Character of the Warden and the General Management of the Iowa Penitentiary at Fort Madison together with A Report Concerning the Jail System of Iowa with Recommendations*. Des Moines: Emory H. English, 1912, p. 11.

6. Federal Writers' Project of the Works Progress Administration for the State of Iowa, p. 113.

7. *Journal of the House of Representatives of the Thirteenth General Assembly of the State of Iowa, Which Convened at the Capitol in Des Moines, Iowa, January 10, 1870*, p. 355. Heisey left Fort Madison in 1872 and became involved in the construction of the new penitentiary at Anamosa, where he served as warden from 1873 to 1876.

8. Edward M. Roberts, *Illustrated Fort Madison: A Volume Devoted to the Interests of Fort Madison, Iowa*. Fort Madison, IA: Roberts and Roberts, 1896, p. 70.

9. Federal Writers' Project of the Works Progress Administration for the State of Iowa, p. 113.

10. *Daily Iowa Capital*, June 5, 1897, p. 5.

11. J. W. Campbell, "Fragmentary History of the Fort Madison Penitentiary," *Bulletin of Iowa Institutions* 2.2 (April 1900), pp. 172–73.

12. Cosson et al., p. 16.

13. *Adams County Union*, October 4, 1894, p. 1.

14. Cosson et al., p. 11. The original source is *Journal of the Senate of the Thirty-first General Assembly of the State of Iowa*. Des Moines: Bernard Murphy, 1906, p. 84.

15. *Vinton Eagle (VE)*, December 1, 1908, Section 3, p. 1.

16. Correspondence from Governor Carroll to David Brant, September 8, 1910, State Historical Society of Iowa, Des Moines, Governor's Criminal Correspondence file.

17. *VE,* December 1, 1910, Section 3, p. 1.

18. *Iowa City Citizen,* December 2, 1908, p. 4.

19. *Cedar Rapids Evening Gazette (CREG),* June 12, 1908, p. 16.

20. Correspondence from Brant to Carroll, September 3, 1910, State Historical Society of Iowa, Des Moines, Governors Criminal Correspondence file.

21. Correspondence from Brant to Carroll, September 3, 1910.

22. Correspondence from Carroll to Brant, September 8, 1910.

23. Correspondence from Carroll to Brant, November 16, 1910.

24. The description of Brant's character is from *The Annals of Iowa: A Historical Quarterly.* Volume 12, 3rd series. 1915–1921. Edited by Edgar R. Harlan, curator. Des Moines: The Historical Department of Iowa, p. 391.

25. *Algona Courier,* June 23, 1911, p. 2.

26. *CREG,* August 22, 1911, p. 2.

27. *DMDN,* July 6, 1906, p. 1.

28. McNamara's first article ran on July 18, 1911, and was given a prominent position above the fold.

29. *DMDN,* July 20, 1911, p. 2.

30. *DMDN,* July 21, 1911, p. 3. Of course, Novak was not in a roadhouse playing a violin when he was arrested, according to Perrin.

31. *DMDN,* July 21, 1911, p. 3.

32. *Waterloo Reporter,* September 5, 1911, p. 2.

33. *CRDR,* September 27, 1911, p. 9. Although his name was never linked to this anonymous writer, one suspects that it was probably M. J. Tobin. Perhaps only Tobin, with his extensive knowledge of the case and the appeal, could have written such an eloquent and concise summation of the case.

34. *VE,* September 8, 1911, p. 6. His sighting in Des Moines was mentioned in *CRDR,* September 20, 1911, p. 7. There is no evidence that Novak ever established a photography business or any other business in Cedar Rapids after he was released from Fort Madison. One could speculate from a few newspaper ads cited below that he was trying to earn a living by selling some photographs of life at the Fort. He may have made a number of prints while he was still incarcerated.

35. *CREG,* November 9, 1911, p. 11. Also, see the *Marion Register,* November 28, 1911, p. 4. Novak had indeed set up a business in Fort Madison. This paper added an additional comment to the story: "there are those who never believed he was guilty."

36. *CREG,* December 28, 1911, p. 2. In fact, Sanders would become the focus of an investigation after Novak was released. The state's Department

of Justice published a report in 1912 that examined several charges against the penitentiary warden. The report explored "First, the personal integrity and moral character of the warden. Second, the physical and sanitary conditions of the institution," and "third, the general management of the institution." The progressive warden had a number of supporters, including Maud Ballington Booth, who was especially pleased that the warden let the prisoners use the yard for "base ball and other games." Overall, while the warden was found innocent of a lack of moral character, he was castigated for improprieties in managing the prison and tolerating its poor conditions overall. See Cosson et al., p. 16.

37. Cosson et al., p. 17.

38. For "laid Novak out," see *CRDR*, January 2, 1912, p. 10. The *Republican* referred to the convict as "Dimick." The other information and quotation is from the *Waterloo Evening Courier*, January 2, 1912, p. 4.

39. *Emmetsburg Democrat*, January 10, 1912, p. 5.

40. *CRDR*, November 2, 1913, p. 12. Also, see *Pioneer Recollections*, p. 141. It's possible that she was one of the many women who had kept a steady correspondence with Novak when he was in the Vinton jail.

41. John W. Tobin, *With No Intention . . . and Other Stories*, p. 134.

42. Conversation with Lani Novak Howe, January 15, 2013. For information on Novak's death, see "Illinois, Deaths and Stillbirths, 1916–1947," index, *FamilySearch* https://familysearch.org/pal:/MM9.1.1/N3HW-JK4: Frank Elfred Novak, 12 Jul 1930; citing reference rn 19545, FHL microfilm 1892492.

43. *DMDN*, November 11, 1897, p. 1.

19. The Measure of Their Lifetimes

1. *WDC*, April 17, 1903, p. 1.

2. Novak was declared indigent at the time of the trial. Milner was supposed to be compensated twenty dollars a day for his services. It took two years, but Benton County eventually paid him nine hundred dollars in legal fees.

3. *WDC*, April 18, 1904, p. 7. Milner was jokingly referring to Russell Sage, an extravagantly wealthy nineteenth-century financier who amassed a considerable fortune in the stock market as well as ownership of several railroads and Western Union. See http://encyclopedia2.the freedictionary.com/Sage+Russell.

4. *CREG*, August 19, 1912, p. 10.

5. Another insurance newsletter, *The Baltimore Underwriter*, carried Perrin's diary. Even as late as 1958, Travelers featured an article on the case in one of its publications, *Protection*.

6. Some incorrect accounts of the Novak case had Red Perrin marrying Nellie Murray Shea, a young widow and one of Edward Murray's sisters. In fact, Shea had given Ed Murray the blue woolen shirt with the star-and-crescent moon pattern that he wore on the night of the murder and testified about the garment before the coroner's jury.

7. *Cedar Rapids Sunday Republican*, November 20, 1904, p. 9. Also see *CREG*, November 15, 1904, p. 7.

8. *Documents of the Assembly of the State of New York, One Hundred and Twenty-Seventh Session*, 1904. Albany: Oliver A. Quayle, 1904, vol. 1, p. 720.

9. Lydell was approaching the stretch of track between Batavia and Buffalo where the famous steam engine 999 had set a purported speed record of one hundred twelve miles per hour in 1893. This portion of track was especially fast and in fact had all of the curves removed prior to the 999's record run. Perhaps Lydell knew he could make up some time once he reached that portion of the route.

10. *Syracuse Herald*, January 13, 1911, p. 1. For the Masonic bracelet found under the body, see *Middletown* (NY) *Daily Times*, January 13, 1911, p. 1.

11. Perrin and his wife are buried at St. John's Cemetery in Cedar Rapids.

12. On one visit to Vinton, Betsy Fischer Hadley and her husband, Rick, showed me a walking stick that had been passed down from her mother, Patricia Tobin Fischer. Elaborately carved, the stick features M. J. Tobin, along with four other prominent Republicans from the turn of the century: President William McKinley, Theodore Roosevelt, Iowa Governor Leslie M. Shaw, and Congressman Jonathan P. Dolliver, who later became a U.S. senator. Tobin's likeness occupies a place of honor on top of the staff and bears a laurel wreath along with the epithet, "Hero of Vinton."

13. While it is difficult to prove whether the Novak case was in fact the first murder conviction in Iowa based solely on circumstantial evidence, the legal ramifications from the verdict are still felt today. A search in the LEXIS database shows that the Novak case and subsequent appeal was cited in thirty-four legal documents and journals.

14. John Tobin never received a law degree from the University of Iowa, although he had taken several years of law classes as an undergraduate. After consulting with the head of the law school, Tobin was told that since he had already passed the bar and was a practicing lawyer, there was no need for

him to go back and get a law degree. See the *Cedar Rapids Gazette*, June 14, 1970, Features Section, p. 1.

15. Conversation with Elizabeth Fischer Hadley, July 10, 2007.

16. Conversation with Karl W. Fischer Jr., August 11, 2007.

17. *Cedar Valley Daily Times*, May 21, 1945, pp. 1 and 3.

18. www.cobentoniaus.com/Upperframe.html.

19. Conversation with Elizabeth Fischer Hadley, July 10, 2007.

20. Conversation with Karl W. Fischer Jr. and Patricia Tobin Fischer, August 11, 2007.

21. "Leo 'Ooch' Novak: 'The Man with the Most Fight Wins,'" *Coe College Newsletter*, 2006, p. 3. Novak and Rockne were good friends. In fact, Novak served as a pallbearer at the Notre Dame coach's funeral in 1931. See http://www.public.coe.edu/historyweb/alumni_novak_leo.html.

22. www.search.com/reference/Norway,Iowa.

23. Conversation with Pat Erger, Norway Public Library, July 26, 2007.

SELECTED BIBLIOGRAPHY

Adney, Tappan. *The Klondike Stampede*. Vancouver: Univ. of British Columbia Press, 1994.

Albert B. Cummins Memorial Address. Delivered on February 27, 1927. Washington, D.C.: Government Printing Office, 1927.

Albert Lea Evening Tribune.

Algona Advance.

Algona Courier.

Algona Republican.

Algona Upper Des Moines.

Anamosa Journal-Express.

Anamosa Prison Press.

Anamosa State Penitentiary Records.

Anita Republican.

Appelbaum, Stanley. *The Chicago World's Fair of 1893: A Photographic Record*. New York: Dover, 1980.

Arizona History and Archives Division, Archives and Public Records, Phoenix, AZ.

Arizona Republic.

Associated Press.

Bearss, Edwin C. *Proposed Klondike Gold Rush National Historical Park*. Washington, D.C.: U.S. Office of History and Historic Architecture, 1970.

Bell, Suzanne. *Crime and Circumstance: Investigating the History of Forensic Science*. Westport, CT: Praeger, 2008.

Belle Plaine Union.

Bergman, Marvin. *Iowa History Reader*. Ames: State Historical Society of Iowa in Association with Iowa State Univ. Press, 1996.

Berton, Pierre. *The Klondike Fever: The Life and Death of the Last Great Gold Rush*. New York: A. A. Knopf, 1972.

———, Frank Newfeld, and Barbara Sears. *The Klondike Quest: A Photographic Essay, 1897–1899*. Erin, ON: Boston Mills, 1997.

Bettmann, Otto. *The Good Old Days – They Were Terrible!* New York: Random House, 1974.

Blomberg, Thomas G., and Karol Lucken. *American Penology: A History of Control.* Hawthorne, NY: Aldine De Gruyter, 2000.

Bode Bugle.

Booth, Maud Ballington. *After Prison–What?* New York: F. H. Revell, 1903.

Boyden Reporter.

Brands, H. W. *The Reckless Decade: America in the 1890s.* Chicago: Univ. of Chicago, 2002.

Bruce, Miner Wait. *Alaska: Its History and Resources, Gold Fields, Routes and Scenery.* New York: G. P. Putnam's Sons, 1899.

Bryan, Patricia L. "John Wesley Elkins, Boy Murderer, and His Struggle for Pardon." *Annals of Iowa* 69 (Summer 2010): 261–307.

Burlington Hawk-Eye.

Butler County News.

Campbell, Captain J. W. "Fragmentary History of the Fort Madison Penitentiary." *Bulletin of Iowa Institutions* 2.2 (April 1900): 171–78.

Campbell, W. Joseph. "Not Likely Sent: The Remington-Hearst Telegrams." *Journalism and Mass Communication Quarterly* 77.2 (Summer 2000): 405.

———. *The Year That Defined American Journalism: 1897 and the Clash of Paradigms.* New York: Routledge, 2006.

Carlson, Phyllis Downing, and Laurel Downing Bill. *Aunt Phil's Trunk: An Alaska Historian's Collection of Treasured Tales.* Anchorage, AK: Laudon Enterprises, 2006.

Carmack, George W. *My Experiences in the Yukon.* Seattle: Marguerite Carmack, 1933.

"Catholic Encyclopedia: Confraternities of the Cord." *NEW ADVENT: Home.* <www.newadvent.org/cathen/04357a.html>. 22 March 2010.

Cedar Falls Gazette.

Cedar Rapids Daily Republican.

Cedar Rapids Daily Times.

Cedar Rapids Evening Gazette.

Cedar Rapids Sunday Republican.

Cedar Rapids Weekly Gazette.

Chicago Inter-Ocean.

Chicago Times-Herald.

Chicago Tribune.

Christianson, Scott. *With Liberty for Some: 500 Years of Imprisonment in America.* Boston, MA: Northeastern Univ. Press, 1998.

Clark, Henry W. *Alaska: The Last Frontier.* New York: Grosset and Dunlap, 1930.

Clinton Mirror.

Coffin, N. E. *Proceedings of the Iowa State Bar Association's Third Annual Meeting, Held at Cedar Rapids, Iowa, July 7th and 8th, 1897.* Des Moines: Kenyon, 1898.

Cohen, Stan. *A Klondike Centennial Scrapbook.* Missoula, MT: Pictorial Histories, 1996.

Cohen, Stan. *The Streets Were Paved with Gold: A Pictorial History of the Klondike Gold Rush, 1896–1899.* Missoula, MT: Pictorial Histories, 1977.

Cohen, Stan, and Candy Waugaman. *A Klondike Centennial Scrapbook: Movies, Music, Guides, Photographs, Artifacts, and Personalities of the Great Klondike Gold Rush.* Missoula, MT: Pictorial Histories, 1996.

Constantine, Charles C. *Report to E. L. Newcombe, Deputy Minister of Justice, Ottawa.* Library and Archives Canada, Ottawa. 1897 Inventory No. 13-12. Extradition Files R188-42-8-E.

Constantine, Veronica. "Booth, Maud Ballington Booth." *Learning to Give.* <http://learningtogive.org/papers/paper213.html>. 1 July 2011.

Corbit, Robert M. *History of Jones County, Iowa, Past and Present.* Chicago: S. J. Clarke, 1910.

Cosson, George. *The Report of the Committee Appointed to Investigate the Character of the Warden and the General Management of the Iowa Penitentiary at Fort Madison, Together with a Report concerning the Jail System of Iowa, with Recommendations.* Des Moines: E. H. English, 1912.

The Daily Huronite.

Daily Iowa Capital.

Davenport Leader.

Decatur Daily Republican.

Des Moines Daily Capital.

Des Moines Daily News.

Documents of the Assembly of the State of New York, One Hundred and Twenty-Seventh Session, vol. 1. Albany: Oliver A. Quayle, 1904.

Dornfeld, A. A., Tom Vickerman, and Archibald Leckie. *"Hello, Sweetheart, Get Me Rewrite!" The Story of the City News Bureau of Chicago.* Chicago: Academy Chicago, 1988.

Dubuque Herald.

Dunbar, Robin. *The Detective Business.* Chicago: Charles H. Kerr, 1909.

Dykstra, Robert R. *Bright Radical Star: Black Freedom and White Supremacy on the Hawkeye Frontier.* Cambridge, MA: Harvard Univ. Press, 1993.

Edge, Laura Bufano. *Locked Up: A History of the U.S. Prison System.* Minneapolis, MN: Twenty-First Century, 2009.

Elgin Echo.

Elizabeth Fischer Hadley. Telephone interview. 10 July 2007.

Emmetsburg Democrat.

Erusha, Robert C. Letter. 29 August 2007.

Estherville Weekly Northern Vindicator.

Farley, Mary M., and Marcella E. Dillon. "Biography of John F. Farley." Unpublished scrapbook on John F. Farley.

Faulkes, F. W. Letter to Governor Albert Cummins. 14 January 1903.

Fifield, James Clark. *The American Bar: A Biographical Directory of Contemporary Lawyers of the United States and Canada.* Minneapolis: Fifield, 1918.

Fort Wayne Evening Post.

Fort Wayne News.

Freedman, Estelle B. *Their Sisters' Keepers: Women's Prison Reform in America, 1830–1930.* Ann Arbor: Univ. of Michigan, 1984.

Gates, Michael. *Gold at Fortymile Creek: Early Days in the Yukon.* Vancouver: Univ. of British Columbia Press, 1994.

Glenwood Republican.

Grand Lodge of British Columbia and Yukon. <http://www.freemasonry .bcy.ca>. 3 April 2010.

Grinnell Herald.

Gue, B. F., and Benjamin Franklin Shambaugh. *Biographies and Portraits of the Progressive Men of Iowa: Leaders in Business, Politics and the Professions, Together with an Original and Authentic History of the State.* Des Moines: Conaway and Shaw, 1899.

Habenicht, Jan. *History of Czechs in America.* St. Paul, MN: Czechoslovak Genealogical Society International, 1996.

Haeber, Jonathan. "The 1893 Fair That Changed the World—Bearings." *Terrastories–Places That Tell Stories.* <http://www.terrastories.com /bearings/chicago-worlds-fair>. 25 January 2009.

Harrison, E. S. *Nome and Seward Peninsula History, Description, Biographies and Stories.* Seattle, WA: E. S. Harrison, 1905.

Hartman, John C. *History of Black Hawk County, Iowa, and Its People.* Chicago: S. J. Clarke, 1915.

Haskell, William B. *Two Years in the Klondike and Alaskan Gold-Fields,*

1896–1898: A Thrilling Narrative of Life in the Gold Mines and Camps.
Fairbanks: Univ. of Alaska, 1998.

Heller, Herbert L. *Sourdough Sagas.* New York: Ballantine, 1972.

Henry, George T., and Mark W. Hunter. *Cedar Rapids: Downtown and Beyond.* Charleston, SC: Arcadia, 2005.

Hill, Luther B. *History of Benton County, Iowa: From Materials in the Public Archives, the Iowa Historical Society's Collection.* Chicago: Lewis, 1910.

The History of Lee County, Iowa Containing a History of the County, Its Cities, Towns, &c. Chicago: Western Historical, 1879.

Holmes, Bayard P. Letter to Dr. J. B. Lewis. 9 Mar. 1897.

Hull Index.

Humboldt County Independent.

Humboldt Independent.

Humeston New Era.

Iowa: A Guide to the Hawkeye State. New York: Viking, 1938.

Iowa Citizen.

Iowa City Daily Press.

Iowa City Republican.

Iowa City State Press.

Jarchow, Merrill E. "Social Life of an Iowa Farm Family 1873–1912." *Palimpsest* 50.2 (April 1952): 123–54.

Johnson, James Albert. *Carmack of the Klondike.* Seattle: Epicenter, 1990.

Kalona News.

Karl W. Fischer Jr. Telephone interview. 11 August 2007.

Klondike: The Chicago Record's Book for Gold Seekers. Chicago: Chicago Record, 1897.

Kysila, Karel. "Emigration to the USA from the Policka Region in 1850–1890." *Proceedings of Genealogy Seminar of the Czech Heritage Society of Texas, Hillsboro.* 1999.

LaGrange, Connie. "Tilford Academy, 1872–1916." Unpublished manuscript, 1971.

Larson, Erik. *The Devil in the White City: Murder, Magic, and Madness at the Fair That Changed America.* New York: Crown, 2003.

Legislative Documents Submitted to the Twenty-Ninth General Assembly of the State of Iowa, Which Convened at Des Moines January 13, 1902. Des Moines: B. Murphy, 1902.

Leonard, John William. *The Gold Fields of the Klondike: Fortune Seeker's Guide to the Yukon Region of Alaska and British America.* Whitehorse, YT: Clairedge, 1994.

Lewis, Dr. J. B. Letter to Bayard P. Holmes. 8 Feb. 1897.

Lewis, Dr. J. B. Letter to Northwestern Mutual Life Association. 1 Mar. 1897.

Lewis, Dr. J. B. Letter to U.S. Casualty Company. 11 Nov. 1897.

Library of Congress, Manuscript Division, ID #MS536301, Administrative File, 1857–1899, Box 32. Washington, D.C.

Loerzel, Robert. *Alchemy of Bones: Chicago's Luetgert Murder Case of 1897*. Urbana: Univ. of Illinois, 2003.

London, Jack. *The Road*. Salt Lake City, UT: Peregrine Smith, 1978.

London, Jack. "Through the Rapids on the Way to Klondike." In *Jack London's Tales of Adventure*. Garden City, NY: Hanover House, 1956.

Lukas, J. Anthony. *Big Trouble: A Murder in a Small Western Town Sets off a Struggle for the Soul of America*. New York: Simon and Schuster, 1997.

Mackay, James A. *Allan Pinkerton: The First Private Eye*. New York: J. Wiley and Sons, 1997.

Marion Register.

Marion Sentinel.

Marshalltown Times-Republican.

McKay, Joyce. "Reforming Prisoners and Prisons: Iowa's State Prisons—The First Hundred Years." *Annals of Iowa* 60.2 (2001): 139–73.

McKeown, Martha Ferguson. *The Trail Led North: Mont Hawthorne's Story*. New York: Macmillan, 1948.

McLaren, M. N. Letter to Dr. J. B. Lewis. 28 Oct. 1897.

The Milepost: All-the-North Travel Guide. Anchorage, AK: Morris Communications, 2005.

Monkkonen, Eric H. *Police in Urban America, 1860–1920*. Cambridge: Cambridge Univ. Press, 1981.

Morgan, Murray. *One Man's Gold Rush: A Klondike Album*. Seattle: Univ. of Washington, 1967.

Morn, Frank. *"The Eye That Never Sleeps": A History of the Pinkerton National Detective Agency*. Bloomington: Indiana Univ. Press, 1982.

Music of the Alaska–Klondike Gold Rush: Songs of History. Jean Murray, 2003. CD.

Neese, Bob. *Prison Day by Day*. Fort Madison, IA: Penal, 1957.

Neese, Bob. *Prison Exposures: First Photographs Inside Prison by a Convict*. Philadelphia: Chilton, 1959.

Neufeld, David, and Frank B. Norris. *Chilkoot Trail: Heritage Route to the Klondike*. Whitehorse, YT: Lost Moose, 1996.

New York Observer.

New York Sun.

New York Times.

Oelwein Reporter.

Ogilvie, William. *Early Days on the Yukon.* Whitehorse, YT: Wolf Creek Books, 2002.

Oswego Daily Palladium.

Patricia Tobin Fischer. Telephone interview. 11 August 2007.

Perry Daily Chief.

Philadelphia Evening Telegraph.

"Photographic Technology Patents." *Scott's Photographica Collection.* <http: //www.vintagephoto.tv/patents.shtml>. 23 August 2011.

Pisciotta, Alexander W. *Benevolent Repression: Social Control and the American Reformatory-prison Movement.* New York: New York Univ. Press, 1994.

Portrait and Biographical Album of Benton County, Iowa, Containing Full Page Portraits and Biographical Sketches of Prominent and Representative Citizens of the County, Together with Portraits and Biographies of All the Governors of Iowa and of the Presidents of the United States. Chicago: Chapman Brothers, 1887.

Proceedings of the Twenty-Eighth Annual Session of the Iowa State Bar Association, Held at Sioux City, Iowa, June 22 and 23, 1922. Des Moines: Iowa State Bar Association, 1922.

Ramsland, Katherine M. *Beating the Devil's Game: A History of Forensic Science and Criminal Investigation.* New York: Thorndike, 2007.

Ransom, Harley. *Pioneer Recollections: Stories and Pictures Depicting the Early History and Development of Iowa County, Selected from the Family Albums and Libraries of the Descendants of the Pioneers of the County.* Cedar Rapids, IA: Historical Publications, 1941.

Roberts, Edward M. *Illustrated Fort Madison: A Volume Devoted to the Interests of Fort Madison, Iowa.* Fort Madison, IA: Roberts and Roberts, 1896.

Roberts, John W. *Reform and Retribution: An Illustrated History of American Prisons.* Lanham, MD: American Correctional Association, 1997.

Ross, Julie K. "Welcome To the Fair." *American Studies @ The University of Virginia,* 1996. <http://xroads.virginia.edu>. 25 Jan. 2009.

Rothman, David J. *The Discovery of the Asylum: Social Order and Disorder in the New Republic.* Boston: Little, Brown, 1971.

Runyon, Tom. *In for Life: A Convict's Story.* New York: Norton, 1953.

San Francisco Chronicle.

Satterfield, Archie. *Chilkoot Pass, the Most Famous Trail in the North.* Anchorage: Alaska Northwest, 1988.

Schwieder, Dorothy. *Iowa: The Middle Land.* Ames: Iowa State Univ. Press, 1996.

Seattle Post-Intelligencer.

Second Biennial Report of the Board of Control of Iowa, for the Biennial Period Ending June 30, 1901. Des Moines: B. Murphy, 1901.

The Sibylline. Mount Vernon, IA: Cornell and Edson Fish, 1888.

Sioux Valley Bee.

Sioux Valley News.

Siringo, Charles A. *A Cowboy Detective: A True Story of Twenty-two Years with a World-famous Detective Agency.* Lincoln: Univ. of Nebraska Press, 1988.

Skagway Alaska. <http://www.skagway.com>. 11 Apr. 2010.

Snavely, Richard, and Steve Wendl. *Anamosa Penitentiary.* Charleston, SC: Arcadia, 2010.

Spirit Lake Beacon.

Starr, Douglas P. *The Killer of Little Shepherds: A True Crime Story and the Birth of Forensic Science.* New York: Alfred A. Knopf, 2010.

State Historical Society of Iowa. Governor's Criminal Correspondence, 1838–1910. Des Moines.

State of Iowa v. Frank A. Novak. Benton County District Court. 1898. Court Transcript.

Steele, Harwood. *Policing the Arctic.* London: Jarrolds, 1936.

Steele, Samuel B. *Forty Years in Canada: Reminiscences of the Great Northwest, with Some Account of His Service in South Africa.* Toronto, ON: McClelland, Goodchild and Stewart, 1915.

Swailes, Jean Newland. *Belle Plaine, Iowa: 1862–1962: Centennial History Book.* Belle Plaine, IA: Belle Plaine Century Corporation, 1962.

Swartzendruber, Dellis. *A History of the Anamosa State Penitentiary.* Anamosa: IPI Graphics Arts, 2006.

Syracuse Herald.

Syracuse Post-Standard.

Thiel, G. H. Letter to M. J. Tobin. 4 April 1897.

Thornburg, Frank. Letter to Dr. J. B. Lewis. 8 Feb. 1897.

Tilstone, William J., Kathleen A. Savage, and Leigh A. Clark. *Forensic Science: An Encyclopedia of History, Methods, and Techniques.* Santa Barbara, CA: ABC-CLIO, 2006.

Tobin, John W. "Murder: A Persistent Pursuit." *Palimpsest* 51.10 (October 1970): 417–21.

———. "Murder: Circumstantial Evidence." *Palimpsest* 51.10 (October, 1970): 422–27.

———. *With No Intention . . . and Other Stories.* Cedar Rapids, IA: Laurance, 1979.

Tobin, M. J. Letter to Dr. J. B. Lewis. 20 October 1897.

———. Letter to G. H. Thiel. 16 Apr. 1898.

———. Letter to B. W. Garrett. 26 January 1903.

———. Letter to W. I. Endicott from M. J. Tobin. Referenced in Travelers Archives, p. 12.

Travelers Archives

The Travelers Record.

Van Wormer, Andrew. Letter to Dr. J. B. Lewis. 3 March 1897.

———. Letter to Dr. J. B. Lewis. 8 March 1897.

Vinton Eagle.

"Visible Proofs: Forensic Views of the Body." *National Library of Medicine–National Institutes of Health.* <http://www.nlm.nih.gov/visible proofs/galleries/technologies/bertillon.html>. 22 April 2010.

Waterloo Daily Reporter.

Waterloo Daily Times-Tribune.

Waterloo Evening Courier.

Waterloo Semi-Weekly Courier.

Way, John L. Letter to Dr. J. B. Lewis. 4 Feb. 1897.

Webb, Melody. *The Last Frontier.* Albuquerque: Univ. of New Mexico, 1985.

Webster City Tribune.

Welty, Susan Elizabeth Fulton. *Look Up and Hope! The Motto of the Volunteer Prison League: The Life of Maud Ballington Booth.* New York: T. Nelson, 1961.

Wheeler, Martin P. *Judas Exposed Or, The Spotter Nuisance: An Anti-secret Book Devoted to the Interests of Railroad Men.* Chicago: Utility Book and Novelty, 1889.

Wigmore, John Henry, comp. *The Principles of Judicial Proof, As Given By Logic, Psychology and General Experiences and Illustrated in Judicial Trials.* Boston: Little, Brown, 1913.

Williams, R. S. "Botanical Notes on the Way to Dawson City, Alaska." *The Plant World: A Monthly Journal of Popular Botany.* (August 1899): 178.

Zuehlke, Mark. *The Yukon Fact Book: Everything You Ever Wanted to Know about the Yukon.* Vancouver, BC: Whitecap, 1998.

INDEX